W9-AXV-517

GRACELAND

THE LIVING LEGACY OF ELVIS PRESLEY

GRACELAND

THE LIVING LEGACY OF ELVIS PRESLEY

CollinsPublishersSanFrancisco

A Division of HarperCollins*Publishers*

This book is dedicated to the memory of E L V I S   P R E S L E Y

whose remarkable life and art made this very special project possible

The publishers would like to thank the management and staff at Graceland for their assistance in making this book possible, with special thanks to:

Carla Peyton, Worldwide Licensing Director
Debbie Johnson, General Manager
Todd Morgan, Communications Director
Danna Lee, Licensing Account Manager
Steve Marshall, Media Coordinator
Shelley Ritter, Archivist
Greg Howell, Archival Assistant
and Delta Presley Biggs, Elvis' aunt residing at Graceland

Graceland text by Chet Flippo.

All caption information and quotes (except where otherwise indicated) derived and adapted from information provided by Todd Morgan.
Special thanks to Gil Michael and Pauline Cuevas at Gil Michael Photography, Memphis.

Editor: Mike Evans
Design: Ashley Western
Production Controller: Michelle Thomas
Picture Research: Jenny Faithfull

Picture Acknowledgments:
Special photography for this book by Gil Michael,
all other photographs supplied by the Graceland photographic archive, with the exception of the following:
Hudd Andrews & Associates, Memphis 68, 78, 80, 88, 90, 126, 216;
Archive Photos 10, 20 bottom; Mike Evans 33, 51, 137 top;
Hulton Deutsch Collection Ltd 20 top, 37 top, 37 bottom, 38 top, 39 top; Hulton Deutsch / Bettmann 25 top; Kobal Collection / MGM 168 top, 168 center right, 168 bottom right; Kobal Collection / Paramount 27 center, 151 left; Kobal Collection / Twentieth Century Fox 27 top, 151 right; London Features International 3, 172, 196 left, 196 right; MGM 54, 240 left; Pictorial Press / Escott 15, / Keese 19 bottom, 26 bottom; Snap / Katz Pictures Ltd 97 left, 97 center; Syndication International 49 bottom left, 49 bottom right, 173 top, 173 bottom; Topham Picture Source 179 top left.

First published in USA in 1993 by
Collins Publishers San Francisco
1160 Battery Street
San Francisco CA 94111

First published in 1993 by Mitchell Beazley,
an imprint of Reed Consumer Books Limited, Michelin House,
81 Fulham Road, London SW3 6RB
and Auckland, Melbourne, Singapore and Toronto

Text and design Elvis Presley Enterprises, Inc. and Reed International Books Limited Copyright © 1993

Elvis, Elvis Presley and Graceland are registered trademarks of Elvis Presley Enterprises, Inc. The rights of publicity to the name, image, and likeness of Elvis Presley are exclusively owned by Elvis Presley Enterprises, Inc. All rights reserved. Copyright © 1993
All rights reserved, including the right of reproduction in whole or in any part or form.

Library of Congress Cataloging-in-Publication Data

Flippo, Chet. 1943-
        Graceland / Chet Flippo
        p. cm.
        ISBN 0-00255250-7
        1. Presley, Elvis. 1935-1977–Homes and haunts–Tennessee–
Memphis–Pictorial works. 2. Graceland Mansion (Memphis, Tenn.)-
Pictorial works. I. Title
ML420. P96F6 1993
782.42166'092-dc20   93-15057
                                             MARC Partial
                                                      MN

Produced by Mandarin Offset
Printed and bound in China
2 4 6 8 10 9 7 5 3 1

Even though he is gone, it is still possible to get close to Elvis Presley, to understand who he truly was as both an artist and a human being.

The best way is to listen, really listen, to his recordings, and to study the videotapes of his performances. Elvis put so much of himself into his work and communicated on such an intimate level with his audience.

A very close second, a must to complete the study, is to visit Graceland, his beloved home in Memphis, Tennessee, the home within whose walls so much of his life took place, the private world of the most famous and influential person in entertainment history. Beyond the fascinating rooms and all the treasures and wonders within, there's just something in the air, a presence, a warmth, an indefinable feeling that makes even the most casual visitor feel as though he were dropping in on a dear old friend. It's also a lot of fun. Savoring this book is almost like being there.

Never before has the Estate of Elvis Presley allowed photographers and writers such liberal access to Graceland. Never has the Graceland staff been so closely and personally involved with an Elvis-related book project.

GRACELAND – THE LIVING LEGACY OF ELVIS PRESLEY results from a year of great commitment from all the people who were part of making it happen – a solid year of photographing Elvis Presley's home and its treasures in a way that has never been done before, a year of creative brainstorming, a year of studying and writing and rewriting.

Filled with splendid, completely unique, new original Graceland photography by Gil Michael of Memphis, a fresh and fascinating text by noted rock and roll writer Chet Flippo, a generous selection of historic photographs and documents from the Presley Estate archives, and lots of inside information and creative input from the Graceland staff, this book is a treasure all its own. Enjoy.

TODD MORGAN

FOR THE ESTATE OF ELVIS PRESLEY

Can there possibly be a more peaceful spot on earth than Graceland on a soft, dewy morning? As the first rose-hued fingers of sunrise poke through the stately oak and elm trees that form a soaring natural cathedral and begin to gently illumine the Meditation Garden, I turn to study my fellow travelers. It is "walk-up" time, when the gates are opened for 90 minutes or so before the shuttle tours begin, to allow visitors to take a leisurely walk up the drive and sit in the Garden. Interestingly, that's the only time during the day — because of the shuttle tours — that "walkers" are allowed on the grounds. Elvis himself used to ride his favorite horse, a beautiful palomino, Rising Sun, out here and would sometimes canter down to the gates to admit the fans into the grounds and sign autographs from horseback. Last night I watched videotapes of old home movies of Elvis riding Rising Sun just past the Meditation Garden. Could he have even suspected that he was riding past his final resting place?

My fellow travelers this gentle dawn were a woman from St. Louis, a couple from Minneapolis, and a teenager from Birmingham. They sat with their private thoughts on the concrete steps behind the eight-columned pergola. To our backs was the curved brick wall with its four nineteenth-century Spanish stained-glass windows. Their content is open to interpretation; I myself would hazard a guess that one is a straightforward depiction of a Moorish town, one is the same thing but closer up, one depicts a black Madonna with a baby in its crib, and the last shows the Three Wise Men visiting baby Jesus. As I say, this whole matter is open to interpretation (as are many things hereabouts.) There is no hard and precise history of the Meditation Garden. The official history has it

From the roadside of Highway 51, the Graceland mansion is hardly visible through the stately trees that reach up to an open sky that touches Arkansas to the west and Mississippi a mile due south.

that Elvis commissioned a man named Bernard Grenadier to build it in the mid-Sixties. It was, though, one of Elvis' favorite places to come and sit. My companions said that they had come to Graceland to try to be close to Elvis. They had liked his music, they said, and that was important, but they were discovering that Elvis as a person and, even more so, as a persona was what drew them to Memphis and to Graceland. They wanted, they said, to enter the walls of the house that he inhabited, to walk the earth he walked upon, to breathe the air he breathed, to sit under the trees he sat under, to meditate by his grave, and to try to contemplate the things that he contemplated. Mainly, they wanted to be close to him. These pilgrims were open and totally unashamed about it. They were drawn, they said, by a presence. Some used the word "spiritual," some did not. All said that rock and roll had very little to do with it. From these and other faithful travelers with whom I spoke, I began to glean something that should have occurred to me long ago. It especially should have struck me when I was reading through mounds of Elvis newspaper clippings and yellowing magazines and stacks of books about him and countless newsreels and thousands of photographs (literally millions are available). A lot is known about Elvis. Supposedly. We have this huge physical pile of stuff in which he figured prominently. What do we really know? Pick up twenty different Elvis books at random; you will find twenty different Elvises. Many facts, dates and places, quotes, et cetera. But what do we really know? One of the pilgrims voiced it quite eloquently: "With Elvis, we know more than we understand. That's why I came here. To try to understand."

THE ROCK

Home was, for the first years of his life, a tenuous notion for Elvis. The concept of home as a permanent, solid and very palpable and real foundation of life was nonexistent for him as a child. The many moves, the poverty, the memory of his father's constant struggle to make ends meet, the uncertainty of a day-to-day life, the memory of Gladys marching off to pick cotton, the memory of Gladys working all day in a steaming-hot laundry — all of these contributed to Elvis' desire for some permanence in an uncertain world, for a rock on which to stand, for a refuge and a safe harbor. That refuge was to be Graceland. He lived there for twenty years, brought his family and

"A refuge and safe harbor" for Elvis. From his early fame in the Fifties he sought a sanctuary in a real home, which he found in Graceland. He returned home in a different sense when he made a triumphant appearance in his native Tupelo (below) in 1956.

friends together there, took his new bride there, and it was there that they raised their daughter. They enjoyed the seasons, rode their horses and played with their many pets, frolicked in the snow, decorated the grounds for Christmas, had ferocious fireworks battles in the backyard, had spats and disputes and made up, and generally conducted a fairly public life that fascinated millions of people. Graceland, understandably, came to represent much more than Elvis' home. It stood for a Southern way of life, for a new sensibility in popular culture, but it also represented a certain value that was missing in pop culture. It stood for the superstar who stayed home amidst his friends and neighbors, who

shunned Hollywood and its attendant trappings and didn't want a guarded citadel in Malibu and an elaborate penthouse on Sutton Place, who in short didn't get above his raising. Which in itself is a very Southern characteristic. Graceland has become the Plymouth Rock of pop culture, the home church of rock and roll, the rallying point for a generation with no other home base. A brush arbor for the soul, as one fellow traveler at the Meditation Garden told me. Not a bad metaphor. There has been scarce else to fulfill such a function in our culture. Elvis bridged rock and roll, rhythm and blues, gospel and country music as no one else did (or has since), and more importantly, came to be an icon even more than a musician. He caused more social change in this country and indeed around the world than most world leaders. And I'm not just talking about sideburns and rocking and rolling and attitude. He returned the democratic ideal to a business— you really can't call it an art form when it's driven by marketing— that had been run from the top down. Tin Pan Alley dictated what Americans could listen to. With "Heartbreak Hotel" he broke Tin Pan Alley's lock grip over pop music. Before Elvis, pop music depended on the sales of sheet music for its success. With Elvis came torrents of teenagers buying 45 RPM records. Those teenagers are now touring Graceland.

TUPELO

Vernon and Gladys were married on June 17, 1933, in Lee County, Verona, Mississippi, having purchased a marriage license in Pontotoc County, where they listed their ages for the circuit clerk as twenty-two for Vernon and nineteen for Gladys. In fact, they had eloped off to Pontotoc (where Gladys was from) because too many people knew them in Tupelo and knew that Vernon was under legal marrying age — he was actually seventeen, and Gladys was twenty-one. She had no birth certificate, since they were not legally required in Mississippi until some months after her birth in April of 1912.

They had no place to live: each had been living at home but there was no room for a married couple at either the Smiths' house on Kelly Street or the Presleys' on Old Saltillo Road, on the east side of Tupelo. Each home was full to bursting with extended family, not unusual in poor Southern communities. For the first few weeks of their marriage, they slept on a pallet on the floor in the modest home of Vernon's friends, Marshall and Vona Mae Brown.

Vernon borrowed $180 from Orville Bean, the Presley landlord who also owned the tract next to the Presley house on Old Saltillo, to build the little two-room shotgun shack on that site, the little house where Elvis would be born on January 8, 1935, and where his twin brother would be stillborn. Jesse Garon was born first, Elvis Aron came thirty minutes later, at 4:35 a.m. The name "Elvis" was of course Vernon's middle name; "Aron" was after Vernon's good friend Aaron Kennedy (the whole business of the spelling of "Aron" versus "Aaron" — especially on Elvis' gravesite — has been dealt with exhaustively elsewhere). "Jesse" was after Vernon's father J.D. (with whom Vernon was not

Vernon, the young Elvis and Gladys during the itinerant years when they moved to various places in and around Tupelo, including short spells with members of the Presley family and a brief stint in Pascagoula, Mississippi.

close) and "Garon" was simply to rhyme with "Aron," a Southern custom, to rhyme twins. Jesse was buried in an unmarked grave. They were identical twins.

Before Elvis was three years old, his father was involved in a strange crime that has never been fully explained. Apparently, Orville Bean — the Presley landlord, whose land Vernon's father farmed — accused Vernon, Gladys' brother Travis Smith, and another man, Lether Gable, of forgery. Talk was that Vernon, after a drink or two, had been talked into it by Gable and Smith.

Apparently, Vernon had sold a hog to Orville Bean for $4 and felt cheated by the transaction. He, with the aid and abetment of the other two men, had either altered that check or forged a new one to raise its amount to $40. At any rate, all three were indicted for forgery. According to Elaine Dundy's thorough book, *Elvis and Gladys*, the three men were jailed after pleading not guilty. Even though Vernon's uncle, Noah Presley, was mayor of East Tupelo, apparently he could or would do nothing. Gladys tried to raise support from Noah and from church groups to persuade Orville Bean to drop charges. He would not; he wanted to teach some lessons. Bail of $500 was posted for Gable by relatives.

The same bail for Gladys' brother, Travis Smith, was posted by Vernon's own father, J.D. Presley (along with J.G. Brown). J.D. was still one of Orville Bean's tenant farmers. Vernon was apparently left to sit in jail for six months to await trial.

Elvis, although only three years old, was not ignorant of what was going on around him. He made attempts to be the man of the house, getting Gladys a glass of water and otherwise trying to look after her (in childhood, he started referring to Gladys and

Vernon as his "babies"). He could not have escaped hearing the talk about his father and his uncle, Travis Smith. (Many years later Smith came to work at Graceland as a gate guard, living on the grounds; after he left the job, the little house he occupied was demolished to make more pasture land for the horses. The story goes that when Elvis grew impatient with the demolition team's progress, he climbed aboard a bulldozer and finished the job of flattening the still-furnished house himself.)

After a speedy trial in May of 1938, the three men were sentenced to three years each in Parchman, the now-legendary prison farm. While Vernon went away to prison, Gladys was forced to go on welfare. She and Elvis lived on what were then called federal commodities. Federal fat and junk food. Surplus cheese.

Many people at that time, through improper laws and maladministration of justice, were sentenced to terms at Parchman for mundane crimes that were little more than financial misdemeanors usually triggered by poverty. Subsequent accounts of Elvis' early life have often implied that there was an element of family neglect on Vernon's part, but the truth is that Elvis was as loved as any other child of a family of meager means.

Two Sundays a month, Gladys and Elvis would board a bus to visit Vernon in prison. Apparently because of good behavior and the hardship his sentence entailed for his family, Vernon was released after serving nine months.

During the period of Vernon's prison stay, Gladys had apparently felt sufficiently uneasy living next door to J.D. that she and Elvis left and moved in with her cousin Frank Richards and his wife on Maple Street. Gladys began working full-time in a local manufacturing company.

Upon Verson's release, they moved back to the east side of Tupelo. It was then that relatives noticed that all three Presleys occasionally sleepwalked, sometimes together, sometimes singly. The sleepwalking was referred to by the relatives as "action nightmares." The family never returned to the little house on Old Saltillo Road. For several months in 1940, the Presleys lived in a one-room cabin in Pascagoula, Mississippi. Vernon had found work with the Works Progress Administration in the wartime expansion of the shipyard there. But the Presleys apparently

wearied of the living conditions, the heat and the hard work, and returned once more to Tupelo, staying first with the Richards again, then moving in with Vernon's brother Vester and his wife Clettes – who was Gladys' sister – and their daughter Patsy, on Reese Street.

Elvis started school in 1941, at East Tupelo Consolidated, a short walk away on Lake Street. Nonetheless, this was a short walk on which he was never to be alone: Gladys began her Elvis escort service, walking him to and from school every day – whenever she could – for the rest of Elvis' school days.

Vernon found his return to Tupelo a rough readjustment. He got sporadic work on city projects around town. He worked for a brief time on a war prisoners' camp being built at Como, but work was generally unavailable for most people in the Presleys' financial position. Finally, as the war escalated, he went to work in factories in Memphis, spending the week there and coming home to Tupelo only on weekends.

It was during these days that Elvis somehow found a way to slip away from Gladys and wander around with an itinerant country singer named Mississippi Slim. And it was during that time that Elvis came near to dying from tonsillitis and came through whooping cough and measles. It was also during those days that seven-year-old Elvis accompanied Gladys to Tupelo Hospital where she had a miscarriage.

For either his ninth or tenth birthday (probably the tenth, because it was in the fifth grade that he began performing "Old Shep" at school), Gladys took Elvis into F.L. Bobo's hardware store to get his present. He wanted an air rifle, but Gladys finally talked him into getting a little guitar. That fall, he got up at the Mississippi-Alabama Fair and Dairy Show and won second prize – $5 plus free admission to all the carnival rides – for singing "Old Shep." There, purely by singing, in one fell swoop he managed to accomplish a great deal: he had made his mother proud of him, he had earned a lot of money, he had won the girls' notice and admiration, he had proven that he was capable of achieving a kind of greatness, and he had sudden control over all the fun in sight, all those thrilling rides to be ridden. One cannot help but wonder if his Master Plan for Life was already starting to take form in his brain.

MIGRANTS

With the war ending, things began to look up for the little family. Although Vernon had lost his job in Memphis, at least they were all together again in Tupelo. Vernon became a deacon in the First Assembly of God Church. Most importantly, Vernon had managed to save up enough money to buy a modest house. In August of 1945, he made a down payment of $200 toward a four-room house on Berry Street. The total price was $2,000. The owner? Orville Bean. Payments were $30 a month plus six percent interest. Vernon got a job in the Deake and Goodlet lumberyard, earning $72 a month. Not much was left over after the house payment. Then Vernon's father, J.D., deserted Minnie, so Minnie moved in with them. A cousin, Harold Loyd, stayed there occasionally.

Less than a year after the triumphant purchase, Vernon was forced to sell out. He had apparently been unable to keep a steady job and had missed a payment. Orville Bean later sold the house.

The Presleys ended up sliding down the scale again, landing in a hovel on Mulberry Alley, near the city dump. Vernon found work again, driving a truck for L.P. McCartey, a wholesale grocer, for $22 a week. The job also carried a side benefit: Vernon could bring home "damaged" groceries to feed his family.

Elvis went off to his new school, Milam Junior High, where he was noticed, but not liked, for his talent and his clothes, particularly his overalls, the neighborhood he lived in, and the unfair stigma attached to his family, primarily because of Vernon's financial plight.

Vernon kept his truck-driving job and Gladys went back to work at the Mid-South Laundry. The combined income allowed them to move to a two-family house at 1010 North Green Street. It was while they lived there that Gladys took Elvis down to the Lee County Library and Elvis got his library card. He used it often.

Things would likely have continued along in this modestly upward vein except something untoward happened: Mr. McCartey fired Vernon from the driving job for taking the vehicle on a Sunday after work hours for his own personal use. That was it for Vernon in Tupelo: no more church deacon, no more respected employee. Just unemployed – again.

Around the first of October of 1948, as Elvis later said, "Dad packed all our belongings in boxes and put them on top and in the trunk of the 1939 Plymouth. We left Tupelo overnight. We were broke, man, broke." On his last day at school at Milam, he sang for his class the song, "A Leaf on a Tree" (with its familiar refrain of "The green grass grew all around"). Goodbye, Tupelo.

MEMPHIS

Memphis proved to be no promised land for the Presleys as they hit town with Gladys' brother Travis, his wife Lorraine, and their sons, Bobby and Billy. They first shared cramped quarters in a Washington Avenue boarding house, then they all moved to 572 Poplar Avenue, near downtown. The building was a four-story house that had been converted into sixteen one-room apartments, four shared bathrooms and no kitchen. Vernon later told one of the Graceland secretaries, Becky Yancey, that they cooked on a hot plate in their one room and shared a tiny bathroom with three other families. He described the cockroaches: "Some of them were a couple of inches long at least and there wasn't nothing we could do to get rid of them. You could kill a few but before it got dark they would be right back."

Elvis spent eighth grade at the Christine School on Third Street. He would not be enrolled in L.C. Humes High, on Manassas Street, until 1949, when he began ninth grade there.

Gladys went to work almost immediately, sewing at Fashion Curtains. It would take Vernon much longer to find gainful work, on the loading dock at the United Paint Company on Winchester Avenue. Travis worked there, too. It was just down the street from the Presleys' new home, the 433-unit Lauderdale Courts, at 185 Winchester Avenue. It was a federal housing project, with a waiting list. So they considered themselves fortunate to have a private bath and kitchen, two bedrooms and a living room all to themselves: Vernon, Gladys, Elvis and Minnie.

Unfortunately, for the four or so years that the Presleys lived there, it seemed that they were forever at odds with the housing authorities as to whether or not they continued to meet the financial criteria for being allowed to stay. Vernon's back would go out, and then family the income would dip and Elvis would mow lawns and Gladys took a job as nurse's aide at St. Joseph's Hospital (it was there that she glimpsed her first pink Cadillac and told Elvis about it at great length). Then their income would exceed the minimum, and the fussing would begin all over again. Their rent was $35 a month. Vernon himself was earning eighty-three cents an hour, and with raises he eventually got up to $53.22 a week.

Elvis worked as an usher at Loews' State Theater until he was fired for fighting, and how Hollywood missed including this potent scene in any of his movies shall remain a mystery. The scenario: The candy counter girl admires Elvis, resplendent in his trim usher's uniform, and, in an attempt to telegraph her love, begins slipping him some of her counter's largesse. Tootsie Pops, jawbreakers, licorice whips, multi-hued gumdrops, and Red Hots pass through her hot little hands to Elvis' own waiting palms. Little did she know that all those years of deprivation in East Tupelo had built up a massive sweet tooth. Meanwhile, another pair of eyes glows green there in the cool Loews' darkness. In a jealous rage, another usher rushes to the manager to rat on the young lovers, to spill the sordid story of the purloined sweets. Confronted with the awful secret, Elvis rushes out of the manager's office, his jaw clenched, his resolve firm. He tracks down the little rat fink usher and decks him with one punch as his little heroine applauds. Unfortunately, the manager, far from admiring his pluck, fires him on the spot for being a troublemaker. In a trice, he's out there alone, standing in the alley, after having been forced to hand in his uniform.

It's the first such noted episode in his life. Perhaps all those years of maintaining a calm, courteous facade in the face of grinding poverty, ridicule, and the growing notion that his was, after all, a dead-end world — just as Vernon's proved to be — finally caused Elvis to boil over.

Vernon was laid up half the time, with his back out or maybe not. All he had to show for his life was a beat-up old Lincoln with cardboard in one window where the glass used to be, subsidized housing on a shaky status, and a wife and son who clung to each other. Elvis was painfully aware of each visit by the housing authority, of each eviction threat, and he once dictated a letter in Vernon's name to send to the authority: "Have had illness in family. Wife is working to help pay out of debt. Bills pressing. Don't want to be sued."

Gladys had also told Elvis that she had been doing so well in her nurse's aide job that her supervisor told her the hospital would nominate her to attend nursing school, if she cared to go. Well, that was a laugh, she told her son. If only they weren't going to teeter on the poverty fence for the rest of their lives, if only Vernon could work full-time, if only she'd had the education it would take to get into nursing school, if only...

Vernon supported his son's decision wholeheartedly when Elvis became despondent and threatened to quit school in his senior year, as many kids in his position did. As Vernon said, Elvis didn't need no education to drive no truck or work construction or even sing. Gladys, tight-lipped and furious, would have none of that. And, in fact, she won Elvis over.

He went back to school. She went back to work. First was the seasonal job of picking cotton in September. After Elvis took an evening job in a metal shop to help the family income, she made him quit when he began falling asleep in class. To take up the slack, she went back to her old job at the hospital.

At Humes High School, his majors were English, history and shop. He belonged to the history club, the speech club, ROTC, the English club, and he also worked in the library. He graduated in 1953.

Perhaps that library card had been his biggest legacy from Tupelo. It represented much more, obviously, than just permission to walk into the Lee County Library and walk out with any book he wanted. With that card, Gladys lifted him above all the rest, all the Smiths and Presleys and the rest of the hard-scrabble pack in East Tupelo for whom life was nothing but daily drudgery. Not that he became a scholar, but Elvis never got out of the reading habit, despite the hoopla about all his TV sets. Elvis often spoke later in his life about the power of the ability to dream and that library card certified his license to dream, validated his dreams that had begun with comic books as a kid. Now he could discover T.E. Lawrence, Lindbergh or Edison. Life was not limited to four barren wood walls on a tenement farm.

In Tupelo, Elvis had had the beginnings of a musical education; but he had no best friend and had yet to discover the proper approach to the opposite sex. Gladys had been all that he had known as a close friend.

All that gradually changed with each move in his life. The Lauderdale Courts, for example, with its 433 families, exposed him on a daily basis to people and things, and music and ways of speaking, that were far more worldly than anything he had encountered before.

He had acquired his first high school friend – for better or for worse – when Red West came to his aid in the boys' room at Humes and stopped a group of Elvis-bashers from pummeling him. Around the same time George Klein, the president of his class, became his second friend.

He changed more than Gladys and Vernon realized. Midway through his senior year at Humes, he began to show a true back-bone, rather than being the one who got his way by being – in effect – everyone's teacher's pet.

Christmas of 1953, the housing authority squad came around as usual and told the Presleys that, now that Gladys was working again, they were making too much money to stay there. It happened in one form or another every Christmas. Elvis snapped. He announced flatly to his parents, "We're getting out of here." He was seventeen years old.

They left January 7, 1953, and apparently stayed with relatives on Cypress Street until April, when they took an apartment on Alabama Avenue, number 462, not far from Lauderdale Courts.

MUSIC

At the beginning of his second senior semester, Elvis entered the annual Humes Minstrel Show and, winning the contest, was the only entrant allowed to do an encore. Apparently his first number was "Cold, Cold, Icy Fingers" and his encore was the sturdy "Till I Waltz Again With You." Elvis was so buoyed by the reception he received that he started wearing his guitar to school (he owned no guitar case but he did have a strap).

Jim Denson lived in the Lauderdale Courts and attended Humes High, and he also knew Elvis because his parents ran the Poplar Street Mission. He claimed that the Presley family shopped there often.

Denson's brother, the guitarist Jesse Lee Denson, wrote the song "Miracle of the Rosary" which Elvis recorded in 1971. Jim Denson recalls that his brother hung around the Lauderdale

Courts with the Burnettes, Dorsey and Johnny. "My brother taught the Burnettes how to play guitar and he taught Elvis, too."

The Burnettes in 1952 were driving trucks for Crown Electric during the day and playing gigs at night. They were local heroes to the teenage boys and when the Burnettes deigned to drop in on the kids' outdoor jam sessions at the Courts, it was like royalty coming around. Elvis had already met bassist Bill Black, whose mother Rudy lived in the Lauderdale Courts and who became friends with Gladys. Bill Black was playing in a local band called Doug Poindexter's Starlite Wranglers and had done work for Sam Phillips ever since Phillips opened his Memphis Recording Service, back in 1950. It was Bill Black who more than anyone introduced Elvis to the world of professional music.

Elvis was getting out around town, hanging out on Beale Street and in white honky-tonks such as the Eagle's Nest. Occasionally Jesse Lee Denson and Bill Black's brother Johnny would let Elvis sit in with them when they played the Girls' Club at Lauderdale Courts. He would show up at Saturday afternoon matinees sponsored by radio station KWEM, with bands playing from car dealers' lots and so on. One song that Elvis reportedly was doing then was "Keep Your Hands Off Of It (Birthday Cake)." He also played at parties in the basement of the Hotel Chisca. Radio station WHBQ had its offices in the building and its star DJ, Dewey Phillips, often dropped in.

CELEBRITY

The most celebrated of Elvis' first romances was with the viva-cious Dixie Locke, but Denson remembers Elvis going with a girl named Betty Anne McMahon. (He also recalls that there was a tough lesbian in the neighborhood named Betty, nicknamed "Little Fish," who liked to chase Elvis — with the aim of fighting him. "Me and Jesse had to protect him from her.") "He had other friends, too. I remember Billie Wardlow was one and Paul Durer was another."

Denson also remembered, as was common knowledge, that Elvis had terrible facial acne for a while. Such was the preoccupation with Elvis' sudden success that Denson can relate with all seriousness that "everyone" who had known Elvis at the Lauderdale Courts gossiped that Elvis had gone off and had a facelift – "had skin grafted from his rear end" – and a nose job.

To Gladys' great joy, Elvis was graduated from Humes High on June 3, 1953. According to Elaine Dundy, just days before that ceremony, Elvis had been standing on a stage in Mississippi, winning second prize in yet another talent show. The occasion was the first Jimmie Rodgers Festival in Meridian. Part of the show was a talent show for Mississippians only. Two of the organizers of that show — reporters for the *Meridian Star* — told Dundy that Elvis showed up, said he had hitchhiked from Tupelo, and was broke. They paid his hotel room, he won a guitar in the contest, and he left town. The reason that Elvis never mentioned this episode in his life, Dundy speculates, is that in 1956 (probably 1955, when he was still on the Louisiana Hayride tour) Elvis returned to Meridian as part of the scheduled show. He was roundly booed by the country audience when he performed

"Baby, Let's Play House" and he vowed he'd never mention Meridian again.

After high school, Elvis went to work for the Parker Machinist Shop. He also continued going to gospel singings and to the First Assembly of God Church and it was there that he met Dixie Locke, whom he later described as "kind of small with long, dark hair that came down to her shoulders and the biggest smile I've ever seen anywhere." He was a working man with a girlfriend – albeit a girlfriend who was fifteen years old.

SUNSTRUCK

He soon changed jobs, to the Precision Tool Company. That summer, 1953, he decided to finally take Bill Black's advice – in response to Elvis' wondering aloud what his voice sounded like – and dropped in at the Memphis Recording Service (also the home

The teenage Elvis with one of his first regular girlfriends, Betty Anne McMahon, on a Memphis sidewalk.

of Sun Records) to cut a record. Making such vanity records for self, family or friends was not unusual and was a large part of Sam Phillips' business. Phillips was out and his assistant Marion Keisker recorded Elvis' versions of "My Happiness" and "That's When Your Heartaches Begin." The cost: $4. Elvis naturally made friends with her and she made note of his name and address.

Then came what Elvis considered a major break. He got Johnny Burnette's old job as well as his truck at Crown Electric. Nothing changed at home, at 462 Alabama. Vernon and Gladys worked from time to time. Gladys was beginning to let it be known that Dixie Locke was somehow not quite the right girl for Elvis. Elvis started taking electrician's courses at night.

In January of 1954, he decided to go back to 706 Union Avenue. This time Sam was there, along with Marion. Elvis recorded "Casual Love Affair" and "I'll Never Stand in Your Way." Sam was noncommittal but made sure that Marion still had Elvis' phone numbers, including the one at work.

The call came in early May. Marion Keisker later said that Elvis ran in the front door before she had hung up the phone. And he had been at home when she called.

The "Class of '53." Elvis Presley graduated from L.C. Humes High School on June 3, 1953. On April 9, 1953, Elvis had performed in the school's annual Minstrel Show. Singing "Keep Them Cold Icy Fingers Off Of Me," he got the loudest applause from the student audience, which allowed him to sing an encore, his version of Teresa Brewer's "Till I Waltz Again With You."

In 1955 he gave a benefit show at the school, and years later – 1973 – the high school marching band played "Happy Birthday To You" in front of Graceland to honor his thirty-eighth birthday. Today, Graceland staff work with this inner-city school on various projects to benefit the students.

The commonly accepted story is that Sam had a song called "Without You" that he wanted Elvis to try. It didn't work out, but Sam sensed something and paired Elvis up with Bill Black and guitarist Scotty Moore. They worked for several weeks, until, as is widely known, Elvis began noodling one day in the studio with "That's All Right (Mama)," a song originally recorded by Arthur "Big Boy" Crudup. The rest, as you know, is hysteria.

Elvis blossomed incredibly quickly, both as a stage performer and as a singer. He still hadn't learned everything. After "That's All Right (Mama)" and the flip side, "Blue Moon of Kentucky," were released on July 19, 1954, the record was doing well but Sam wanted to get Elvis touring to provide support for the sales. One of the first such appearances was as opening act for country singer Slim Whitman in Memphis on July 30. A couple of days before the show, Marion took Elvis over to the local *Press-Scimitar* for his first press interview. The interviewer, Edwin Howard, said that Elvis was "absolutely inarticulate and limited himself to 'Yes sir' and 'No sir.' Marion filled in everything else." He said that "the boy's hair looked as if it had been cut by a lawn mower, but the trademarks were already there — flat-top, ducktail and sideburns."

Something happened at the Slim Whitman show at Overton Park Shell, though. In the afternoon show he did only ballads. That night, however, he speeded it up a bit and began to shake it a bit, wiggling around a little. He knew something had happened. He later said, "Everyone was screaming and everything, and my manager – Colonel Tom Parker – told me they was hollering because I was wiggling."

THE COLONEL

Not only did the Colonel – who came to be known informally as just 'Colonel' – come and steal her baby away from her for good, he had the nerve to enter Gladys' own house and perform the deed under her very roof. August 15, 1955, in the Presleys' rented home at 1414 Getwell Street: the date might as well have been written with her blood. She had sent the Colonel away once, distrusting him with a mother's instinct. He had sent in bland, amiable Hank Snow to plead troth. That was not enough. In came the trusted Bob Neal to say that things were not as they seemed. Still, she resisted. Like when she had stuck to her guns over Elvis quitting high school, she knew she was right then and she knew she was right now. But her resistance was not as strong; she was not as strong. Elvis was legally a minor: he had to have his parents' permission to sign a contract. Once with the Colonel, he was effectively gone from her forever. This she told her friends.

A picture of Gladys and Vernon taken by William Speer, a Memphis photographer. He had done some of Elvis' earliest promotional photo sessions. This picture was in Elvis' private suite upstairs before being brought down to the living room for visitors.

Even as success swirled all around Elvis, things remained on a tolerable human level through mid-1955. As the money first started rolling in the year before, they actually had fun with it. The first thing he had bought was clothes for his parents. They, pleased, went out and had a studio portrait taken of the two of them and they proudly presented it to their son. It would be the last picture taken of Gladys smiling that genuinely, with a sparkle in her eye.

Elvis bought jewelry for Minnie, and for Gladys jewelry and a pink car – a Ford, for he hadn't yet made the leap for the pink Cadillac. He bought two Mixmasters for Gladys, so she could have one at each end of the kitchen counter. Only then did he finally buy himself all the fine clothes he had been admiring down at Lansky Brothers, the flashy shop on Beale Street, where the blues singers bought their threads. Bernie Lansky became friends with Gladys and laughed about how he had never thought the skinny kid who was always window shopping at his emporium would one day come to be its favorite – and most affluent – customer.

And, just for himself, Elvis ate. He had been hungry for so many years, that now that he could indulge himself, he did so. He told *Country Song Round-up* magazine that he could polish off, in a single sitting, eight deluxe cheeseburgers, two bacon-lettuce-tomato sand-

SPECIAL AGREEMENT between ELVIS PRESLEY, known as artist, his guardians, Mr. and/or Mrs. Presley, and his manager, MR. BOB NEAL, of Memphis, Tennessee, hereinafter referred to as the Party of the First Part, and COL. THOMAS A. PARKER and/or HANK SNOW ATTRACTIONS, of Madison, Tennessee, hereinafter known as the Party of the Second Part, this date August, 15, 1955.

COL. PARKER is to act as special adviser to ELVIS PRESLEY and BOB NEAL for the period of one year and two one-year options for the sum of two thousand five hundred dollars ($2,500 per year, payable in five payments of five hundred ($500) each, to negotiate and assist in any way possible the build-up of ELVIS PRESLEY as an artist. Col. Parker will be reimbursed for any out-of-pocket expenses for traveling, promotion, advertising as approved by ELVIS PRESLEY and his manager.

As a special concession to Col. Parker, ELVIS PRESLEY is to play 100 personal appearances within one year for the special sum of $200 (two hundred dollars) including his musicians.

In the event that negotiations come to a complete standstill and ELVIS PRESLEY and his manager and associates decide to freelance, it is understood that Col. Parker will be reimbursed for the time and expenses involved in trying to negotiate the association of these parties and that he will have first call on a number of cities, as follows, at the special rate of one hundred seventy-five dollars ($175) per day for the first appearance and two hundred fifty dollars ($250) for the second appearance and three hundred fifty dollars ($350). San Antonio, El Paso, Phoenix, Tucson, Albuquerque, Oklahoma City, Denver, Wichita Falls, Wichita, New Orleans, Mobile, Jacksonville, Pensacola, Tampa, Miami, Orlando, Charleston, Greenville, Spartanburg, Asheville, Knoxville, Roanoke, Richmond, Norfolk, Washington, D.C., Philadelphia, Newark, New York, Pittsburgh, Chicago, Omaha, Milwaukee, Minneapolis, St. Paul, Des Moines, Los Angeles, Amarillo, Lubbock, Houston, Galveston, Corpus Christi, Las Vegas, Reno, Cleveland, Dayton, Akron and Columbus.

Col. Parker is to negotiate all renewals on existing contracts.

wiches, and three milkshakes. The article, entitled "Folk Music Fireball," also told the reader that Elvis liked nothing better "than to spend an afternoon practicing football with some of the youngsters in his neighborhood."

Early in 1955, the Presleys left Alabama Avenue for a modest rented four-room house on Lamar, then after only six months they moved into a two-story brick rental house – with a real lawn – at 1414 Getwell Street.

And it was there that Elvis took pen in hand and doomed himself, in Gladys' eyes. This was Elvis' first contract with the Colonel, but it has received little attention.

It wasn't too long before both Hank Snow and Bob Neal were missing in action *vis-à-vis* Elvis. November 20, 1955, when the Colonel finished finessing the deal in which he essentially bought Elvis from Sun for $30,000 and sold him to RCA for $40,000, found Hank Snow suddenly out of the picture. (Neal was gone by March of 1956.)

Increasingly distant, too, to her grief, was Gladys. As she saw her boy growing into a more confident, assertive man, she was also losing him: losing him to Colonel Parker, to the constant touring which left Elvis drained and pale and which forever blurred for him any distinction between day and night, and to the voracious demands of his new public. He was obviously torn between what in effect was a totally new life and his need for home and love. It was a struggle. An early victim of that struggle was his

Elvis in 1954 with his very first Cadillac, a secondhand Forties sedan. It wasn't his first car – that was a '51 Lincoln Continental.

girlfriend, Dixie Locke. As his absences grew longer and his phone calls shorter, she decided not to wait forever. One day toward the end of 1955, she went to Gladys and asked her to pass on the news to Elvis: Dixie was getting married. Though Elvis never really talked about it, relatives said he was both furious and deeply depressed by this summary rejection.

"ELVIS, SCOTTY AND BILL"

Still, his public waited. Elvis and Bill Black and Scotty Moore were out there in the boonies every week, knocking 'em dead. Touring on their own and with Louisiana Hayride package tours (going back to Elvis' first appearance on the Hayride on October 16, 1954, after his only appearance at Nashville's Grand Ole Opry on September 23 resulted in his not being asked back). They crossed and criss-crossed every highway from Alabama to Texas. They started out crammed in Scotty's wife's Chevrolet. Then Elvis bought a 1951 Lincoln Continental, which Bill Black wrecked. His next car was his first Cadillac, which burned up. He got the four-door 1955 Cadillac Fleetwood, which is now famous as the Pink Cadillac (it was blue when he bought it and he had it painted "Studebaker pink"), and another Cadillac.

During the first four months of 1956, Elvis' pace graduated to an even more frenetic scale: he had his first recording session in Nashville (resulting in "Heartbreak Hotel" and his first album), he appeared an unprecedented six times on *Stage Show* on CBS with the Dorsey Brothers, he had a screen test for Hal Wallis and Paramount Pictures and signed a seven year movie contract, and appeared on ABC's *Milton Berle Show,* from the deck of the aircraft carrier U.S.S. *Hancock.*

AUDUBON DRIVE

And he finally bought his mother a real house in one of Memphis' best neighborhoods, just off Park Avenue and near Audubon Park. They made it their home in March.

Home: July 4, 1956. Elvis returned by train to Memphis from New York City, to whence he had journeyed to appear on the Steve Allen TV Show and where he had recorded "Hound Dog" and "Don't Be Cruel" and "Anyway You Want Me" at the RCA studio at 155 East 24th Street. He went by train because he was still hesitant to fly. He returned to 1034 Audubon Drive, the first house he ever bought. He had paid $40,000 for it. Cash money. It was his first serious attempt to get a real home for Gladys and Vernon and

himself, something that was obviously very important to him now that he was bringing in some considerable income.

He didn't realize that a suburban ranch house was not ideally suited to the Presleys and their radically new lifestyle. Neither had Gladys realized just what a major step up the social rung this house represented: it never occurred to her that they should buy new furniture for their first real house. She had intended to just haul along all the mismatched and odd pieces of furniture they had acquired over the years. A woman friend of hers convinced her otherwise. She and Elvis went on a mammoth shopping spree buying all the modernistic pieces of furniture Memphis ever dreamt of, and then some. Even so, Gladys brought all her old furniture along.

Number 1034 Audubon Drive was the embodiment of the Fifties: a spic-and-span green rancher with black shutters and a tiled gray roof and a lush lawn. There was no front porch: an irony, because in Tupelo a porch was a status

The Audubon Drive house *(above)* received a constant stream of sightseers, a noisy mixture of genuine fans plus the just plain curious. Elvis always made them welcome, as he did throughout his life whether from the confines of army life *(top)* or the gates of Graceland.

symbol. Here, it was just the opposite. In true suburban fashion, yards blended into one another uninterrupted; no fences or walls separated neighbors.

There were now two Cadillacs in Elvis' carport, along with a constant crowd of neighbors and fans — young boys and girls, but mostly young women, some toting their babies and their Brownie cameras along with them. The fans' insistent presence would persist throughout the rest of Elvis' life. It never occurred to him that they should be or could be totally shut out.

Photographer Alfred Wertheimer accompanied

Vernon and Gladys in the carport at Audubon Drive, where already the incredible Presley automobile and motorcycle collection was beginning to take shape.

Elvis on this trip and later wrote his impression of life, Elvis-style, in mid-1956. (Wertheimer was on assignment for RCA Records and later said that all 3,800 of his pictures of Elvis were on black-and-white film because RCA didn't have enough confidence in Elvis' future to spend the extra money on color film and processing). He recalled that he was let in through the side door — the front door was seldom used — by a "graceful young blonde" who let him into the kitchen, which was the central gathering place, as in any Southern home. It was a big, casual kitchen with Formica countertops and veneered cabinets. Bowls and glasses filled the counterspace: this was a constantly busy and bustling kitchen.

Elvis, wrote Wertheimer, "had changed from his coat and tie into a collarless shirt and motorcycle cap. He had his arms around a stout woman in a baggy housedress. Her features, round and soft from age, deepened her eyes."

That was, of course, Gladys, already suffering from the excesses of success. Elvis introduced her to the photographer and she offered to get him a glass of milk or a soda. All he needed was a

place to deposit his equipment bags for a while. Gladys led him into the den. It was, he remembered, "a ranch-style room with a beamed stucco ceiling, dark wooden walls, venetian blinds and an odd mixture of Victorian and Fifties overstuffed furniture. It looked like the catchall for what didn't fit in the rest of the house. On a card table next to a standing ashtray was a portable phonograph buried under a litter of record jackets and notebooks. Newspapers filled a metal rack. A sewing table supported potted plants and paper bags. The walls held a plastic kitchen clock, a corn-cob pipe, a set of longhorns and Elvis' high school diploma."

Gladys showed Wertheimer around the house. He described the living room as a "showcase of popular contemporary design: wide, thick chairs overlaid with fabric designed with bamboo leaves or tumbling ferns, blond split-level tables, a blond hi-fi console. More brass standing ashtrays, two television sets (another was in the den) and white drapes splotched with some abstract design borrowed from Joan Miró. Scattered around were stuffed animals: tigers, monkeys, bears, dogs. Hanging on the blond, paneled wall next to the drapes was an oil copy of the 'collector's edition' publicity photo, a dreamy Elvis with his cheek resting against his clasped hands, his lips full, his eyes looking intimately at the viewer. A lamp was attached to the top of the gilt frame."

Gladys proudly pointed out to Wertheimer some of Elvis' awards hanging on the living room wall: *Cash Box* proclaiming Elvis "Most Promising Up and Coming Country Male Vocalist" for 1955, *Billboard*'s 1955 award for "Heartbreak Hotel," and the pride of Gladys' eye: the gold record for "Heartbreak Hotel." The

21

little gold disc framed on a background of green felt represented the phenomenal surge in Elvis' career. The record sold 300,000 copies in the three weeks following its release on January 27, 1956, was number one on the pop charts for eight weeks, went to number one country and number five on the R&B chart. It was Elvis' first million seller, although the RIAA — the Recording Industry Association of America which certifies gold and platinum records – was not formed until 1958, RCA awarded gold records itself to its artists. When the "Jailhouse Rock" EP sold more than a million copies in 1957, RCA gave Elvis a splendid trophy instead of a gold record: a fake gold column atop a gleaming black marble base, on which sat little figurines of Nipper, the trademark dog, and his gramophone. He received a similar trophy for his second album, "Elvis."

But Gladys treasured that first little gold record. Wertheimer said he saw in her at that moment "the excitement of a mother's pride [that] lifted her deep eyes and, for a moment, gave Gladys Presley a joyful youth she seemed to have missed."

Elvis tipped his biker's cap and went outside to ride his big Harley-Davidson. A crowd of about thirty people watched from their vantage point in the carport — apparently their designated place, just as the area outside the gates at Graceland would later serve the same function — as he tried and failed to turn over the big Harley's engine. At last Vernon walked out and found a wrench and fixed whatever was wrong while Elvis signed a few autographs as he sat on the Harley.

On June 30, just a few days before, Elvis had given a show in

Drinks on the patio. From virtually abject poverty, Vernon and Gladys found themselves catapulted into a lifestyle of leisure, entertaining, and generally being host and hostess. No doubt their circle of "friends" grew amazingly, but for a while life was definitely sweeter than it had ever been.

Richmond, Virginia, at the Mosque Theater and afterwards had sat for a press conference. Besides the usual questions about girlfriends ("Well, when the right one comes along, maybe I'll settle down, but right now I haven't found the right one. I like all girls. I like 'em all."), he was asked if he had a fence around his house.

"No sir," he answered, "we just have a big front lawn." Well, then, he was asked, did it bother him when the fans came round?

"It's not nice when they trample down the grass, but I don't mind people coming up into the driveway. Sometimes Ma will invite them in to have some sandwiches or sit around the pool."

That afternoon he rode out to the approving nods of the fans who said things along the lines of "Doesn't he look good?"

After giving a ride to an adoring young neighbor, Elvis took Wertheimer out for a spin on the Harley and promptly ran out of gas on a country road. Wertheimer offered to hike off to try to find a gas station but Elvis told him to stay put and wait and not worry.

Sure enough, the first young woman who drove by slammed on her brakes when she spotted Elvis standing by the side of the road. He had plenty of gas in no time. Elvis' currency: a kiss. Back at 1034, Gladys sat worried, keeping a vigil out in the yard. "We ran out of gas," Elvis told her and that's all he said.

His fans stood around and waited, as Wertheimer said he felt at the time, for the "next event." It was as if Elvis was already on twenty-four-hour call. Elvis as Spectator Sport. He drank a cold Pepsi out of the bottle on the patio with Vernon and his cousin Bobby Smith. Then he went inside and soon reappeared in swimming trunks. The pool was new and the pump wasn't working, so Vernon was filling the pool with a garden hose and it thus was only partially full. Gladys and Minnie sat in the shade as Elvis and a few young friends dove in. Suddenly Elvis called out: "Ma!" She hurried down to the edge of the pool to see what was wrong.

"Ma, I left my watch on."

He removed it and handed it to her and looked on anxiously as she dried it with her dress.

"Ma, is it still working?"

She shook it and held it up to her ear. "I think it'll be fine, son. I'll take care of it."

Thus reassured, he dove back underwater. He tried and tried and finally convinced his father to try the pool. Vernon advanced only as far as the water was thigh-deep and stood there, rather rigid, before leaving. Elvis was letting go after his road trip. Vernon seemed to never let go. The picture Wertheimer took of that moment tells much about Presley père et fils. Elvis looks younger than his 21 years and seems to want to just bang around in the pool like a teenager. Vernon is standing almost at attention, ramrod-stiff, defensive, apprehensive, paranoid even.

Things lightened up as the "event" moved inside. A bunch of the kids came in. As Elvis was going off to shower to get ready for that evening's show at Russwood Stadium, Gladys presented her son with a clean pair of white jockey shorts that she had ironed for him. He gave her a kiss and a thank-you.

While Elvis was showering, Wertheimer asked Gladys if he could photograph the family photo album. He was surprised when she agreed. "She was just being polite," Wertheimer wrote, "but I wondered how a house this open could remain a home."

From down the hall, Wertheimer heard the strains of "Don't Be Cruel." Elvis had returned from his shower and was standing by his blond hi-fi console set. He was wearing only slacks and dark socks and his hair was uncombed.

Grandmother Minnie, with her elegant marcelled hair, long dress, and turn-of-the-century black lace-up shoes, leant forward on the big sofa and strained to make out the words of the song that she was hearing for the first time. Next to her on the couch sat Elvis' current girlfriend, Barbara Hearn. She was very pretty, with short brown hair and she had decked herself out in a white

with blue polka-dots, form-fitting sleeveless dress, dark, heeled pumps and white cluster earrings. She sat leaning forward during the song, legs crossed demurely at the ankles, her purse on her lap. There was a large teddy bear on the couch behind her.

"Let's dance," Elvis said to her. She demurred. He persisted. "Come on. It's okay."

Minnie got up and made for her bedroom, to get ready for Elvis' show that evening.

Elvis and Barbara began dancing, she very reluctantly. Oddly, although this session with Wertheimer was Elvis' first exposure to having a camera trained on him at virtually all times, he seemed able to completely tune out the photographer's presence. He was truly able to live out his life in public.

Barbara sat down, saying she wanted to listen to the record. Elvis pouted momentarily. His mood lifted when she told him how much she liked "Don't Be Cruel."

"Do you want to hear the other song?"

He put on "Any Way You Want Me" and gathered her in what Wertheimer remembered as an "awkward embrace." He decided to leave them alone and went to take a peek at Elvis' bedroom.

The room struck him as having "more color than Technicolor Cinemascope. On pastel-yellow wallpaper speckled with blue and orange hung leaping ceramic minstrels on black oval plaques. White-quilted bedspreads painted with pink and blue flowers covered the twin beds and overflowed into rose satin trim. Blue puppies rested against the blond headboards of the twin beds."

Once again, Wertheimer cursed RCA for limiting him to black-and-white film.

Although Colonel Parker was in town for the show that evening, he very pointedly stayed away from the house, as he would do during the rest of his association with Elvis. Elvis had clearly drawn a dividing line there. The Colonel did show up at 1034 that evening, but only to collect his "boy" and make sure he got to the show. He had a black-and-white police car waiting out by the curb, engine running, an officer at the wheel. Elvis, Colonel Parker and Wertheimer rode in the police car and Vernon, Gladys, Minnie and Barbara followed in a Cadillac. Tom Diskin, Parker's right-hand man, was waiting to guide the Presley entourage to good seats. It was a benefit show for St. Jude

Children's Research Hospital, with 14,000 present and it was the first time Wertheimer got to see Elvis really pull out all the stops on stage. Elvis was wearing a striking black suit with a black shirt and a flaming red tie and he was a nonstop blur of movement on the stage. That crowd didn't need any Fourth of July fireworks after Elvis.

The minute he was gone from the stage and the police had him in a squad car, tires burning, squealing out of the parking lot, Colonel Parker broke open a package of souvenir pictures of Elvis. "Getcher souvenir photographs!"

He was selling them for a dime apiece and soon collected pocketfuls of dimes. He and Diskin and Wertheimer rode back to their motel in a station wagon crammed with boxes of pictures and souvenir programs. Wertheimer wondered aloud why there were no prices marked on them.

The Colonel took his unlit cigar out of his mouth and looked off down the road before answering.

"Wertheimer," he finally said, "you never want to put a price on anything. In Vegas, we might sell them for two dollars. Here, we sell them for a dime. People only appreciate something they pay for. If you give it to them for nothing, it won't be appreciated."

Wertheimer realized the Colonel was "just looking out for his boy's best interests. I never got close to Elvis again." In fact, in the fall of 1956, at the Colonel's specific request, control of all of Elvis' publicity shifted from RCA to the Colonel and he was given all of RCA's

Vanity case, purse and wallet – typical examples of the Elvis merchandise boom. Below, Elvis is presented with some souvenir sneakers by beaming manufacturers.

publicity files. Access to Elvis became the Colonel's exclusive prerogative and he guarded it as tightly as he did the handfuls of dimes earned from those souvenir pictures.

Elvis soon had to install a fence around 1034 Audubon and a gate to discourage the growing numbers of fans who were showing up twenty-four hours a day. Neighbors began complaining, not only about the crowds of people and cars, but also about Gladys' practice of hanging laundry out on a clothesline in the backyard. If only they had known that Gladys wished she had a bigger yard, so she could keep chickens. She had always enjoyed having chickens in the yard and missed that. The neighbors got their heads and wallets together and actually offered to buy Elvis out, if the Presley clan would just pack up and leave. Elvis had a little research done and discovered that he was the only one on the block who owned his home outright. So he offered to buy all of them out. Things were not pretty.

HOLLYWOOD

Still, they had barely moved in, so decided to see how things would go. Besides, Elvis was constantly busy. That August, he left for Los Angeles to begin shooting his first movie, *Love Me Tender*, for Paramount. Elvis moved into the Beverley Wiltshire Hotel for an extended stay. When he had come out to L.A. for a screen test with Hal Wallis on April 1 and for an appearance on *The Milton Berle Show* on ABC, he had stayed at the Knickerbocker (in New York City, home away from home had been the Warwick Hotel on West 54th Street). Hotel living was

already beginning to wear on him: his two-week engagement at the New Frontier Hotel in Las Vegas from April 23 to May 9, 1956, had not been a one hundred percent success due to the age and temperament of the audience, plus he was virtually trapped in a hotel room the entire time.

Still, during the course of the first four movies, made before he went into the army (*Love Me Tender* in 1956, *Loving You* in

Elvismania knew no bounds in the mid-Fifties, but right up to the point where it became a physical danger, Elvis was anxious to meet his fans face to face.

1957, *Jailhouse Rock* in 1957, and *King Creole* in 1958), the Beverley Wiltshire was home away from home. Fans packed the lobby and room service was Elvis' greatest adventure.

At a rare press conference in Memphis, in a break from *Love Me Tender*, he allowed a crack to show in the facade: "I feel like a bird who's been let out of his cage and wants to fly a little. I want to flap my wings. I want to feel sure I'm free again. I never know what I want to do, but I sure want to do something that has nothing to do with this [movie] business."

When Elvis came back from filming his first movie, *Love Me Tender* he brought an aura of Hollywood with him that Gladys found off-putting. He also brought along as a sort of sidekick the actor Nick Adams (who had introduced Elvis to all the hip young actors, such as Sal Mineo and Dennis Hopper and Natalie Wood. Especially

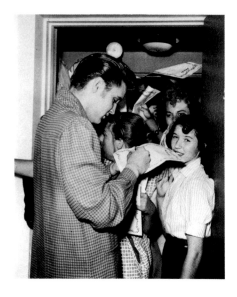

Natalie Wood). Adams had performed a similar role for the actor James Dean, who had been killed the year before when his Porsche crashed, but there's also reason to believe Colonel Parker put him on the payroll and assigned him to the growing Elvis entourage (which for a time included the Colonel's own brother-in-law, Bitsy Mott) to keep an eye on Elvis, even at home.

Even when the Presleys made their triumphant return to Tupelo on September 26, 1956, for "Elvis Presley Day" at the Mississippi-Alabama Fair – the guitar-shaped "Key to the City" Elvis was presented with is on display at Graceland – Nick was on stage with Elvis, mumbling into the microphone that he had known James Dean.

That could have been Gladys' proudest day—she had sewn a pretty blue velvet shirt for Elvis and wore what became her public outfit: a brocade dress and a souvenir pendant with a picture of Elvis engraved on it.

Elvis gave his proceeds from the show to the City of Tupelo to start funding a future Elvis Presley Youth Center to be located beside his birthplace. There was one catch: Elvis' donations (he played the fair again in 1957) were contingent upon Orville Bean selling the old Berry Street site to the city for $500. That happened in 1957, to the Presleys' great satisfaction.

Elvis and all went home long enough

for Elvis to make local headlines by punching out a gas-station jockey, who had slapped him on the back of the head and told him to move on out of his gas station. Elvis had been stuck there signing autographs. He blackened Ed Hooper's eye nicely. Elvis was cleared of any charges.

He went off to play *The Ed Sullivan Show* for the second time and got back in time to pick up Natalie Wood at the Memphis Airport on Halloween Day in his new Continental Mark II. His hair was dyed jet black when he got home. Gladys was about to get her first Hollywood

Newspaper ads for Elvis at the Mississippi–Alabama Fair and Dairy Show in 1956 and 1957, a stark contrast with coast-to-coast prime-time television *(below)* on *The Ed Sullivan Show.*

house guest. It was fairly anticlimactic. Natalie was a "nice girl" who was obviously crazy about Elvis. They spent most of their time doing the things Elvis liked to do: riding his Harley around town, going for burgers at different joints, and causing mob scenes by driving the Mark II down to the Chisca Hotel and visiting Dewey Phillips during his radio show.

Natalie returned to Hollywood on November 8 and Gladys had Elvis all to herself for all of November and December. It was a luxury she hadn't enjoyed in some time and one which she would never have again. They talked about the future and how he would cut back on the touring. He said it would be nice to buy

a big farm somewhere outside Memphis, where they would always be together and the relatives could all come and visit and Gladys could have her chickens and farm animals again.

In late December, Hal Kanter, who was to write the screenplay for Elvis' next movie, *Loving You,* came to visit and traveled with Elvis to Shreveport for a Hayride concert. Kanter later wrote in *Variety* about an anonymous young pop star and what was happening to him during his meteoric rise to fame: "But after a year, there were no more clothes to buy; there was no more good food to be wanted; there was no room for more Cadillacs or motorcycles; the home appliances were all bought and paid for; the future was assured; Mom and Dad had nothing left to desire, for they had all they could ever use."

The Presleys enjoyed a quiet Christmas at home. On December 31, the *Wall Street Journal* reported that sales of Elvis merchandise had reached $22 million only six months after first appearing.

On January 4, Elvis had his pre-induction physical at the Kennedy Veterans Hospital, not far from the Presleys' old house on Getwell Street. He was 1-A.

On the 6th, he made his third *Ed Sullivan* appearance. He was shown only from the waist up; interesting that he be censored so relatively late in his TV career. Sullivan made his famous statement that "this is a decent, fine boy," which was some comfort to Gladys, especially after that unpleasant episode in 1956 when a Baptist preacher had denounced Elvis in the pages of *Life* magazine as an apostle of "degeneracy."

Elvis left for Los Angeles to begin preproduction work on *Loving You.* He left behind a mother who was ecstatic because Elvis had invited her to come join him in L.A. for a month. On the other hand, she had to get up out of a hospital bed to make the trip: she was bloated and apparently had gallstones. She declined surgery, heading instead for Lowenstein's Department Store for some new clothes suitable for Hollywood. She and Vernon decided to ask their new friends Carl and Willy Nichols to go with them. Carl was the contractor who had installed their new swimming pool. They took the train across the country and had a big time. Gladys sang a lot: she had a lovely voice. They went on the movie set and Elvis showed them the stars' homes,

Both his debut film, the Civil War drama *Love Me Tender (above),* and his second movie, *Loving You (below),* were in a far superior league to the formula-driven films that Elvis got saddled with in the Sixties.

especially Red Skelton's, which apparently impressed Gladys greatly.

Gladys went home in a better frame of mind, ready to find their dream farm.

GRACELAND

Graceland was built with music poured into its very foundations. Dr. and Mrs. Thomas D. Moore finished it in 1939, on a hilly, heavily wooded thirteen-and-three-quarter-acre site then way out in the country on the two-lane Highway 51 that connected Memphis and Jackson, Mississippi. The site is actualy closer to the Mississippi state line than it is to downtown Memphis proper.

Although the name "Graceland" came to refer specifically to the house, originally it applied to the entire 500-acre spread, which was established as a Hereford cattle farm in 1861, by S.E. Toof, the publisher of the Memphis *Commercial Appeal.* It was named "Graceland" after his daughter, Grace Toof. Ruth Moore, who built Graceland the house, was Grace's niece. Over the years, various pieces of the farm were developed into Graceland subdivision and the Whitehaven Plaza Shopping Center.

"Our entire home is centered around music," a proud Mrs. Moore told a reporter from the Memphis *Commercial Appeal* in 1940. "We planned it for our daughter, Ruth Marie, who has played the harp and piano since she was four. The rooms have been designed with an eye to future musical evenings, and space was essential, not only for seating purposes but for tone volume." Ruth Marie was fourteen when the family moved in to the house and she confidently posed for a picture with her gold-inlaid concert grand harp in the drawing room, which would one day be Elvis Presley's living room. Ruth Marie went on to join the prestigious Memphis Symphony Orchestra.

A *Commercial Appeal* headline for Sunday, October 27, 1940, heralded the "Colonial Courtliness of Georgian Style Exemplified in Stately 'Graceland.'" A subhead declared that an "Air of Subtle Elegance Pervades Moore Manor."

The *Commercial Appeal*'s reporter, Ida Clemens, gushed enthusiastically that "Much like a poem which echoes the loveliness of trees and sky — and architectural perfection — is enchanting 'Graceland,' country home of Dr. and Mrs. T.D. Moore. Located well back from Highway 51 in a grove of towering oaks, it stands proudly on land that has been in the family nearly a century. As you roll up the drive, you sense the fine heritage of the past in its general feeling of aristocratic kindness and tranquility."

Like the White House, the neoclassical facade of Graceland has become the trademark of a national institution. Little could its original owners imagine that it would come to embody an aspect of American popular culture.

Clearly inspired, the pensmith continued her detailed account of the Moore residence: "Polished with the quiet manners characteristic of today's beauty, the palatial home is a noteworthy example of the Georgian Colonial style. White Tishomingo stone was shipped in for its construction, and it is shuttered in contrasting green. Symbolic of the Georgian is its front entrance of majestic Corinthian columns. Coach lamps in gold bronze flank the hospitable door and a larger lamp lights the porch.

"An air of subtle luxury that pervades the exterior seeps through the walls and penetrates every room in the house. Extending across the entire front are the reception hall, drawing room and solarium. When I tell you that the four rooms [sic] can seat an audience of 500, you have an idea of their spacious proportions."

After what sounded like an awestruck description of the many and wondrous antiques in the house, the reporter resumed a blow-by-blow tour of the wonderland. "Adding to the graciousness of the [dining] room are cornices for decorative display of more fine china and glassware, and a picture window framing the trees on the grounds beyond. Draperies of French blue damask draw cozily together at night but leave the enchanting view unobstructed by day. Taking a reluctant leave of the dining room, I entered the drawing room and immediately winced at the futility of trying to capture such loveliness in the written word. Center of interest is the

fireplace carved in Colonial motif and faced in white marble. A wall of glass blocks separates the drawing room from the solarium (which would later serve as Elvis' Music Room). Also included in the first-floor plan are a guest room, breakfast room, kitchen, and service rooms. The basement houses a den, library and two game rooms. Four bedrooms and four baths on the second floor complete this family manor, one of the most outstanding homes in Memphis." The glass blocks referred to were first of all covered with drapes by Elvis, then much later were taken out completely and stored in the barn when the stained glass peacocks were installed in the room division in 1974.

REAL ESTATE

The process of Elvis' purchase of Graceland naturally took on a certain amount of high drama. His neighbors on Audubon Drive were mounting a whispering campaign against the Presleys. Several months earlier, in September of 1956, Gladys had told friends that Elvis was receiving over a thousand letters a week at 1034 Audubon Drive and that fully

There had been Frank Sinatra's "bobby soxers" in the Forties, and the Johnnie Ray fanatics of the early Fifties, but fan hysteria reached near-riot proportions when Elvis took to the stage.

half of them were addressed to her and Vernon, accusing them of fomenting juvenile delinquency, and worse, through their "obscene" son. She was shaken to her very core: how could Gladys defend her son against such an unseen enemy? To make matters worse, Elvis had reverted to his childhood practice of sleepwalking. That was the main reason for the presence of someone with Elvis all the time, which later built into such an

entourage: Gladys insisted that Elvis never be alone. At first, it was her sister Levalle's children, Junior and Gene Smith. Junior had accompanied Elvis every step of the way on his last New York trip. Elvis had to be protected, Gladys dictated.

There was also the memory of the first full-fledged "Elvis riot," which had taken place at the Gator Bowl in Jacksonville, Florida, May 13, 1955. Police protection completely broke down and hundreds of screaming girls chased Elvis into his dressing room and tore his clothes from his body. They scratched lascivious messages into the paint of his car and wrote on it with lipstick. Elvis later made light of the episode, telling a reporter, "Mom and Dad still haven't gotten over all this hoopla about me. Mama was down in Florida once when the girls mobbed me and she was afraid they were hurting me. Shucks, they were only tearing my clothes. I didn't mind a bit. I told her, 'Mama, if you're going to feel that way, you'd better not come along to my shows because that stuff is going to keep on happening — I hope.'" Gladys only worried the more after she and Vernon went with Elvis to a performance at a dance — previously she had been only to her son's concerts — in Mississippi. When things got heated up, the girls left their partners and rushed the stage, eager to get to Elvis. Gladys fought through the crowd to "rescue" her son. It was an uneasy moment for both Gladys and Elvis. He didn't want to be rescued.

I hope it does not surprise you to learn that the realtor who sold Graceland to Elvis wrote a book about the transaction. A booklet, actually. There wasn't all that much to say, I guess, about the real-estate deal itself. Still, Virginia Grant, the realtor, found a great deal of drama in her dealings with the Presleys, and I don't blame her one bit. She named her booklet *How Elvis Bought Graceland: Exactly As It Happened.* Copyrighted and all that.

Our story begins, if I may quote from Virginia Grant, "at exactly 1:55 p.m., on Tuesday, February 11, 1957. I was in Lowenstein's East, one of Memphis' major department stores. The appointment with my client was for 2:00 p.m., at which time I was to meet him at the main entrance of the store, for the purpose of showing him some property. As I stepped outside to see if he had arrived, I saw directly before my eyes one of the most gorgeous pink Cadillacs I have ever seen. Now, I have always had a secret ambition to own one of these fabulous automobiles, so naturally, I would look to see who is inside this beautiful vehicle."

Well, after several hundred words, we learn that it is none other than Gladys sitting in this fabulous car.

After he had it specially sprayed that color, Elvis' pink Cadillac became a universal symbol of rock'n'roll.

After Grant raps on the closed window to get Gladys' attention, they chat for a while and Gladys learns that her new friend is in fact a realtor, who remarks, "I heard that you folks would be interested in finding a good farm." Gladys said that was untrue but that they actually would like to find a few acres with a big house somewhere out of town. Grant said that she had a nice seven-acre site. Gladys said that she and Vernon — who was inside buying luggage — were leaving that very day for Los Angeles to visit with Elvis but they would welcome any referrals upon their return.

Then, wouldn't you know it, on Grant's day off, Saturday, March 17, when she's just cancelled her weekly appointment at the beauty salon because she's stuck in bed with a virus, the phone rings and it's Presley. Vernon, that is, and he wants to see this house she had talked about. Well, as you can imagine, the rest of the day is something of a blur of hurried arrangements to meet the Presleys at Lowenstein's South, as opposed to Lowenstein's East, the site of their first preliminary negotiation.

Then the fateful journal entry: "3:30 p.m. The white 1956 Continental turns into the entrance of Whitehaven Plaza Shopping Center. It's a beauty and cost Elvis $11,650. I'd know it anywhere, and think it is safe to say that it is the only one of its kind in the South. At least, it's the only one I've seen, and I always look at cars. Like houses, they fascinate me. So, I'm happy again! They did keep their appointment after all, and right on time, too! Even though I so graciously offered to drive them out in my two-tone Pontiac Catalina, they suggested that they follow me out to see the property which we had come to see, and after a vague interest on their part, which I could also detect, Mrs. Presley informs me that if they should buy this property, they would have to build a large Colonial home as that is the type of home Elvis wants. The ranch-style home of more than 3,500 square feet, which heretofore had looked fine to them, would be used as a stable for their horses, as it sits back in the woods quite a distance from the road. I have always heard that to undersell your client is as dangerous as overselling, but not being accustomed to dealing with this type of client in my everyday business, I had made the error of showing them property of a much lesser value than they expected to buy.

Fortunately for me, I discovered my mistake immediately, so not too much damage was done. Just then, Mrs. Presley turned to me and asked, 'Don't you have anything to show us with a Colonial home?' Without hesitation, and as if God Himself put the thought in my mind and the words on my tongue, I immediately picked Graceland as the home for them, though I had never been in the house myself. 'Oh yes,' I said, 'On Highway 51 South as you approach Whitehaven Plaza, there is the most beautiful Colonial mansion which a friend of mine has for sale — thirteen beautiful acres, too!'"

Naturally, Gladys wanted to see it that very day. The listing was with another realtor, Hugh Bosworth, and so the beleaguered Mrs. Grant had to find Bosworth on Saturday afternoon, "which I have often found hard to do."

The private swimming pool — long the status symbol of the rich and famous.

So off they drove to Graceland, which was vacant, apart from being temporarily used for church services by the Graceland Christian Church. Mrs. Ruth Brown Moore was separated from her husband and had moved to 2405 Union Extended and not only was letting the congregation use her house for worship, but had just donated four and a half acres of land for the church's future site. (After Graceland Christian Church was built, right next door to Graceland, it became a bit overworked, as tourists and visitors from everywhere automatically assumed that it was "Elvis' church" and wandered in and out, using the facilities at will, changing clothes and bedding down and what not. During the week of Elvis' death and funeral, it came under siege and the church's grounds were totally denuded of grass and leaves. Recognizing the old real estate adage that "location is everything," the church moved. (The site is now the headquarters of Elvis Presley Enterprises.)

Gladys loved the house, and so Vernon had to too. As Mrs. Grant observed, "I could think of nothing more perfect for the Presleys, and a perfect spot for a swimming pool which Elvis must have wherever he goes."

By 6 p.m., an increasingly ebullient Mrs. Grant had their offer tucked away firmly in her briefcase, "together with the proper amount of earnest money. Elvis will be home from Hollywood Monday and the offer is contingent on the approval of Elvis Presley, not later than 8:00 p.m.,Monday, March 19th."

Vernon later said it was a very good deal, in that they got $55,000 for the house on Audubon Drive and "that was just about what we had in it." So, with the trade-in, Elvis paid only $45,000 for the house and grounds. Surely it must have been the best investment of his life.

It wasn't until Mrs. Grant returned to her office that the sheer enormity of her task fully settled upon her shoulders: "Oh Lord! What have I done? It was unbelievable! It seemed that I had found a home for the great Elvis Presley, for sure! I stayed on 'Cloud 9' all weekend."

On the Monday, Elvis unexpectedly showed up very early in the morning, further taxing Mrs. Grant's wits and her ability to beat the Memphis speed limit. She recalled: "I simply refused to be late! Now, I have seen Elvis every way except in person, so this is the big day! I had heard of the soul-shattering effects of meeting in person that human A-Bomb, Elvis Presley! I found him to be quite as his mother had described him to me — very polite, quiet, and very loving and respectful toward his parents. I think he's the greatest!"

SETTLERS

Elvis Presley walked slowly through Graceland for the first time and sat down to play the piano. He got up and remarked that the place "sure needs a lot of work done on it." Mrs. Grant's heart sank. He continued, "This is going to be a lot nicer than Red Skelton's house when I get it like I want it." Mrs. Grant's heart soared. Elvis was ready to sign, and wanted to close the deal as soon as possible.

Naturally, that meant that Mrs. Grant had to drop by the house on Audubon Drive at least once, and she got to see Elvis modeling his new gold suit.

She was also awakened one morning by a reporter from the Memphis *Press-Scimitar*, who wanted the scoop on Elvis and his new house. Mrs. Grant told her it was a secret. "It's all over the morning paper," the reporter told her.

"Well," said Mrs. Grant to herself, "if that's true, I might as well let her in on the 'goodies,' so I proceeded to give her a good story, and I'll say this for her — she really gave us wonderful coverage every day for almost a week."

Elvis told the reporter, "I want the darkest blue there is for my room, with a mirror that will cover one side of the room. I probably will have a black bedroom suite, trimmed in white leather, with a white rug." He also said he intended to have a hi-fi receiver in every room and that he wanted the entrance hall painted to resemble the sky, with clouds on the ceiling and dozens of tiny lights for the stars.

Gladys for her part said, "I think I am going to like this new home. We will have a lot more privacy and a lot more room to put some of the things we have accumulated over the last few years."

Vernon, predictably, complained that "we just had the old place fixed up like we wanted it. Now we have to start all over again. Moving is going to be a problem." He did find one bright spot: "A moving company has said they will move us free of charge."

Elvis remarked that the bathrooms in the basement were marked "Boys" and "Girls" (How soon Colonel would muzzle all these unauthorized interviews!) and that he thought the first thing the house needed was "a swimming pool on the south side of the house, with a large sunken patio leading up to the pool." He also said he wanted a six-foot stone fence across the front and up the sides of the property. He further said that he had already ordered purple wallcovering with gold trim for the living room, dining room, and sun (music) room, with white corduroy drapes.

Gladys said she wasn't so sure about purple, that she might prefer some lighter colors.

Elvis also noted the house had garage space for only four cars (in what became an apartment on the north end of the house). At the time he had his Mark II Continental, three Cadillacs, a three wheel Messerschmidt (which he later traded to Bernie Lansky for a mess of clothes) and his Harley motorcycle.

So, all that press coverage all week thrilled Mrs. Grant until Sunday. She was in Raleigh, showing a house, when she got a panicky call from her husband. It developed that Memphis' teenagers still read newspapers and figured out where Graceland was and they were out there swarming all over the place, hauling off everything they could find as an Elvis souvenir.

So the police got their first taste of life at 3764 U.S. Highway 51.

On closing day, Mrs. Grant and Mr. Bosworth went by Audubon Drive to take the Presleys downtown to the law offices of Evans, Petree and Cobb, in the Commerce Title Building.

Imagine their astonishment to find the Presleys entertaining guests while Elvis — with his new monkey, Scatter, perched on his shoulder — was shooting pool out in the den.

Mrs. Grant just could not get them to follow realty protocol: "It so happened that Mr. and Mrs. Presley decided to go to the closing in one of the fleet of Cadillacs, and Elvis chose to drive alone in his little red sports car with no top, his latest purchase before buying Graceland. We had hoped that he would ride with us so that we might protect him from the usual mobs of screaming teenagers, as we felt certain that he would be detained along the way for many hours — until much, much too late to have a closing."

People found it hard to believe that Elvis loved the mobs. Only a couple of nights before the closing on the sale of Graceland, Elvis was bored. He jumped in his Mark II, alone, and drove around town for a while. The *Press-Scimitar* reported that "Elvis tooled his 1956 Continental Mark II $11,575 auto into the parking lot across from Hotel Chisca at 10:30 last night, just as the Traffic Safety banquet was breaking up. A typical Elvis jam session resulted, with so many teenagers about that the car couldn't be moved for some time. Commissioner and Mrs. Stanley Dillard and Capt. and Mrs. Joe Griffin (he is a school safety officer) came out of the safety banquet and watched the scene with amazement. Mrs. Dillard and Mrs. Griffin wanted to get closer. Soon Commissioner Dillard was shaking hands with Elvis and Mrs. Dillard said she got him into it. Stanley said he admires Presley. Elvis will leave Wednesday for Chicago to open a 10-day road trip. So there won't be any jam scenes with teenagers until he returns. And the mustache may be a lot more noticeable by the time he gets back (he was toying with growing a mustache.)

Back at the closing, Elvis made his way there on his own, to Mrs. Grant's relief. Elvis picked up a newspaper and began reading about his purchase.

"Of course," Mrs. Grant harumphed, "the Presleys preferred to have no publicity on the purchase of Graceland before it was actually transferred, but news of Elvis has always leaked out fast, and there was no way to keep it out of the papers."

There was a side deal involved that didn't quite go through. An (unidentified) chewing gum company wanted to buy all the wood paneling from the house on Audubon Drive and cut it up into little gum-size pieces: buy a pack of gum, get a piece of Elvis' house inside the pack, absolutely free! Vernon went off to call Colonel, who nixed the offer: he already had a different gum company lined up for a different deal. Elvis said that was too bad, because "It was a cute little gimmick."

HOME

The Graceland that the Presleys moved into in late April of 1957 was vastly different from what the house and compound became over the years. The front of the house looks very much the same. The only physical addition to the front of the physical plant itself was the addition of iron grillwork over the doors and windows.

But in 1957, there was just the house, the barn, and the little smokehouse or wellhouse behind the house. Nothing else. No stone fence, no gates, no outbuildings, no carport, no swimming pool, no Meditation Garden, no Trophy Room, no bath house, no racquetball court, no Jungle Room addition: just open land.

After the walls and gates went up, Gladys got to have her chickens again and got to hang out washing behind Graceland.

The interior of the house changed slowly. When Elvis took occupancy, the house covered 10,266 square feet (compared to 17,552 today, excluding the racquetball court).

Elvis took the second floor as his private domain, as it was to remain over the years, except for his grandmother's room which eventually became Lisa Marie's nursery in 1968. People could come and go downstairs pretty much as they pleased, but there was an invisible — but very real — line drawn across the great stairway leading up from the entrance hall. His bedroom was much as he had described it to the *Press-Scimitar* reporter: blue, with the black and white furniture and white rug.

He didn't get his wish

The barn, which now houses the horses' stables, is an enduring reminder of the rural origins of Graceland.

with the purple walls downstairs. Gladys' more understated taste prevailed, and long marked the Graceland decor. Sadly, Gladys didn't get to fulfill her dream of slowly decorating the house with Elvis. He was off making his third movie, *Jailhouse Rock.* Instead, Goldsmith's department store became her surrogate decorator. She was, by most accounts, a bit bewildered by all that had happened. Now she was surrounded by cooks and maids and couldn't walk down the street to go to the grocery store (and she never did drive). She would go out in one of her house dresses and feed the chickens and carry a lawn chair down to the gate to visit her brother Travis when he worked the day shift there. She would sit there and dip snuff and watch the world go by. In those days, letting the fans onto the grounds was commonplace, especially when Elvis was out of town. Gladys would sit out in the shade and be completely unrecognized by the fans strolling by. Sometimes, she would introduce herself and show them through the house. Relatives later said that she complained about being virtually left alone by Elvis and by Vernon. Her health became a matter of concern. What would apparently later kill her (there was no autopsy, at the wish of Elvis and Vernon) was hepatitis, exacerbated by alcohol consumption and diet pills. Her doctor thought it was gallstones bothering her and urged her to enter the hospital. She refused.

During the infrequent periods when Elvis was home, he became impatient with the slow pace of reconstruction and decorating. He wanted everything done immediately, which is the way he had gotten used to things happening when he was out on

Just as Graceland came to symbolize Elvis, so the gates came to symbolize Graceland. Never mere prison bars for some reclusive star, they are now a way for ordinary folk to enter the world of the king of rock'n'roll.

the road or on a movie set.

By some accounts, Elvis spent upwards of half a million dollars on Graceland the first year alone, inside and out. The wall surrounding the grounds, made of Alabama fieldstone, was $65,000. The iron gates, designed for Elvis by Abe Saucer and custom-built by Doors Inc. of Memphis, were $2,400. He also had the pool put in, and enlarged the patio considerably.

He was away so much that first year that each time he got home, the place looked different. After that, redecorating became natural for him, a way of life. D.J. Fontana, the drummer who worked for Elvis off and on from 1955 to 1969, later recalled Elvis' love of colors. "White shoes, white belt, black pegged pants. He was like that from the first day I met him. That was the way he dressed. He'd put together colors that would look awful on you or me, but he could pull it off; it would look right on him." Even people who didn't know him in high school remarked on that. Bill Leaptrott, who became friends with Elvis after both graduated from Humes High, remembered that "We all wore Levis — but I remember that Elvis had two pairs of pants, both made of gabardine: one pair was black with a white stripe down the side, and the other was black with a pink stripe." Fontana recalled how Elvis would "invite me over to his place in Memphis and say, 'Come on in, I want you to see the house.' And I'd say, 'But, Elvis, I just saw it three weeks ago when I was here.' 'No, no,' he'd reply. 'I just redecorated it!' On one occasion my wife went over with me to the house. After we left, she said, 'You know, those colors just don't go together. But the way he does it looks right!' "

The Christmas of 1957 found Elvis and his family at last settled comfortably into Graceland. And if ever a house was perfectly suited to the celebration of Christmas in a totally traditional style, Graceland was it.

The white carpet was finally down in the Dining Room, the Living Room and the Music Room. The fireplaces were glowing and the big white tree was up in the north end of the Dining Room. It was covered with red ornaments, and presents were piled high around it. The big kitchen was full of the delectable aromas of turkey and dressing.

As friends and relatives gathered for Christmas, it was a perfect scene of warmth and gaiety.

Christmas at Graceland has been a major event before and since Elvis' death.

ABSENCE

Still, a certain malaise hung in the air, owing mainly to Gladys' obvious unease. Elvis had been gone most of the year, just when she thought the family would finally coalesce around Graceland. He had toured extensively, mainly through the Northwest, Canada (his only shows outside the United States), and Hawaii. They would be his last tours until the Seventies, although, of course, no one could know that.

Then there was the unspoken matter of the movie *Jailhouse Rock*, which Elvis finished before moving into Graceland. Its story line uncomfortably intertwines the supposed life story of Elvis with Vernon's own stay in prison, the secret the Presleys had been sitting on for eighteen years. The movie's world premiere was in Memphis but neither Elvis nor his family attended. They very carefully had nothing to say about the film. Those were different times and it's difficult to speculate on what the public's

reaction would have been to learning that Elvis' father had a prison record. It's possible that, had Vernon made a clean breast of it, it would have blown over. On the other hand, it might well have blown up in all their faces. It didn't take much in those days for a performer to be effectively blacklisted; witness Jerry Lee Lewis and Charlie Chaplin, to name but two. Rock and roll was still regularly under attack by bigots and puritans throughout the country and records were still being burned. On October 28, 1957, when Elvis played the first of two sold-out nights at the Pan Pacific Auditorium in Los Angeles, it became obvious that official society and the powers-that-be in the United States were still scrutinizing Elvis and the supposed effect he was having on the nation's youth, pretty carefully.

On that first night, Elvis concluded a full-blown show by rolling around on the stage with a larger stuffed version of Nipper, the RCA dog. By morning, newspapers all but accused him of simulating sex with an animal. One reviewer reviled him as a "sexhibitionist." The Los Angeles Police Department (remembering the Jacksonville, Florida, police department's filming of Elvis to see if he should be arrested for obscenity) sent film crews down to the Pan Pacific the next night, to be ready to catch evidence of any obscene acts.

There was also a simmering interest in certain quarters of the gossip media concerning the Selective Service draft board "going soft" on Elvis. This of course was not the case, as the next few months would prove.

But at the time all this helped exacerbate the growing unease concerning the filming of *Jailhouse Rock*. Elvis was known not to like the film, though whether this was actually due to the association with his father's brief and largely blameless prison incarceration during his childhood is open to speculation.

For whatever reason, Elvis had walked out on *Jailhouse Rock* the first day and something or someone convinced him to return. He said openly that he didn't like the movie and was described by co-workers as being uncharacteristically testy and quick tempered. Notwithstanding whatever reservations he might have had, he finished the movie and then did his best to forget and ignore it. In fact, it would become a rock movie classic and would be considered one of his best performances.

But, the movie had been hanging over their heads. There was also the knowledge that this would likely be Elvis' last Christmas with his family for a couple of years. In October, the local draft board had said that Elvis probably would not be called up for the draft for another year or so. Then, suddenly, on December 20, the chairman of the draft board himself hand-delivered to Graceland Elvis' induction notice: he was to present himself for military service on January 20. That news dealt Gladys a crushing blow.

The RCA Victor trademark dog, known as Nipper, first appeared listening to an ancient wind-up phonograph on the British HMV – "His Master's Voice" – label at the end of the last century, and was a perfect publicity gimmick for Elvis to promote "Hound Dog." Coupled with "Don't Be Cruel," it was his first double-sided chart-topper.

It also disturbed producer Hal Wallis and Paramount Pictures since they were already in preproduction on Elvis' next movie project, *King Creole*, and planned to film it in January. Wallis wrote to the Selective Service, pleading for a deferment long enough to allow Elvis to make the film. Selective Service replied that it might consider a plea if it came direct from Elvis himself.

Accordingly, one of Elvis' tasks that Christmas Eve in 1957 was to sit down at his office upstairs and write a letter to the draft board. Their reply was that they would consider the matter after the holidays.

That sword hung over the festivities, only adding to Elvis' usual determination to have a merry Christmas. It was always his favorite holiday period and he went at it nonstop, as he did with most things he enjoyed.

He had sent Vernon to the bank with $21,000 to get him ten $100 bills and twenty $1,000 bills. He and his cousins Billy and Bobby Smith first drove down to the nearby Whitehaven Plaza shopping mall to buy yet more presents for Gladys and Vernon, then they headed south into Mississippi to buy hundreds of dollars' worth of fireworks.

Back at Graceland, Elvis posed with his draft notice in front of the family Christmas tree for a crowd of photographers that had been summoned from the local newspapers. He later distributed $1,000 bills to a few of his employees and $100 bills to the cousins.

Elvis also left several $1,000 bills spread out on his bed upstairs as a test of the honesty of certain of his employees and friends. According to Dundy's quote of Billy Smith, one hapless individual did fall prey to temptation. Elvis let him keep the money but thereafter subjected him to a long, slow banishment from Graceland.

WAR

Then came "war," which is what Elvis dubbed it. All the fireworks were hauled out to the backyard and distributed to the unwary. Two teams were selected and then Elvis led the charge with a sputtering Roman candle. Rockets soon joined the fray and it became a real war with real fireworks bouncing off people. Hair sizzled, shirts smoldered, skin was scorched. No one was seriously burned. Eventually, one of the cousins dropped his cigarette lighter into the ammunition dump and the whole thing blew up with the impact of several bombs going off. Rockets arced into the henhouse and there was general confusion everywhere. Elvis loved his "war" and made it an annual affair.

Despite making the often-repeated point that he wanted to be treated as an ordinary soldier, it was inevitable – and both Colonel Tom Parker and the RCA publicity machine did nothing to prevent it – that the world's press would cover Elvis' army service as closely as possible.

The night of March 23, 1958, Elvis rented the Rainbow Rollerdome on Lamar Avenue, one of his favorite places in Memphis, and gave himself a farewell party.

Early the next morning, Elvis, Gladys and Vernon arrived at the draft board. He had gotten a delay to finish shooting *King Creole* and to record the soundtrack. Upon his return to Memphis, he had performed two farewell shows on March 15 at Russwood Park. He had owned Graceland just over a year and thus far had spent less than half that time at home. There was no doubt though, even then, that he intended to make it his permanent home. Friends and staff alike said that Graceland seemed to go into a state of suspended animation when he was away. Everyone waited for "The Boss" to come home and make things happen again. A telegram now in the Graceland archive testifies to this; from some of his friends, it reads "Welcome home. Graceland shall rock once again!"

There can be little doubt that his absence had profound effects on Gladys — but it also had to do with his maturing, with his need to stake out his own life. He and Gladys had been so close, with their own vocabulary of baby talk, their own dream world. Now, that was clearly coming to an end.

Gladys held back her tears until the army bus took her Elvis away to his basic military training.

After the first induction at Fort Chaffee, Arkansas, Elvis spent four months in basic training at Fort Hood, Texas, and did his best — as he would the rest of his life — to sort of set up a mini-Graceland wherever he was. At first, he ran into an old friend, Eddie Fedal, a former DJ and announcer in Dallas, who was then living in Waco. Elvis spent many weekends at Eddie's house, where he was sometimes joined by his girlfriend, Anita Wood. Elvis had met her in 1957 when she was a Memphis radio and TV personality and they began dating.

Elvis got two weeks' furlough at the end of May and drove back to Memphis in his Mark II with Anita and the Colonel. They all went to a preview showing of *King Creole*, Elvis held roller-skating parties at the Rainbow Rollerdome, and life returned to normal for a few days at Graceland. He slipped over to Nashville on June 10 and 11 for a recording session — his first with Chet Atkins — which produced "I Need Your Love Tonight," "I Got Stung," "Ain't That Lovin' You Baby," "A Fool Such As I," and "A Big Hunk o' Love."

Back at Fort Hood, Elvis could now live off base and he made preparations for the Presley clan to join him. He initially rented a trailer, then found a four-bedroom house at 906 Oak Hill Drive in the nearby town of Killeen. A Judge Crawford rented it to him for $1,400 a month, a steep price, but the place resembled the house on Audubon Drive and Elvis wanted something right away.

Vernon and Gladys and Minnie arrived in the Fleetwood, pulling a trailer full of household goods, and they set up house.

Elvis had never traveled further than Hawaii. His posting to Germany was traumatic for family and fans.

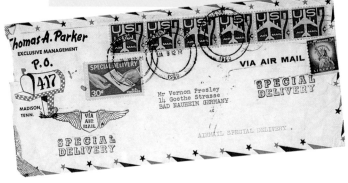

GRIEF

It was obvious that Gladys was not happy, and she began a sudden physical decline. In early August, even she finally admitted that she needed help and she called her doctor in Memphis and asked him to come to Texas. He was not licensed to practice out-side Tennessee, so he told her to see a local doctor. She did so, but he was unable to produce a diagnosis. She was becoming jaundiced and obviously failing fast. Elvis decided she must return to Memphis for treatment. She would not fly, so he drove her and Vernon to Fort Worth to catch the train for Memphis.

That was on Friday, the 8th of August. When she got home the next afternoon, Dr. Evans took one look at her and put her in Methodist Hospital immediately. Specialists who were called in announced that she had hepatitis, but they weren't sure as to its cause. Gladys got steadily worse. On Tuesday, Elvis — who had only a week of advanced training left before being posted to Germany — tired of being unable to get emergency leave and announced that he was going to see his Mama anyway. Emergency leave was suddenly granted.

He sat with her from Tuesday night through Wednesday night, when Gladys told him to go home to Graceland to get some rest. Vernon awoke him in the middle of the night with the news of her death.

Elvis was inconsolable.

Even his grief was made public when Colonel arrived and opened Graceland's gates to the press. They rushed up the hill to find Vernon and Elvis sitting on the front steps, weeping. The next few days were the worst of his life — beginning with Vernon and Colonel arguing over whether the funeral should be held at Graceland or at a funeral home. The Colonel prevailed. Services were at the National Funeral Home, although open casket viewing was held in the living room at Graceland. A very emotional burial service was held at Forest Hill Cemetery. Elvis physically tried to get into the grave and follow her. Then he took to his room for days of uninterrupted grief.

Always before, the dragons had been out there, in the world, beyond the safe confines of his walls and his gates. Gladys, his protector and his one true friend, was at his side no longer. Now, he was safe at home no longer, and the dragons still lay in wait out beyond those shielding gates.

PRISCILLA

Elvis held his now-famous "welcome home" Army discharge press conference in Vernon's little office out behind Graceland on March 8, 1960.

In many ways Elvis really never left home. His twenties, the formative years in any young man's life, were spent getting over Gladys' death, going into the army and then making quickie movies. He was never really out on his own, much less alone. He was lonely, but not alone. Even in the army, he had his Graceland entourage: Vernon, Red West (Red's father had died the day after Gladys did, so he and Elvis felt a close bond), Lamar Fike (the fat boy who had shown up one day at the house on Audubon Drive, ingratiated himself into Elvis' life and never really left) and Grandmother Minnie. Plus domestic help. And the odd girlfriend or two, even though Anita Wood was faithfully waiting at home. When word got out in the American press that Elvis

Elvis' draft was eagerly covered by the media *(above)*. His discharge was welcomed in a letter from Parker assistant Tom Diskin *(below)*.

was seeing a sixteen-year-old Bardot look-alike named Margrit Buergin — whom Elvis nicknamed "Little Puppy" — Anita got her back up. Elvis actually wrote her a letter purporting to explain all to his "Wittle Beadie," as in beady eyes. Elvis was big on nicknames for everyone.

Elvis' version of Graceland in Germany had been no picnic. After living in a series of hotels in Bad Nauheim, he and his crew settled in a three-story house, Goethestrasse 14. It was a five-bedroom, white-stucco structure renting for $800 a month. Frau Pieper, the domineering landlady, decided to stay on as housekeeper and general overseer, so they were stuck with her in her little room just off the kitchen.

The house was oppressively dark and full of the smell of years of sauerkraut and sausage (both of which Elvis loved). After the first crush of fans, Vernon had erected a sign outside in German and English that read: Autographs between 7:30 and 8:00 p.m. only.

Besides the Little Puppy, Elvis briefly dated Elisabeth Stefaniak, an army brat whom he met in Grafenwohr when his unit was on maneuvers there. He took her back to Goethestrasse 14 as a secretary, to handle the thousands of fan letters he was receiving weekly. He paid her $35 a week (which was a standard Presley salary for a while; its significance being that Elvis had earned $35 a week at Crown Electric, his last real job). She also was expected to help Minnie with the cooking and shopping and anything else that Vernon felt was essential.

Elvis also became friends with two men who would become essential parts of his life. Joe Esposito was a street-savvy Chicago native who could get things done in a hurry, a skill which Elvis always appreciated. The other was a diminutive guitar player and singer from Alabama who had been in Red Foley's band before the army. This was Charlie Hodge, who would live at Graceland for seventeen years as part of Elvis' entourage.

And, of course, Elvis met Priscilla. She was then in the ninth grade and living in Wiesbaden with her mother and stepfather, Captain and Mrs. Joseph Paul Beaulieu. Priscilla met Elvis through a friend of his, Special Services NCO Currie Grant (whose wife Carole was singer Tony Bennett's sister). Currie spotted her sitting in a park with her brother Don one day late in 1959 and felt that she was per-

Back from the army to "welcome home" presents, March 1960. The tree is from Christmas 1957.

fect for Elvis. He persuaded her to accompany him and his wife to an evening at Goethestrasse 14. She, of course, had no idea of what to expect.

She was put off by the half-nude Bardot poster on the living-room wall and by Elvis' exclaiming "You're just a baby" when they were introduced, but then Elvis began playing the piano and singing, to impress her she thought. He sang "Rags to Riches," "Are You Lonesome Tonight" and "End of the Rainbow."

Then he invited her into the kitchen to meet Minnie, who was frying bacon at the stove. Priscilla was too nervous

to eat, but Elvis chowed down on "five gigantic bacon sandwiches, each one smothered with mustard" as he asked her, "Who are the kids listening to?"

She thought he was joking and told him so, adding: "Everyone listens to you." Even so, he said he was unsure about his fans and he wondered about Fabian and Ricky Nelson. Then it was time for Currie Grant to chaperone her home to her parents.

A few days later Elvis called Currie and asked for a return engagement. Priscilla couldn't believe it. But she was happy to return, and found the evening went as before: singing and eating pretty much occupied everyone's time. But then Elvis asked her to come upstairs, to his room. "There's nothing to be frightened of, honey," he said soothingly.

She found his bedroom as plain as the downstairs had been: some books, some records, his army uniforms, some love letters from girls on the night table. Some of them, she noticed, were signed "Anita" and later confessed she would have liked to have read them.

Elvis appeared and asked her to sit next to him on the bed. They cuddled. He said, "I just wish Mama could have been here to meet you." He told her all about himself, Gladys' death and Graceland and how he dreaded returning there without Gladys. He also talked to her about the worry he had about this married Stanley woman that Vernon had been dating and what was going to happen about that.

He said he couldn't bear anyone trying to take Gladys' place.

They kissed — "my first real kiss" — and she sensed that one kiss would not be the end of this.

Elvis was not in uniform when he held his press conference on March 8, 1960, in Vernon's little office out behind Graceland.

Reporter: "Any romance? Did you leave any hearts, shall we say, in Germany?"

Elvis: (laughing)"Not any special one. There was a little girl that I was seeing quite often over there that — her father was in the Air Force — actually they only got over there about two months before I left and I was seeing her and she was at the train — at the airport when I left and there were some pictures made of her but there was no big romance. The stories came out about the girl he left behind and all that. But it wasn't like that (laughing). I have to be careful when I answer a question like that."

(This extract is now screened on a video in the office as part of the visitor's tour, and still raises a laugh from everyone, including Priscilla.)

Reporter:"Do you have any advice for the boys your age who are now going to have to spend a certain amount of duty with the service?"

Elvis:"Well, the only thing I can say is to play it straight and do your best because you can't fight 'em (laughing). They never lost yet. And you can't fight 'em. So you can make it easy or you can make it hard on yourself. I mean, if you play it straight and get the people on your side and let 'em know you're trying, you — as the army would say, you've got it made. But if you're gonna try to be an individual or try to be different, you're gonna go through two years of misery."

Reporter: "Are you going to keep Graceland; do you have plans

for moving away from Memphis?"

Elvis:"No sir, I have no plans for leaving Memphis."

Reporter:"Are you going to keep Graceland?"

Elvis:"I'm going to keep Graceland as long as I possibly can."

Reporter:" Elvis, this is not in the form of a question, but I'd like to take this opportunity to welcome you home for everybody in Memphis and in the South."

Elvis:"Why, thank you. You'll never know happy I am to be here. Somebody asked me this morning what did I miss about Memphis and I said everything."

WELCOME

During March of 1960, Elvis eased back into civilian life, getting reacquainted with Graceland, cutting songs in Nashville, earning a first-degree black belt in karate, and taping a "Welcome Home, Elvis" special with Frank Sinatra for the latter's ABC-TV variety show. Only three years earlier, Sinatra had greatly hurt Gladys' feelings when he lambasted rock and roll as — among other things — "a rancid-smelling aphrodisiac." Which had changed? Sinatra or rock and roll? Or Elvis? Or the world? Now Sinatra was singing "Love Me Tender" on TV; Elvis was doing Sinatra's "Witchcraft," and Elvis and Frank duetted at the end of "Love Me Tender." Just like that, Elvis became an "entertainer."

His first studio session since leaving the army yielded "Stuck on You," among other songs. He also recorded "Soldier Boy," which had been his and Anita Wood's song when they were separated during his army days. (Things with Anita may have changed for the worse when Elvis learned from photographer Bill Leaptrott that the reason Bill seemed to be always around taking pictures of Elvis and Anita out on dates was supposedly that Anita

At the "homecoming" press conference, immediately behind Elvis is Memphis photographer Bob Williams.

had been tipping the photographer off.) On April 3 and 4 he cut twelve songs in Nashville, including "Are You Lonesome Tonight" and "It's Now or Never." The latter song remains in many listeners' minds as a conscious choice by Elvis to finally transcend the limitations of being labeled a rock and roll singer and to establish his own middle ground, from which he could easily move in any musical direction. The song, of course, is based on the 1901 Italian composition "O Sole Mio." Elvis knew it from records by Caruso and Mario Lanza, but the recorded version he studied while in Germany had been Tony Martin's 1949 English language rendition with the title "There's No Tomorrow." He asked Hill and Range for new lyrics and a new arrangement. The resulting "It's Now or Never" went on to sell more than twenty-two million copies worldwide. It was also a song that showed off to best advantage the maturing of Elvis' voice.

Next Elvis was off in a special train car to resume his Hollywood career. He called Priscilla in Wiesbaden to tell her that his latest movie, *GI Blues*, was a "joke" and that "the Colonel's requested better scripts."

When he got back to Graceland from shooting *GI Blues*, something happened, apparently. Vernon and Dee Stanley and her three children were living in Graceland, the couple in Vernon and Gladys' old room. Gladys' clothes were still in that closet and her pictures were still up on the walls. Vernon and Dee would be married on July 3, 1960, but according to Gladys' sister Lillian, as quoted by Elaine Dundy, Elvis came home and had a major fit. Lillian reported that she had been sitting in the kitchen, drinking coffee, when she heard a door slamming upstairs and Elvis

The ultimate accolade? Elvis' show business respectability was confirmed on his return from the army with his 1960 appearance on the Frank Sinatra TV program.

yelling, "Don't you come out!" Then she heard the sound of furniture being thrown around in the living room and the ripping sound of curtains being pulled off the walls. Lillian, who was at that time working in the Graceland office, said she was not at all surprised to see Elvis' reaction to Dee's attempts at redecorating. A truck soon arrived from Goldsmith's department store. The driver loaded all of Dee's stuff onboard. She said he "stuffed cats into that van for fifteen minutes." Cats! At Graceland! Meanwhile, Vernon, Dee and her three sons left for Hermitage, where they stayed until they found a suitable place on Dolan Drive at the back of the Graceland grounds. Vernon did not live at Graceland again until after Elvis died and he had separated from Dee.

In Dee Stanley Presley's book, she wrote that "eventually Vernon also began to recognize the necessity of moving his new family into a home of their own. They moved before Dee had a chance to do much redecorating at Graceland."

GRACELAND WEST

Elvis sent for Priscilla in the summer of 1962, to visit him in Los Angeles. He had spent the past year and a half shuttling between Graceland and Hollywood, making movies. (He performed on two occasions, two shows on February 25, 1961, at an Elvis Presley Day in Memphis to benefit local charities; and one show on March 25, 1961, to benefit the building of the U.S.S. *Arizona* memorial at Pearl Harbor. Those would be his last live, in person shows until 1969, not counting the '68 TV special.)

Elvis' first version of Graceland West, after he moved out of the Beverley Wiltshire Hotel — he was encouraged to move out after complaints about roughhousing by his guys — was a Frank Lloyd Wright house at 565 Perugia Way in Bel Air. The Shah of Iran had once owned it, as had actress Rita Hayworth. From there, Elvis moved to 1059 Bellagio Road, also in Bel Air; then back to Perugia Way.

Priscilla found him at the Bellagio Road house, which was fashioned after a Mediterranean villa. A butler admitted her and she found Elvis, as usual, the center of attention in a roomful of people. After two years, she found that Elvis had quickly grown from "sensitive" and "insecure" to "self-confident to the point of cockiness." That night, Elvis made her stay with George and Shirley Barris, so the wrong word wouldn't get back to her parents. (It was George Barris, a well-known custom car designer, who customized a forty-foot Greyhound bus for Elvis; his first rolling Graceland. Barris was also responsible for the famous solid gold Cadillac, which in fact was mostly used as a promotional item rather than being one of Elvis' regular private vehicles.)

The next night, with Elvis at the wheel (with his yachting cap and racing gloves), the whole crew took off for Las Vegas for the bus' maiden voyage. (Priscilla had left letters for the butler to mail daily to her parents with the L.A. postmark.) At the Sahara, she quickly adapted to Elvis' nocturnal habits. He bought her sophisticated gowns, sent for the hotel's hairdresser to do her hair and makeup, and then they hit every show on the strip. Priscilla was seventeen.

The Nativity tableau has been a Christmastime feature at Graceland for some years. Few houses in the United States – or elsewhere – could boast the kind of extravagant display that greets visitors to the home of Elvis, for whom Christmas was the favorite time of year.

HOMECOMING

Christmas 1962 at Graceland. Elvis was the happiest anyone had seen him since before Gladys' death. Priscilla was coming! She had somehow managed to convince her parents to let her go. Vernon and Dee met her at La Guardia in New York and flew on to Memphis, and drove to their house on Dolan Street (where her parents were convinced she would stay). Elvis had already laid down the law: only he would be allowed to drive Priscilla through those gates into the promised land of Graceland.

She was delighted by the sight that greeted her: "The front lawn was adorned with a nativity scene and the white columns of the mansion were ablaze with holiday lights. It was one of the most beautiful sights I'd ever laid eyes on."

Inside there was a crowd waiting to meet her. Grandmother Minnie was glad to see her again, but cautioned her that Elvis and Vernon were still not getting along terribly well as a result of Vernon's marriage.

Young Priscilla marveled at all that went on that evening and night. It was a sort of boys' club: the guys were shooting pool and watching TV and shooting the bull and pestering Alberta the maid (whom Elvis called "VO5" for obvious reasons) in the kitchen and getting her to fix them burgers and stuff. Priscilla realized that Graceland had no routine: everything revolved around Elvis. It was, she thought, just one big open house.

The downstairs part, that is. At four a.m., when Elvis decided to retire, everything shut down. Elvis took Priscilla upstairs.

It snowed on Christmas Eve, answering Elvis' spoken prayer, and Graceland could not have looked more like a postcard scene. Everyone gathered around the tree and Elvis gave Priscilla a poodle puppy that she christened Honey. She gave him a musical cigarette case that played "Love Me Tender."

The following nights, Elvis would rent the Memphian or the Malco theater for all-night movies. One night they all went to the Rainbow Rollerdome, where they played "crack the whip." No one was hurt too badly. Another night, he would rent out Fairgrounds Amusement Park and do his favorite stunt of standing up in the roller coaster. Or they would ride the bumper cars and try for really vicious wrecks.

For New Year's Eve, Elvis rented the Manhattan Club for his guys, friends and relatives.

Priscilla didn't want to go back to Germany and Elvis didn't want her to go. Elvis and Priscilla began plotting ways that she could stay at Graceland. Eventually, he wore down her father by promising that Priscilla, not yet 18, would live with Vernon and Dee and would attend a good Catholic school.

Priscilla indeed began living with Vernon and Dee and attending classes at Immaculate Conception. Before anyone knew it, Priscilla moved into Graceland. Could it be any more like the story of Pygmalion?

Elvis molded her into the woman he wanted to marry. She wanted to become the woman that Elvis wanted to marry. It was not always easy for her, especially with him gone much of the time making his movies (three a year during this period). She couldn't have girlfriends over, because Vernon forbade strangers. She couldn't visit with Patsy Presley and Becky Yancy, the secretaries in the office, because they had work to do. She was reprimanded by a friend of Dee's for "making a public display" of herself playing with Honey under the trees in the front yard. She was effectively grounded because Vernon chauffered her to and from school. Eventually, she got permission to drive Elvis' beloved Continental Mark II to school and she and Patsy started going out in the evenings to the bowling alley or to a movie or to get a burger.

At home, she was expected to spend time with Minnie, who was very sweet, but who spent much of her time recalling all the misfortunes of the past that the Presleys had suffered and worrying that all of this good fortune was fleeting and could be snatched from them at any second.

And she waited for Elvis to call home. And she worried about whether he was really having an affair with his current leading lady, as all the movie magazines strongly hinted.

Eventually, she and everyone else at Graceland would count the days until he would be home. "With his arrival, Graceland sprang to life," she

marveled. He would expertly pilot the big bus through the gates and past the screaming fans and brake to a halt before the front door. "Where's my Cilla?"

People materialized out of nowhere until there was a noisy houseful. The dining room table could seat only eight, so a side table would be set up to handle the overflow. Alberta would bring in huge platters of steaming cornbread, sizzling pork chops, crispy home fries, and bowls of chowder peas. Elvis talked all night: Hollywood gossip, tales of his co-stars, corny jokes. Toward dawn, he yawned and that was the signal. The crew disappeared and Elvis and Priscilla went upstairs. His world was complete.

Priscilla soon learned that there were certain tasks required of her to ensure Elvis' happiness, safety, security and peace of mind. One was to dress for dinner so that he and she could make a grand appearance coming down the big staircase. Elvis always wore a pistol under his coat and Priscilla tucked her pearl-handled derringer in her bra.

Another was to scout the downstairs after Elvis awakened and before he came down, to make sure there was no one underfoot whom he did not want to see. He hated morbid people and there were apparently plenty of them around. Some of the more blatant hand-out cases had to be removed. Because Elvis was so generous it took a real sponge to overstretch his largesse. Certain relatives who had ridiculed him as a child now suddenly showed up with palms outstretched. Even so, it was hard for Elvis to say no. For

Visitors to Graceland stand in awe at the sheer flamboyance of the Pool Room decor, extravagant in its detail as much as its actual design.

Vernon, it was easier. But Elvis was more tenderhearted.

She had to keep the downstairs warm, keep his bedroom very cold, keep the lights down low, and see that his food was ready when and how he wanted it; in short, she had to see that everything in his world was just right.

VOICES

Priscilla and Minnie began hearing noises one night. Noises up in the attic of Graceland like someone was stirring around up there. Minnie said she was sure it was Gladys, come back to watch over Elvis. Night after night, they heard the stirrings. Hattie, one of the women employees, often stayed with Priscilla and Minnie when Elvis was gone and the house seemed so very empty (Hattie also packed a pistol). Hattie confessed to Priscilla that she could

hear "strange voices" in Graceland that she had never heard anywhere else before and that sometimes it got so quiet in Graceland that it went beyond any stillness she had ever experienced before. But, she reassured Priscilla, whatever spirits were there were good spirits, not bad. Thus comforted, Priscilla went up to explore the attic. She found trunk after trunk of Elvis' past: pink and black clothes, motorcycle jackets, old furniture, records, old TVs. And old love letters. Especially old love letters from Anita to Elvis in Germany. She felt obligated to read those.

And she found all of Gladys' clothes, neatly put away, with her personal papers and pictures. She couldn't resist trying on one of

Gladys' dresses. She began to identify with this strong woman she had never met but felt she knew. Suddenly, she felt overwhelmed with loneliness and grief and began weeping: she felt Gladys' presence there with her.

Hattie came to investigate the noises too, and they both screamed at the sudden sight of each other. Hattie told her to come away: "Child, this ain't no place you should be. Too many sad memories."

It hurt Elvis at first that Priscilla asked him to wait outside the school during her graduation exercises, on June 14, 1963. He was simply too famous, she explained, and it would disrupt things too much. He understood. So he and some of the guys, wearing suits and shades and pistol-packing shoulder holsters, waited outside with the big Mercedes limo while she was awarded her diploma.

He had a party for her afterwards at Graceland and presented her with her first car — a modest red Corvair. Then Priscilla got what she really wanted — time alone with Elvis. He was between movies, so they withdrew to the second floor of Graceland and watched movies, played records, listened to gospel music on the radio, read, had pillow fights and ate whatever they wanted for days on end. Elvis loved *The Way of All Flesh*, a sentimental movie about a man who, after losing all his money, becomes a derelict and one day happens upon his wife and children in a happy scene on Christmas night. She invites the poor drifter in, not recognizing him, but he turns away to spare his family his shame. Elvis identified with its message and talked about doing a remake of it.

Up on the second floor away from all cares, Priscilla wrote, "Elvis could become a little boy again, escaping from the responsibilities of family, friends, fans, the press, and the world. Here with me, he could be vulnerable and childlike, a playful boy who stayed in his pajamas for days at a time."

When floodlit at night, the Meditation Garden takes on an almost spiritual quality, particularly on occasions like the anniversary of Elvis' death when it is the scene of a candlelight vigil by fans.

Ultimately, the outside world beckoned to him again: time to pay the bills. He was off to film *Viva Las Vegas* with Ann-Margret and decided that Priscilla should stay at Graceland and keep the home fires burning. Priscilla was not pleased with that and soon started making the West Coast trips with Elvis, to protect him from the likes of Ann-Margret and others. When Priscilla's parents visited Los Angeles, she moved all her stuff, including a number of stuffed teddy bears, into Charlie Hodge's room (which he vacated).

She could see that Elvis was growing increasingly frustrated with his acting career and that he could plainly see that things were not likely to change for the better. Also, she, along with everyone from the Colonel to Vernon and all the guys, became very uneasy and worried after Larry Geller went to work as Elvis' hairstylist in 1964 and gradually became his spiritual adviser. Elvis invited Geller and his wife to come to Graceland. Everyone was jealous of Elvis' attention, after all, and when he went off to meditate and to read his spiritual books and the Bible, he ignored them all. As with everything he approached (from karate to cars), Elvis went at it full-tilt.

He had the Meditation Garden added to Graceland around 1965, the same year he added the den that would later become the Jungle Room. The origins of the Meditation Garden are somewhat hazy — some say it was designed and built in 1963 by Marty Lacker's sister, Anne, and her husband Bernard Grenadier. Geller maintained that he and Elvis and Marty Lacker designed it in 1964 and completed it in 1965, centering it around a circular pool and a statue of Jesus. Vernon and the guys thought it a very odd sort of thing at first, but it soon became a popular spot to go and sit. It remains much as it was, except of course for the gravesites of Elvis and his family.

INVENTORY

During the period of 1964–1965, when Marty Lacker briefly replaced Joe Esposito as Elvis' "foreman," Lacker — with Elvis' input, apparently — drew up a rough set of responsibilities for some of the guys. Elvis obviously did nothing for himself, so there, in painstaking detail, were written down such obscure but essential duties as buying five copies of *TV Guide* each week and putting them in the right places, "being in the den with Elvis as much as possible," maintaining Elvis' scrapbook, "keeping Elvis' black kit stocked with needed items and carry for him if he needs it," taking care of all the cars, caring for Elvis' clothes and shoes and razor, supplying Elvis and Priscilla with "large cups of water at movies," calling the Memphian Theater to arrange "movie nights," and taking care of Elvis' "cigar boxes." These were little storage cabinets and one had to be in the den, one in Elvis' car and one available during movie nights. Each box was stocked with the following: "wood tipped cigars — El Producto Diamond Tips, plain cigars — El Producto Atlas, tube of Blistex, Tareyton cigarettes (2 packs), small bottle of Dristan, small bottle of Super Anahist, one card package of Contac, one tin of antibiotic Sucrets (red box), small bottles of eyedrops, two emery boards and fingernail file and cleaner, matches (4 to 5 books), (in L.A.) one jar of Occuline eye pads, Gum: Spearmint, Doublemint, Juicy Fruit (3 each), four or five pieces of candy (sour balls, hard peppermint),

gloves and sunglasses if not wearing them."

Additionally, the following items were to be kept freshly stocked in the Graceland kitchen at at all times: "fresh lean, unfrozen ground meat, one case regular Pepsi, one case orange drinks, rolls (hot rolls — Brown 'n' Serve), cans of biscuits (at least six), hamburger buns, pickles, potatoes & onions, assorted fresh fruits, cans of sauerkraut, wieners, at least three bottles of milk & half cream, thin lean bacon, fresh handsqueezed cold orange juice, banana pudding (to be made at night), ingredients for making meat loaf & sauce, brownies (to be made at night), ice cream — vanilla & chocolate, shredded coconut, fudge cookies, gum, cigars, cigarettes, Dristan, Super Anahist, Contac, Sucrets, Feenamint Gum, matches."

Marty's own duties in Memphis were these: "Personal bookkeeping for Elvis, transact personal business for Elvis as needed, responsible for all personal expense money, oversee services and food to Elvis by maids in absence of Mr. V. Presley, receive Elvis' personal mail (other than what Mr. Presley takes care of), transact business and correspondence with the Colonel's office for Elvis, purchase records for Elvis, responsible for organization, whether in bad or good situations, to Elvis."

In Los Angeles, his duties shifted somewhat: "Personal bookkeeping for Elvis, writing and mailing all checks, transacting business for Elvis, with the Colonel's staff, working with studio and picture dept. heads for Elvis, maintaining script and marking daily scenes, plus receiving and processing daily call sheet; responsible for all personal household expense money for Elvis, transact personal business for Elvis, weekly grocery shopping for entire house, compiling weekly food menu, maintaining purchase order number system for all charges in Elvis' name." (He was authorized to keep purchase records and to file them.)

Priscilla tried to divert Elvis with other interests. In 1965, she bought him a little slot car racing set. He became fascinated with it, got the guys psyched into racing the cars with him, and before Priscilla could turn around, Elvis had added an entire room on to the house just for his slot cars. He played night and day for a while and then, after he had mastered whatever there was to master with slot cars, he tired of it and put the cars away. The addition became the Trophy Room.

The next passion was horses. It began when Priscilla was looking at the unused Graceland stables and mentioned that she'd love to have her own horse. A couple of weeks later, Elvis presented her with a quarterhorse she named Domino. Elvis had seldom ridden, apart from a few movie scenes, but Priscilla persuaded him to try riding Domino. He was hooked on horses and soon got Rising Sun, the big, beautiful and spirited golden palomino. (Rising Sun outlived Elvis by nine years and died of kidney failure in 1986.)

Soon they were riding daily and then, of course,

Elvis personally supervised where everybody's tack and gear, the saddles and such, would hang and be stored in the barn. His handwriting is still on the wall in the back room ("the tack room"), in red marker, where he determined whose equipment would hang where, including his own, marked as "E.P."

Elvis had to get horses for everyone: Joe Esposito, Jerry Schilling and his wife, Red West, Sonny West, Charlie Hodge, etc. Even Lamar Fike got one. Elvis went around in the barn with a red marker pen, writing everyone's name on the wall next to his or her hook on which to hang tack (the writing is still there). Next, Elvis got Bear, a black Tennessee Walker, and he got a full riding outfit, to show off to the fans.

MARRIAGE

Elvis finally proposed to Priscilla late in 1966, in her dressing room on the second floor of Graceland, a few days before Christmas. "Sattnin," he said ("Sattnin" being a term of endearment he used for Gladys and Priscilla), knocking on her door,

"I have to talk to you." She made him utter the secret password – "Fire Eyes," her nickname for him when he was in a temper – before she would let him in. He had been telling her for years that one day the time would be right. Now, he said, that time had come. He presented her with a ring that sported three and a half carats of diamonds in the center, surrounded by smaller diamonds that could be detached and worn separately. Still in her terrycloth robe, she went racing off downstairs to show Grandma Minnie her ring.

They were married in a style that both later regretted: a quick Las Vegas wedding engineered by Colonel at the Aladdin Hotel on May 1, 1967, at 9:30 in the morning. A State Supreme Court Justice friend of Colonel's performed the ceremony in the suite of Aladdin owner Milton Prell. Priscilla managed to change part of the vows to read "love, honor and comfort," rather than "obey." Colonel controlled the guest list. Attending were Vernon and Dee, Priscilla's parents and her brother and sister, Colonel and his wife Marie, Joe Esposito and Marty Lacker (both were best men) and their wives, Billy Smith and his wife Jo, Patsy Presley Gambill and her husband Gee Gee, and

George Klein.

A photo session, noisy press conference and reception followed, after which Priscilla and Elvis took off in Frank Sinatra's private jet for Palm Springs and Elvis' house there at 845 Chino Canyon Road.

The couple went briefly to the Bahamas, then returned to Graceland for a big reception in the Trophy Room on May 28 for everyone who had not been at the wedding in Las Vegas. Elvis and Priscilla wore their wedding outfits and the champagne flowed for hours. There were still some hurt feelings, but everyone knew it had been Colonel's doing, not Elvis'. (Colonel had already cracked the whip on Larry Geller and his spiritual books which, Colonel said, were "cluttering up" Elvis' mind.) He convened a little assembly of the guys and read the riot act, after Elvis tripped and fell in the bathroom of his rented Bel Air house on Rocca Place and suffered a brain

concussion: "Things are going to change around here. We're going to have to cut back a little. Elvis is spending too much money. Too much money has been going out. Everybody's going to have to take a pay cut. Everybody brings their problems to Elvis. And some of you think maybe he's Jesus Christ who should wear robes and walk down the street helping people. But that's not who he is." He told them that Elvis could not carry all their emotional – and financial – baggage for them. He said it was time for Elvis to concentrate on making movies. The current one – his twenty-fifth – was *Clambake*.

Priscilla and Elvis finished their honeymoon at the "Circle G," the ranch in northern Mississippi he had bought back in February when Graceland was proving too small to contain all the equestrian activity going on. There had been eighteen horses at Graceland

Perhaps predictably, when Elvis married in May 1967 it didn't upset his fans as it would have done ten years earlier.

and a stable staff of nine, all of which were moved to the Circle G. (He later renamed it the "Flying Circle G Ranch," after being reminded that there was already a Circle G Ranch.)

Elvis had literally run across the place when he was out riding his Harley and saw a huge, illuminated concrete cross standing over a small lake, which was spanned by a little oriental bridge. There was a herd of Santa Gertrudis cattle grazing peacefully in the pasture. He was intrigued and toured the 163-acre ranch within days. It belonged to an airplane salesman named Jack Adams who said he would gladly sell the place for $530,000. Elvis and Vernon got the price down to an even half a million dollars and bought it within the week. Vernon had to put Graceland up as collateral for a bank loan. Elvis' record sales were on the decline, as was attendance at his movies. Although income was down, Elvis was never one to economize, especially when it came to family and home comfort.

He christened the ranch the Circle G – after Graceland – and plunged with zest into his new role as rancher. Priscilla, for her part, envisaged Elvis and herself making Circle G their getaway from Graceland — which was their getaway from the world. For that matter, for the last dozen years that he was alive, Elvis rented two rooms year-round at the nearby Howard Johnson's Motor Lodge, a quarter of a mile north of Graceland. The rooms, numbers 127 and 111, were primarily for friends of his to use when they came into town. Even so, when things got too much for him at home, he would slip away to the HoJo and rest there, unnoticed by the world. The manager, Norrine Mitchell, was, of course, a staunch friend of Elvis, and was glad to hide him from the world. Priscilla just wanted her and Elvis to stay in the little ranch house and she could cook and clean and they could ride their horses together.

Elvis had a different vision. In his mind's eye, he saw the Circle G as a kind of perfect commune. He would have the central house, and his guys and their women would be in smaller houses. They would live the way they wanted to, in total privacy, and also run the ranch. It would have taken too long to have the other houses built, so he decided to bring in mobile homes. For the cement slabs to be poured for those and to bring in additional gas and water and electricity, Vernon was kept busy getting zoning

ordinances waived. Next, Elvis bought new trucks for all the ranch hands: $100,000 worth of El Caminos and Rancheros. He was totally immersed in this new life, even shopping at Sears himself for hand tools and overseeing all the work going on at the ranch. He got so busy that he would forget to eat and started carrying around a loaf of bread to have something to munch on while he worked.

For a while, it seemed ideal. The guys and their women and families moved in. They rode their horses, went skeet shooting, held picnics, sang all night and generally had fun and led a carefree life. Elvis named one of the new horses "Mare Ingram," after Memphis Mayor William Ingram, who had been trying — unsuccessfully, as it turned out — to get the name of Mid-South Coliseum changed to "Elvis Presley Coliseum."

Creature comforts were not spared for Elvis and Priscilla: his cook, Mary Jenkins, would come out from Graceland in the mornings and fix their breakfast, then clean the house.

Problems popped up in paradise, though. Fans started showing up in droves, and there was only a low chain-link fence at the ranch. Elvis' little house was clearly visible from the road. He had a ten-foot-high fence erected. The curious just stood on the tops of their cars and vans. Across the street, people gathered on rooftops to watch Elvis. Some of the guys and their families wearied of the communal life. Meanwhile, money began to be a real problem. The ranch had devoured almost a million dollars.

The result was that Vernon called Colonel and Colonel called Elvis and told him he had to go back to work. Elvis went off very reluctantly to make the movie *Clambake* and put more money in the Presley coffers. When he and Priscilla returned to the Circle G to finish their honeymoon, they decided, for privacy's sake, to try one of the mobile homes, a spacious one with three bedrooms. Elvis was intrigued by the idea of living in a trailer and, Priscilla noted, it was "very romantic." He admired the way it was so self-contained, with a washer and dryer and compact little kitchen. She cooked for him, she washed and ironed his clothes, and generally pampered him. His breakfast "began" with a pound of fried bacon, three eggs, and a pot of coffee.

The guys were around, but respected the privacy of the honeymoon couple and they had a fine old time playing house together.

LISA MARIE

When Priscilla discovered that she was pregnant, she at first was not overjoyed. She had so looked forward to the first year of marriage being insulated with Elvis, just the two of them traveling and being together with no other obligations. And she was genuinely fearful that her pregnancy would destroy their romantic life just as the marriage was beginning. (She had set aside any plans for a career of her own when, after she had taken modeling courses and actually worked as a model for a time, at the Piccadilly Cafeteria in nearby Whitehaven Plaza. Elvis forbade her to work). Elvis, for his part, was ecstatic to hear the news.

In early June of 1967, they left in the bus to head for Hollywood and the filming of Elvis' twenty-sixth movie, *Speedway.* It was their last trip in the custom bus before it was sold, as part of the economy move.

The oldest of the horses stabled at Graceland, Mare Ingram still enjoys the rich pastureland that runs to the east and west of the barn.

(The following year the Circle G would also be sold. The Santa Gertrudis cattle had already been sold off, Elvis and Vernon decided that it was unfeasible to try to run the ranch as a money-making venture.) When they stopped one night at an inn in Arizona, Priscilla confessed her fears to Elvis. His resolve to be a father calmed her. They selected possible names from a baby name book: John Baron if it was a boy; Lisa Marie for a girl.

They bought a house in Bel Air, at 1174 Hillcrest Drive in Trousdale Estates, for about $400,000 and Priscilla set to work decorating. Christmas found them back at the Circle G, riding horses and having snowball fights and hay rides. Elvis decided that, instead of them staying out all night on movie nights at the Memphian, they should retire to Graceland after seeing only one movie, instead of three or more.

The Graceland household was of course overjoyed at the prospect of the Presley child, who would also be a Presley grandchild. There was a new Presley aunt in the house. Vernon's sister, Minnie's daughter Delta Mae Biggs, had called Graceland from Florida when her husband Patrick died suddenly. Elvis told her to stay put; he was sending someone for her. He dispatched three guys to Florida; one to fly back with her, and two to attend to matters there and to drive her car to Graceland. She became a member of the household and is living there to this day with her little Pomeranian, Edmond II.

Elvis and the guys had little to do with preparing for the birth – these were still the days when such matters were considered strictly "women's business" –but they came up with something. A typically complicated bit of derring-do: they concocted a plan for racing Priscilla to the hospital when the time came, together with a decoy car to lure all the El fans at the gates who would surely try to follow.

When delivery day came, on February 1, 1968, Priscilla first put on her mascara and eyelashes and teased her hair. Lamar and Joe took off first in the decoy car, then Jerry Schilling and Charlie Hodge drove Elvis and Priscilla. At first they accidentally headed for the wrong hospital – Methodist rather than Baptist – but straightened it out and finally got to Baptist Memorial at 10:40 a.m. Lisa Marie was born at 5:01 p.m. Elvis was too excited to meet with the dozens of reporters and photographers who had gathered at the hospital, so Vernon did so.

At Graceland, Lisa's nursery was all ready upstairs. It was yellow and white, with a custom-made baby crib in the same colors, with a yellow canopy. There was a daybed next to the crib for a nurse, although Elvis and Priscilla often kept Lisa in their bed with them. Elvis received another happy little bundle at the end of February, when he won his first Grammy Award, for "Best Sacred Performance," for "How Great Thou Art." (During that same month, on February 8, Elvis was named to the *Playboy* magazine Music Hall of Fame.)

They soon were back in Los Angeles for the filming of movie number twenty-eight, *Live a Little, Love a Little*. Before long, back at Graceland, Mary Jenkins got a call from Elvis. Could she fly out right away and cook for him? As far as Elvis was concerned, there was no one in Los Angeles who could cook the way she did.

So she was on the next plane out. Elvis asked her to find and hire some good cooks and maids for him, since he knew she couldn't stay out there forever. (She later wrote that she could see that Elvis was happiest at Graceland; Priscilla was happiest in L.A.) At the time, Elvis had a nurse for Lisa and an English couple as household staff, but the three of them – he, Priscilla and Lisa – were forever shuttling back and forth between Palm Springs and Los Angeles.

Mary Jenkins found Elvis' routine in California to be the exact opposite to that of Graceland: up early and off to the studio, home for dinner, play with the baby and go to bed. She cooked all his favorite dishes, one example being beef roast, string beans, creamed potatoes, duck and dressing, mixed vegetables and homemade biscuits.

Colonel started stopping by to join Elvis for breakfast and Mary would cook Colonel's favorite: poached eggs, just the whites, a method of cooking eggs she had never heard of before. Her cooking was such a hit that he invited her to come visit him and Lisa Marie in Palm Springs, which she did.

Elvis wrapped number thirty – *The Trouble With Girls* – in early December and headed home for the holidays. As usual, the Graceland staff and guys were gathered out on the front steps and in the drive to welcome him home. This time, of course, was different: Priscilla held Lisa in her arms to welcome Daddy home.

Christmas of 1968 was undoubtedly his happiest time since Gladys died. His professional life seemed to be back on track now, after the *Elvis* TV special was telecast on December 3, and the soundtrack album and the single "If I Can Dream" were released and hit the *Billboard* charts (the single went to no.12: the album to no.8). He was instantly forgiven for past transgressions and re-crowned as the King of rock and roll. It's not for nothing that the Singer TV special quickly became known as "The '68 Comeback." He started planning some recording sessions, and was eagerly looking forward to them. And, more importantly still, he had a happy family.

Graceland was never more festive, now that they were celebrating Lisa's first Christmas. Vernon dressed up as Santa Claus. The New Year's Eve party was held at the Thunderbird, with B.J. Thomas and Ronnie Milsap entertaining. Elvis and Priscilla stayed late and there was a lot of laughter and smiles: Elvis was on top of the world again.

Elvis stayed in town after the holidays, to record in Memphis for the first time since his Sun Records days. He chose the funky American Sound Studio and used its session players, instead of Nashville cats or L.A. session players. The results can still be heard as some of the strongest, most dynamic performances of Elvis' entire career. In two marathon periods of all-night sessions, from January 13 to 16 and January 20 to 23 (he had tonsillitis in between), he cut twenty-one "keepers." Among them were "Suspicious Minds," "In the Ghetto," and "Don't Cry, Daddy." Elvis was back – not only that, he was back with a vengeance. He and Priscilla and Lisa Marie spent Lisa's first birthday quietly in a private lodge near Aspen, Colorado. Elvis returned to Graceland for another recording bout at American Sound, from February 17 to 22. This time he recorded fourteen songs, including "Kentucky Rain." He accomplished more in three weeks of work than he had done in the previous few years.

In March and April, he returned to L.A. to film what would turn out to be his last movie acting role, in *Change of Habit* with Mary Tyler Moore. He portrayed Dr. John Carpenter, an alias he would later use.

RENAISSANCE

Elvis was at his peak in the years from 1968 to 1972. As Todd Morgan, Communications Director of Graceland, points out, Elvis was at his healthiest, thinnest, and most handsome; his voice had fully matured, and he had recaptured the Elvis confidence – some might say cockiness. He emerged from his years of wandering in the wilderness of the Hollywood sound stages with such a sense

Elvis on stage, 1972. It was an important time for Elvis – the big touring had started in earnest, and it was a very exciting and rewarding time in his career.

of joy and freedom that it fully burst out of him in recording sessions and on stage. It was very obvious that he was in full control of himself, his material, and – importantly – his audience. As Morgan says, many people overlook this era of Elvis' life and career, concentrating instead on the early Fifties rocker or his physical decline in the mid-Seventies. But in these middle years, just after he had become a father and when his marriage and home life were happy and intact, he focused his energy on his work with such intensity that at times it became almost transcendental.

From the *Elvis* television special in 1968 to the American Sound Studio sessions in early 1969 to the epochal Las Vegas shows of July 1969 and to the resumption of touring with the conquest of the difficult Astrodome in February 1970 and on to the final mastery of Madison Square Garden in June 1972, no singer had been hotter or more on target than Elvis in that era. In fact, that era should be stretched a bit to include the spectacular *Elvis – Aloha from Hawaii, via Satellite* television special in January 1973, one of his greatest triumphs. It is also safe to say, with the added wisdom of hindsight, that it was his last great challenge. Any casual reader of Elvis' history knows that Elvis rose to meet and even surpass challenges. It was the ordinary that he couldn't deal with too well.

It was also during this period that Elvis finally began to receive some recognition for his many years of service. It took society-at-large many years to get over its inbuilt resistance and hostility to rock and roll — hence the three Grammy Awards presented to Elvis for gospel music and zero Grammys for rock and roll. Even so, Elvis could not be completely ignored.

Accordingly, on August 28, 1971, the Grammy Awards body, the National Academy of Recording Arts and Sciences, awarded Elvis (between shows in Las Vegas) its prestigious Bing Crosby Award, since renamed the Lifetime Achievement Award. It is not an annual award. Before Elvis, previous recipients had been Bing Crosby, Frank Sinatra, Duke Ellington, Ella Fitzgerald, and Irving Berlin. Elvis' award read, "In recognition of his artistic creativity and his influence in the field of recorded music upon a generation of performers and listeners whose lives and musical horizons have been enriched and expanded by his unique contributions."

Closer to home, Highway 51 South (which was then also known as Bellevue Boulevard) was renamed Elvis Presley Boulevard by the City of Memphis in June of 1971. (Signs didn't go up until January of 1972 and were all, of course, immediately stolen. The solution was to hang them twenty feet above intersections.) The entire stretch of Bellevue was not renamed because the Bellevue Baptist Church, at number 70 Bellevue, didn't want any affiliation with rock and roll or Elvis. Also in June, his birthplace in Tupelo was finally opened to the public, next to the youth center for which he had raised funds.

But the award that probably meant the most to him was given to him in January of 1971 when the United States Junior Chamber of Commerce – known as the Jaycees – selected him as one of the "Ten Outstanding Young Men of the Nation." The others were Walter S. Humann (a developer of the U.S. Postal System), White House aide Ron Ziegler, Harvard biophysicist Dr. Mario Capecchi, Medal of Honor winner and West Point professor Capt. William Bucha, radio station magnate Jim Goetz, National Cancer Institute scientist Dr. George Todaro, Thomas Atkins (the first black city councilman in Boston), Wendell Cherry (a part-owner of the Kentucky Colonels basketball team), and Thomas Coll (founder of the Revitalization Corps, a private sector version of the government's VISTA program).

The awards were presented by U.S. Jaycees president Gordon Thomas in a ceremony on January 16 at Memphis Memorial Auditorium. As far as anyone can figure, that was the only time the adult Elvis attended such a public event. The day before, Elvis had even gone to the Jaycees' prayer breakfast and press conference. The breakfast was attended by about 1,100 persons and was addressed by then-US Ambassador to the United Nations, George Bush. He quipped, "You Memphis politicians had better watch out if Elvis Presley ever decides to enter politics." Elvis took everyone out to dinner that night at the elegant Four Flames restaurant.

During the ceremony the next evening, they of course saved Elvis until last. He developed severe stage fright. "I'm not used to making speeches," he told the event chairman, Frank Taylor. "I'm scared to death."

When he finally got up, in a custom black tuxedo with high collar, he said, "When I was a child, ladies and gentlemen, I was a dreamer. I read comic books, and I was the hero of the comic book. I saw movies, and I was the hero of the movie. So every dream that I ever dreamed has come true a hundred times. . . I learned very early in life that: 'Without a song, the day would never end; without a song, a man ain't got a friend; without a song, the road would never bend —without a song,' So I keep singing a song. Goodnight. Thank you."

A photograph of Elvis during his summer 1970 engagement at the International Hotel, Las Vegas, and which was featured in the MGM film documentary *Elvis : That's The Way It Is.*

After the presentation, the winners all retired to a suite that Elvis had reserved at the Rivermont Holiday Inn and they sat around and chatted, like real people. For once, Elvis was an equal, rather than being fawned upon as the star, and he seemed to enjoy it. Then it came time for him to leave, and the guys and the police escort showed up and it was sudddenly, readily apparent just how different Elvis' life really was.

The most important thing that the award represented for Elvis was the acceptance – the recognition – by the American social establishment. It was a validation of his life and work, especially considering just how far he had come.

STORMCLOUDS

The wheels started to come off his personal life during the Christmas of 1971. On the surface, all was happiness and light. The lifesize Nativity scene was in place in the front yard, the hundreds of blue lights had been strung everywhere and been lit on the first of December, the presents were piled high around the tree, Christmas carols were playing, and the maids circulated with punch and cookies. As usual, movie nights had been held at the Memphian. This year, Elvis' favorites including *Straw Dogs, Diamonds are Forever* (Elvis soon got a .007 9mm gold Beretta with mother-of-pearl handles), and *Dirty Harry* (Elvis soon got a .44 Magnum revolver like Clint Eastwood's).

Priscilla refused Elvis' offer of yet another new car for Christmas (since the Corvair he got her for high school graduation, she had received a Chevrolet, an Oldsmobile Toronado,

The waterfall in the Jungle Room is just one example of how Elvis' taste in interior decor reflected what might be called a "Seventies hotel " style.

a Cadillac El Dorado, and for Christmas 1970, a 1971 Mercedes 280 SL roadster), so instead he presented her with ten crisp new $1,000 bills.

At the party Priscilla ignored Elvis all night and chatted brightly with the women, dwelling at length on the green belt in karate she had just earned. Elvis and the guys had, of course, been touring or in Las Vegas or off on their own in Palm Springs during much of the year (the "no wives" rule particularly galled the women, especially after details of some of their parties began hitting the gossip columns). The party fizzled to a halt when the fountain in the den caught fire and Vernon and Jerry Schilling had to take a sledgehammer to the wall to get to the wiring. Elvis remarked that that was the funniest thing he had seen all night. The next day, Priscilla and Lisa left for L.A. and their Holmby Hills home at 144 Monovale. Elvis and his guys got out their weapons and blasted the hell out of some targets set up against the wellhouse, finally setting the building on fire.

Elvis later got the bad news from Priscilla in Las Vegas, and called home to talk to Grandma Minnie, whom he still called "Dodger" (from an episode in his childhood when he narrowly missed her with a thrown ball). He told her about the separation and said he had taken to his bed, had quit eating, and never wanted to do anything again. Minnie, who could talk straighter to Elvis than anyone else could get away with, told him to get on up out of that bed and get dressed and quit feeling sorry for himself. Minnie, who loved

Priscilla like a daughter, told Elvis that maybe they would get back together and that this wasn't the end of the world.

He wasn't so sure, although he did harbor the hope that they would reunite.

Christmas, 1972. They were still separated, and this year the yuletide stockings hanging on the mantel at Graceland read "Elvis, Lisa, Linda."

Linda Thompson was totally unlike all of Elvis' previous women. Where they were petite, she was showgirl-tall; where they tended to be demure, she spoke her mind; where they were reluctant to call attention to themselves, It was certainly clear to everyone that she was now Elvis' girlfriend. She was, in short, that earthy Southern woman known – affectionately and other-wise – as a good ol' girl.

Linda Thompson met Elvis in August, 1972, introduced by a mutual friend, Bill Browder. He is now known as T.G. Sheppard, the country singer, but at the time he was working as Memphis promotion manager for RCA Records under his real name. When Linda met Elvis, she was twelve hours short of a bachelor's degree in English at Memphis State University. She had been voted best-dressed co-ed at Memphis State and won the beauty titles of Miss Liberty Bowl, Miss Memphis State and Miss Tennessee. She was third runner-up in the Miss USA Pageant.

Her first date with Elvis was for a movie night at the Memphian and she had heard so many wild stories about Elvis that she took along a girlfriend, Miss Rhode Island, just in case. She reported that the evening was pretty tame and that Elvis even tried the old ploy of yawning, stretching his arms and then letting one arm come to rest around her shoulders.

They were soon inseparable. That Christmas, he wanted to show her off to everyone gathered at Graceland. He bought her a full-length mink coat and had had one of his large diamond rings sized down for her. At the party, he asked her to go upstairs and come down wearing her Miss Tennessee crown and banner. She did so, but she also blacked out her front teeth with mascara, without telling Elvis. That of course endeared her to him all the more. She came to be Elvis' buddy, as well as his confidant, his consort, his mother. For a long time, she was the only one who could talk him out of his depressions.

As Elvis had done with Gladys and Priscilla, he communicated with Linda some of the time in an almost impenetrable baby talk.

The Graceland secretary Becky Yancy quoted one of Linda's mailgrams to Elvis in her memoirs: "Baby gullion you are just a little fella. Little fellas need lots of butch, ducklin, and iddytream sure. Sure I said it, Iddytream. Iddytream? Grit. Chock. Chock. Shake. Rattle. Roll. Hmmmmm. . . Grit. Roll again. Hit.Hit. Pinch. Bite. Bite. Bite. Hurt. Grit.. Whew. My baby don't care for rings, da, da, etc. Pablum lullion (in or out of the hospital) P.S. Foxhugh will bite sooties if you say iddytream again. Grit. Grit. Ariadne Pennington (3 years old)."

Some of that is simply untranslatable. "Butch" was Elvis' child-hood term for milk. "Ducklin" was water. "Iddytream" was ice cream. "Foxhugh" was her poodle. "Sooties" were women's feet. (Apparently none of the women around Elvis were immune to the babytalk syndrome. When he was in Baptist Memorial Hospital, his nurse Marian Cocke made "naner puddin" — banana pudding — for him and called his Pepsi-Cola "bellywash." He autographed a picture for her thusly: "To Mrs. Cocke, the sex symbol of the Baptist. . . " Ann-Margret was of course called "Bunny" or "Thumper." And he would talk baby talk with the cooks and maids at Graceland, who spoiled him completely in a slightly dif-ferent vein. There is one quasi-apocryphal story still circulating that stepmother Dee Stanley Presley liked to call Elvis "My Little Prince" – to which he would reply as she walked away, "I've got your little prince right here," grabbing his body in an appropriate spot.) "Ariadne" was the name of a three-year-old girl in Elvis' movie *Follow That Dream.*

Linda was an eater, and, like Elvis, would sometimes eat the same thing every day for weeks on end. For her, a favorite menu was something on the order of tomato gravy, fried chicken giz-zards, fried okra and biscuits. Elvis, meanwhile, would have col-lard greens, cornbread and raw onions. Sometimes he would eat only cornbread soaked in buttermilk – his "soaks."

Linda also loved to dress up and Elvis was happy to indulge her. No blue jeans for her, Linda would have clothing stores bring vanloads of things to Graceland for her to try on. The maids and cooks were astonished once to find that she had ordered them to bring nothing but bikinis, made with leather and feathers and such exotic stuff. Linda always said that people expected Elvis' girlfriend to dress well and even look a little flashy. Although she was well liked by family and friends, the one criticism regularly leveled at Linda was her extravagant spending.

She also loved jewelry and various interested parties have estimated that Elvis spent a million dollars on jewelry – which he called "sparklers" – for Linda in the four years that she was with him. She was also the first woman that he would regularly take on the road with him. Even though Elvis continued to occasionally date during this time – actress Cybill Shepherd was one companion – Linda remained above the fray and would even go on dates with Elvis and a new girl. She was very secure in her role. When Elvis spent eighteen days in Baptist Hospital in 1973, when his colon problems bothered him greatly, she moved into the room with him for the whole time.

She also shared Elvis' love for his animals. In 1975, when his ten-month-old chow, Getlo, became seriously ill, Linda took Getlo and, together with a doctor from Baptist Memorial's kidney dialysis unit, flew by private jet to Boston. The final destination was to have been the New England Institute of Comparative Medicine in West Boylston, Massachusetts, but it was determined that Getlo was too ill to make the remainder of the journey. So she was initially put up at the Copley Plaza Hotel and a medical mobile unit was brought to the hotel for the dog's treatment. Her kidney problems were so bad that the doctors were considering dialysis or even a kidney transplant. But Getlo responded to treatment and spent the next two months receiving intensive care at the home of the Institute's director. The president of the Institute said that Getlo's presence was kept a secret, because of fears that she might be kidnapped. Getlo finally made it home, but passed away a few months later.

The divorce from Priscilla became final on October 9, 1973. Soon Elvis' hospital visits would become more frequent, the health problems more acute and more noticeable. Attempts at self-help and dieting were sporadic and largely ineffectual.

There was a diet list posted in the kitchen at Graceland, for instance, but the cooks could not refuse their beloved Elvis. He would eat only what he wanted to anyway. As one example, when he was in Baptist Hospital with the colon problem, he called Mary

Jenkins at Graceland and asked her to bring him some sauerkraut and wiener sandwiches. She protested, knowing he was on a strict diet. He told her he had to have some sandwiches and how he wanted them fixed: "Boil the kraut and wieners together. Take the wieners out, put them on a hot dog bun, and pile the kraut on top. Then fill them full of mustard. Bring them by to me this afternoon, and tell the guard at my door that you are bringing Linda some clothes." They kept that up for several days until Dr. Nick eventually caught him. Elvis just laughed, like a kid who'd been caught playing hooky.

Back at Graceland, Elvis could not or would not control his appetite. Much has been made of his penchant for cheeseburgers, fries and banana splits, but at home he preferred Southern cooking, albeit with the Presley cholesterol touch. Although Dr. Nick had him on a constant diet, he would call the kitchen and order sausage and biscuits "the way I like them." That way was with the biscuits half dipped in melted butter before the sausage was added. Mary Jenkins tried fixing them with only one stick, instead of two sticks of melted butter. But he could taste the difference immediately and ordered her to fix them the Elvis way. She said she could not refuse her boss.

Not everything Elvis liked was bad for him of course. Mary Jenkins put some of his favorite recipes in a memoir and they show he liked what was typical Southern country cooking: rich cooking that actually evolved on the farm where hard physical labor demanded hearty eating. For breakfast, it was hard for him to break the habit of a pound of fried bacon, with scrambled eggs, biscuits, Cream of Wheat and fresh orange juice. The one California dish that he brought back to Graceland was the Spanish omelette. The luncheon menu included the aforesaid sauerkraut hot dogs, cheeseburgers (with the buns browned in melted butter), B.L.T. sandwiches and homemade vegetable soup – not all for the same lunch of course!

Likewise, his dinner preferences included spaghetti, boneless chicken, almost any kind of steak, meat balls and bacon . . . the list goes on. Dessert favorites were the perennial banana pudding, potato pie, pecan pie, and muffin cakes, while bedtime snacks included the classic, and much-referred to, peanut butter and banana sandwich.

REFUGE

There were fewer and fewer happy times at Graceland. As the concert tours became as routine as the movies had been, Graceland became his refuge more than his joy. Elvis truly brightened up only when Lisa Marie came to visit. The women at Graceland, who probably knew him better than anyone did those last years, were in agreement that Elvis was never the same after the divorce. The boyishness had gone out of him and he spent more and more time by himself upstairs, reading the Bible and his other spiritual books and watching television. Mary Jenkins found that when she took his breakfast tray up on Sunday mornings, he would be watching church services on TV and would ask her to stay and sit and watch the programs with him. He also gave money to her church's building fund.

His last Christmas, Christmas of 1976, was uncharacteristically somber. Gone were the days when the downstairs would rock with music and merrymaking. Elvis had so much wanted, in the old days, everyone to enjoy the festivities that he would send out for sacks of tacos, for example, as he did for Christmas of 1963, so that the cooks wouldn't have to work.

Graceland in 1976 seemed almost empty: there were just Elvis, Lisa Marie (and her new blue electric golf cart), Minnie, Aunt Delta, Mary Jenkins, Charlie Hodge and David Stanley. Vernon was out and about with his nurse-girlfriend, Sandy Miller, although he was not yet divorced from Dee Stanley Presley. Elvis' new on-again, off-again girlfriend, Ginger Alden, was home with her folks mostly, when Elvis wasn't plying her with gifts and buying things for her family. Elvis told Larry Geller that when he looked into Ginger's eyes he could see his mother there. Geller intimated that Elvis was seeing things where there was literally nothing to see. Elvis insisted on seeing what he wanted to see, apparently.

His sense of humor seemed to remain mostly intact, though.

The logo on the fuselage of Elvis' private jet, the *Lisa Marie*, named after his daughter.

Shortly before Christmas, he had one of the guys bring Ginger's mother and one of her sisters up to his bedroom. He solemnly wished them a Merry Christmas and handed them $5 gift certificates from McDonald's. He just wanted to see their reactions, of course. After he was satisfied with the amount of shock he saw registered in their faces, he gave them personal checks, telling them, "All single women need a little money to fall back on."

A few days later, when Ginger's mother's father died, Elvis rallied his guys and arrived with the Alden family in Harrison, Arkansas, in two private jets (his JetStar and a chartered plane, because the runway in Harrison could not accomodate the *Lisa Marie*).

Toward the end of January, Elvis was running alternately hot and cold on the matter of Ginger, but decided to propose to her. He had been studying Cheiro's *Book of Numbers* in his bedroom at Graceland early in the morning of January 26 and decided that the numbers all added up to getting engaged right away. He had one of his guys call his principal jeweler, Lowell Hays, at home in Memphis, waking him up. (Hays over the past couple of years had gone on all the tours because Elvis wanted a jeweler on call at all hours. He used him, too: at the infamous show in Greensboro, North Carolina, when the audience was sitting on its collective hands, Elvis decided to warm them up by giving away an estimated $30,000 worth of "sparklers" to folks in the front rows. That warmed up the crowd, all right. Elvis' other regular jewelers were Harry Levitch in Memphis, who had made Priscilla's wedding ring set, and Sol Schwartz in Beverly Hills. When he was in L.A. Elvis sometimes visited Schwartz' store every afternoon, appropriating Schwartz' office for his own — shaving with an electric razor with his feet propped up on Schwartz' desk. Schwartz' partner, Lee Ablesser, designed the TCB neck charms that Elvis passed out to his workers and friends. The guy who called Hays told him that Elvis wanted a diamond at least as big as the one in his TCB ring. Elvis had paid $55,000 for that, with its 11½ carat stone.

Hays said it was impossible to find a stone like that in the middle of the night in Memphis. Well, Elvis said, what if he flew to New York? Impossible there, too. It would take days. Elvis couldn't wait days. Hays had a brainstorm: he could take the big diamond out of Elvis' TCB ring, fashion it into a proper setting for Ginger, and replace Elvis' stone when a suitable replacement was found. Agreed.

Hays and an employee worked through the night and finally presented Elvis with a spectacular ring. Elvis summoned Ginger into his bedroom and proposed.

She accepted, and then refused to go to Nashville with him while he recorded. He went, sulked and returned home with nothing recorded. He spent the last few months of his life alternately bickering and apparently getting along with Ginger. She did not like to tour. He did five concert tours in the first six months of 1977. On March 3 at Graceland, he signed his will, giving total control of the estate to Vernon and listing only Lisa Marie, Vernon, and Minnie as beneficiaries. The will was witnessed by Ginger, Charlie Hodge and Ann Smith, the wife of Elvis' lawyer, Beecher Smith. Then Elvis embarked on a ten-day Hawaiian vacation, taking thirty-one assorted employees and friends and Alden family members with him on the *Lisa Marie*.

On March 31, he had to cancel a show in Baton Rouge and returned to Memphis, where he was hospitalized at Baptist Memorial and slept for thirty hours straight after checking in to his usual suite on the sixteenth floor. He checked himself out after five days, rested at home a few days, and resumed touring.

After the concert on June 26 at Market Square Arena in Indianapolis, Elvis retreated to Graceland to rest. Nothing was unusual, except that he was quite obviously unwell. The book *Elvis: What Happened?* appeared in bookstores in late July. Elvis had been obsessed by it for some months, especially fearing the effect it might have on *Lisa Marie*. At the end of July, he dispatched *Lisa Marie* the airplane to pick up Lisa Marie the daughter and bring her to Graceland for a visit before the resumed touring on August 16, with the first show on the 17th.

At some point, during one of Elvis' arguments with Ginger, he felt inspired to draw his pistol and fire it in anger. Mary Jenkins was on her way upstairs to retrieve their breakfast trays and turned back when she heard loud, angry voices. Next came the crack of a gunshot. Water came cascading through the ceiling: Elvis had shot out the commode in his bathroom.

The night of August 7, Elvis rented Libertyland (the renovated Fairgrounds amusement park) for a party for Lisa Marie and some friends of the family.

The night of August 10, he rented the United Artists Southbrook 4 Theater (now known as the UA Southbrook 7) at the corner of Shelby Drive and Elvis Presley Boulevard for a showing of *The Spy Who Loved Me*.

He talked on the phone with Larry Geller in L.A. and asked Geller to find him a good book about the Holy Shroud of Turin and bring it to Graceland before they left on tour.

He talked to Joe Esposito about the tour. He played racquetball with Dr. Nick and his son Dean in the racquetball court out back. He supposedly started a fast on August 14.

On August 15, he awoke in mid-afternoon and played with Lisa and her electric golf cart out on the grounds. That night, he had wanted to go and see the movie *MacArthur* at the Ridgeway Theater, but it didn't work out. So he went to his dentist's instead at about 10:30 p.m. – everyone stayed late when Elvis called – in his black Stutz Blackhawk, along with Ginger, Charlie Hodge and Billy Smith. Of all the cars he had gone through in his life, this was the only one he liked to drive anymore. Then there was nothing else he wanted to do, so he came home. He called Dick Grob, his chief of security at Graceland, and gave him a list of songs he wanted added to the repertoire on tour and asked Grob to get lyric sheets for the songs. He sent Al Strada over to the Howard Johnson's up the street to collect from Larry Geller the books he had brought from Los Angeles. They were *The Scientific Search for the Face of Jesus* by Frank O. Adams, *The Second Birth* by O. Mikhail Aivanhov, and *Music: The Keynote of Human Evolution* by Corinne Heline.

He called Mary Jenkins at about two in the morning, this morning of August 16, and asked her to come up and straighten up his bed. When she went into his room, she heard something unfamiliar: total silence. It was the first time she had ever been in his room when he was home and found no TV sets on. She changed the bed linen and took his water bottle and started toward Lisa's bathroom to fill it from the tap there. She found Elvis and Ginger siting on Lisa's bed, sitting there in the dark. He told her he just hadn't felt like having the TV on. She offered to fix him something to eat, and he refused, just as he had done the previous night. She found that unusual.

He took some pills as usual. He played racquetball with Ginger and Billy Smith and his wife Jo, who lived in one of the trailers up in the back forty. He sat down at the piano in the lounge area of the racquetball court to unwind and sang "Blue Eyes Crying in the Rain" and "Unchained Melody," among other songs. Then he read in bed for a while. Aunt Delta brought him a glass of ice water shortly before 9 a.m. Ginger later said that she woke up about 9 and found him still reading in bed. He later went into the bathroom, where he read a little more.

Then he just died. On an ordinary day and in an ordinary way, Elvis just died. Downstairs, Graceland was buzzing with the usual daytime activities. Cooks were cooking, maids were cleaning, phones were being answered, fan mail was being delivered, fans were waiting at the gates for him.

Upstairs, Ginger lay asleep and Elvis lay dead.

At the time Elvis died, the Living Room and Dining Room and Music Room were still in their red velvet mode, as a result of Elvis' last redecoration job with Linda Thompson. It was really red, with the flowing red drapes with gold fringes, hung canopy style in the doorways, the red carpeted entryway with the white

"Many times when I was working here, people would ask 'What colors are you going to have, Elvis?' and he'd reply 'Oh, I'm going to have a red carpet, purple walls and gold furniture' " (George Golden, 1957 Graceland decorator). At the time he settled for the blue scheme, though red took over in the Seventies.

fur rugs dotted about, and the dining room chairs tufted like some kind of vague Las Vegas dream.

Everything stayed just as it was when Elvis died, just frozen in time. Then, in 1981, Jack Soden (chief executive officer of Elvis Presley Enterprise, Inc.) was visiting Graceland to study different feasibilities for opening Graceland to the public. He was talking to Aunt Delta about the red decor. Delta said, "You know, Elvis really didn't like all this red after it was put in. He started using the back stairs so he wouldn't have to look at it. It's a shame we can't have all that nice blue and white stuff that's in storage, that's what he really liked and always used."

Everyone, including Priscilla, was delighted with Delta's revelation. With all the negative press the Elvis legend had been enduring after the publication of some highly-touted, mean-spirited biographies, no one was anxious to offer up these wild red rooms for ridicule as Graceland's front door swung open to the world.

So Priscilla supervised the redecoration back to the way it was. Remaining in the front rooms from the 1974-1977 redecoration booms are the extensive use of mirrors and the stained glass peacock windows separating the living rooms from the Music Room (the windows replaced glass brick, which Elvis had kept covered with drapes. The external stained glass, including the "P" above the front door were added at the same time). Otherwise, the rooms are actually very close to Gladys' first decoration scheme in 1957. The blue and the white had been a constant. The white fifteen-foot-long sofa was custom-made in 1957. It had been in storage since 1974. But, as Aunt Delta remarked to Soden, when Elvis was alive, all of this was part of the very "lived in" furnishing. Priscilla's Great Danes, Brutus and Snoppy, would wrestle on the couch and pull all the cushions off.

It's difficult at first to imagine Elvis actually being here for twenty years, actually living everyday life here, but it becomes very easy after a while. The important realization is that this is all human scale, very human scale, not some gargantuan museum or mausoleum or temple. This was his home, he moved in here when he was twenty-two years old, and it must have seemed the size of a palace to him then. On one of his periodic visits to Tupelo after achieving stardom, he looked at that little birthplace on Old Saltillo Road, amazed at its size. "I could put that whole house in my living room," he said, not believing his childhood memory of the size of the house.

Gold drapes are still up in the Music Room. Elvis had three different pianos in there over the years. The blond TV set dates from 1957. The mirror over the couch had been in the Audubon Drive house. James Brown was the most famous person other than Elvis to play that piano. Many all-night songfests took place here, from the gospel groups to visiting performers to Elvis by himself, singing gospel at dawn. If only it had been recorded.

The Elvis portrait in the living room originally had been thumbtacked − unframed − on a wall in

The Music Room with its gold drapes *(above)*, was the scene of many sessions at the piano. *Below*, Elvis is joined by a gospel group known as the Sunshine Boys.

Vernon's office. Typical of Vernon's death grip on the pursestrings. The secretaries were paid $65 a week − and earned every penny − while hundreds of thousands were paid out to cover Elvis' wildly extravagant gift-giving. During Elvis' time resentment flourished in many corners of the garden of Graceland employees, Elvis' extended family, his different employees and friends. And a lot of those who were not on the receiving end of Elvis' benevolent largesse while he was alive − the cars and houses and jewelry and travel and lavish bonuses − were counting on his will to take care of them after his death. Were they ever surprised. (At least one relative had charged that the will was not genuine, or that it had been altered.)

Elvis' generosity probably worsened Vernon's heart trouble. He would visibly wince when he saw Elvis giving things away from the stage. Most of the spirited arguments Elvis and Vernon had were over Elvis' spending. Vernon would wave the bills at Elvis and rant and rave that they were headed for the poorhouse. Elvis would tell him not to worry; he would just go out and earn some more. An argument over Elvis' buying $30,000 or so worth of guns in L.A. led to Elvis' running away from home to the White House. Elvis used to tell the story of first glimpsing Gary Pepper in his wheelchair at the music gates; he was patiently waiting to meet Elvis. Pepper had cerebral palsy. Elvis invited him in and they became friends. Pepper started the Elvis Presley Tankers Fan Club, and went on Elvis' payroll at $400 a month to handle fan club mail. Elvis also bought him a car.

The foyer was often used for karate practice — especially to get a running jump from the Music Room to break a board in the foyer. After Linda Thompson and Elvis redecorated and transformed the foyer into a vibrant red tunnel, she would often romp and wrestle with the chow Getlo on one of the white fur rugs that adorned the entranceway.

Lisa Marie used to play in here with her dolls and little carriages. One day when she saw Elvis start his descent down the stairs, she threw up her hands and screamed like a crazed fan, "Ailvis! Ail-vis!" Elvis loved that.

The bedroom with bath behind the living room was Gladys and Vernon's, then Minnie's; now it is Aunt Delta's. Minnie was the keeper of the keys and kept the keys to all the cars in a box in her room. There is a small bedroom and bath off the kitchen, usually used as a maid's room.

Vernon bought Priscilla and Elvis a Jenn-Air stainless steel range with a double oven after their wedding and it was installed next to the original one-oven stove. Otherwise, the kitchen had a breakfast nook, where a lot of the guys would eat, a TV, a double stainless steel sink, a red refrigerator and a white one, on opposite sides of the kitchen. There were originally two kitchen windows, but one was covered with curtains after the Jungle Room was added behind the kitchen. Mary Jenkins once estimated that, at the height of the period when the guys were hanging around Graceland all the time (before Priscilla and the Colonel encouraged Elvis to start running them off), Graceland's grocery bills ran between $300 and $400 a day. Elvis may have been eating hot dogs with sauerkraut, but nobody else was at all bashful about ordering up a big, juicy and expensive T-bone steak.

"In 1957 I had complete charge of doing the redecorating, and choosing the furniture" (George Golden)

Roy Orbison was a great friend of Elvis' and visited Graceland often. He learned one major lesson from studying the layout at Graceland. Like Elvis, Roy loved to stay at home and loved to eat and loved his privacy. So, when he built his dream house on the shores of Old Hickory Lake outside Nashville, he installed a dumbwaiter that ran directly from the kitchen to the side of his bed. He also put in several hidden stairwells so that he could literally be invisible in his own house. Elvis could have benefited greatly from similar home embellishments.

Also on the main floor, just off the foyer, is a small room referred to as the "bird room" because a myna bird was kept there. Elvis also kept a small spider monkey there for a time.

Upstairs, Elvis' bedroom was and is above the living room. As you face the front of Graceland, the right two windows open into his bedroom, the smaller center window is in his bathroom, and the two windows on the left open to Elvis' wardrobe room. His bed faced the front of the house. Elvis' bedroom had two TVs mounted in the ceiling above the bed and a large TV console between the windows, with a 3/4" video recorder on top and stereo equipment on the shelves. He also had a security monitor TV screen and he could switch pictures from the gates to Lisa's room to the front grounds to different rooms in the house.

His office, directly behind his bedroom, had a large desk in the right-hand back corner with the nameplate reading "The Boss" on it. The famous photograph of Elvis shaking hands with Nixon in the Oval Office occupied a prominent place on his desk. There was also a crystal ball on a brass stand. He had a gold telephone, two gun cases, a large couch and stereo equipment in the office. Prominent among his books were his well-thumbed *Holy Bible* and his equally used *Physician's Desk Reference*. He also had tiger pictures (his martial arts instructor, Kang Rhee, nicknamed him "The Tiger"). His wall hangings tended toward the inspirational: the poem "The Priceless Gift," written by Tupelo friend Janelle McComb for Elvis to give Lisa Marie on her fourth birthday; an uplifting sermonette called "The Penalty of Leadership"; and a short passage written by Theodore Roosevelt. This is called "The Man Who Counts" and it is not difficult to see why Elvis liked it so: "It is not the critic who counts, not the man who points out how the strong man tumbled, or where the doer of deeds could have done them better. The credit belongs to the man who is actually in the arena; whose face is marred by dust, sweat and blood; who strives valiantly; who errs and comes short again and again; who knows the great enthusiasms, the great devotions, and spends himself in a worthy cause; who at the best knows in the end the triumph of high achievement, and who at the worst, if he fails, at least fails while daring greatly, so that his place shall never be with those cold and timid souls who know neither victory nor defeat."

Behind the office was a dressing room for Priscilla or Linda or Ginger. When Priscilla redecorated Graceland, that was the only room that she made overtly feminine. Otherwise, she said, she knew the house had to stay masculine for Elvis.

Elvis' own dressing room had a bed for bodyguards to use. For a couple of years Elvis had a white circular fur bed in there, similar in style to the "hamburger bed" in Lisa's bedroom. Her bed also had a white fur canopy. Her bedroom and bathroom were white. Her dresser was white and covered with a collection of

Much of the decor at Graceland is pure fun, like the extensive – some would say extravagant – use of mirrors in the TV Room, which was masterminded in 1974 by Elvis, Linda Thompson and decorator Bill Eubanks.

blown-glass clowns. She had a rocking chair with an "Elvis" pillow on it. And a big TV. Her room also opens onto the sundeck above the Jungle Room.

Decorator Bill Eubanks worked closely with Linda (and Elvis, to a lesser extent) on the basement rooms in 1974. Elvis' original decor for the TV Room — known as the Den before he added the Jungle Room — consisted of two sectional sofas, his own chair, which was high-backed and covered in gold leather, blond cocktail and end tables, and draperies adorned with large red flowers amidst greenery. At one point, the basement rooms were brown and white; at another, Elvis had them redone in blue and green. There is no way to determine how many times and in how many ways Elvis had parts of Graceland redecorated.

He always kept his pipe rack on a table by the couch in the TV Room. His favorite pipe had a bowl shaped like a lion's head. The TV Room had always been used for TV-watching, but after Elvis heard that LBJ had three TV sets sitting side-by-side so that he could watch all three networks at once, Elvis decided he had to have the same. The story goes that he preferred to watch three football games at once, with his favorite game on the center screen and the sound turned up on that set — but how often, in the Seventies, were three football games televised simultaneously on broadcast TV (this was pre-cable and pre-satellite)? But the TV Room, with its wildly disorienting mirrored ceiling and the cozy little yellow-padded Naugahyde bar and soda fountain is exactly the way it looked the last day Elvis was in here in 1977, down to the TCB lightning bolt symbol on the wall. We can only imagine the delights that satellite TV, HDTV, high- quality VCRs, and video rental stores would have brought to Elvis. A pity that he departed this vale of tears before they were all introduced for home use. He might have never left his bedroom again if he could have had all the TV toys that now exist.

Behind the TV Room is a bedroom, occupied by various people at different times, Charlie Hodge and Jerry Schilling among them.

Also pristine in its Seventies glory is the breathtaking Pool Room with its ten trillion square feet of an almost psychedelic, quasi-paisley, batik-like fabric forming a gathered and pleated tent of a room (it only looks like several trillion square feet; probably it's about 350 square yards). Bill Eubanks, the decorator who executed the bizarre work, referred to the room as Elvis' "cocoon" and as his emotional "bomb shelter." It was one of Elvis' primary places to retreat. I suppose it could even be referred to as womblike, if a pool table can be considered a natural fixture of such a space.

The Pool Room showed that Elvis was really having fun with decorating. He and Linda had seen a sofa covered with a similar fabric in a decorator showroom and decided to cover the whole room in it, ceiling and all. And, as was very prevalent in the mid-Seventies, they decided to make the furnishings very eclectic, from Louis XV chairs to turn-of-the-century posters to faux-Tiffany lampshades over the table. Elvis liked 8-ball and rotation and supposedly was very good at both. The pool table apparently dates from the Audubon Drive house. Behind the Pool Room is the laundry and a half-bath, and a three-quarter bath that connects to the bedroom off the TV Room.

I hadn't known before that the narrow, steep stairway into the

The monkey-motif runs throughout the Jungle Room, from the huge wooden furniture to delicate china ornaments littered about the tables, as it does about other parts of the house.

basement is mirrored almost completely — ceiling and walls — and the effect upon descending those stairs is akin to that of tumbling ass over tea kettle into a sort of cockeyed wonderland.

The compact bar at the entrance to the TV Room houses a hidden movie projector and a screen is housed in the TV wall, which also has a stereo and a jukebox that holds one hundred 45 singles and is wired for sound throughout the house. From looking at a representative sample of his records, Elvis liked and was knowledgeable about all avenues that American popular music traveled, with the exception of jazz. Blues and gospel were his bedrock, but his tastes ventured far afield. Some representative performers and records: Tom Jones, Ray Price, Jonathan Winters, Bill Black's Combo, the Boston Symphony performing Mahler's Symphony No.1, Mario Lanza, Enrico Caruso, The Clovers, John Wayne, The Blackwoods, The Kingsmen Quartet, Jordanaires, Patti Page, Dean Martin, Allman Brothers Band, Brahms Concerto No.2 performed by the Chicago Symphony, Martin Luther King Jr, Sam Cooke, Peter, Paul & Mary, Buddy Holly, Burl Ives, Ray Charles, the Rambos, The Supremes.

There can be no doubt, though, that Elvis loved his TV. There was at least one set in each room or general area at Graceland. He would sometimes go out to the kitchen to check on the set in there, to make sure the cooks and maids had their TV running right. "I don't want you girls to miss any of your programs, now" he would tell them.

The Jungle Room acquired that name from the staff and media when the Graceland tours opened in 1982; before that it was more commonly called the Den. Measuring fourteen feet wide by forty feet long, it is the largest room in the house (the Dining Room, Living Room and Pool Room are each seventeen feet by twenty-four feet, the Music Room is fourteen by seventeen, and the TV Room is seventeen by twenty-eight). It began life as an added-on screened porch in the mid-Sixties, then it was enclosed as a typical Sixties family room overlooking the backyard and adjoining the kitchen. Then one day Elvis went on a shopping spree at Donald's Furniture Store and brought about the decor that remains there today. The furniture is pine and is difficult to describe: suffice to say great portions of it look like parts of very wild animals. The huge circular chair with the fake fur was too big to come through a doorway, so a picture window had to be removed and it was hoisted in. It was one of Lisa Marie's favorite spots to nap. The furniture was a short-lived regional fad and reminded

green shag carpet on the ceiling and floor surely assisted the acoustics for recording, but that had not been Elvis' intent when he had it installed. It was something of a Californian fashion at the time for recreation rooms, and he just liked it.

Had he lived, given his penchant for frequent change and redecoration, these rooms would now be only memories. As it is, they have become part of the Elvis Presley time capsule.

Elvis kept all his vehicles in the backyard; his snow/grass-mobiles, his golf carts, his go-carts, his three-wheelers. The cars were under a carport. He had an old John Deere tractor that he had once liked driving. He would hook up a wagon to it and take people on wagon rides and try to make the ride so bumpy that they would be bounced off. When Elvis' fireworks battles — his "war" — became more and more official, they

Elvis on a movie set sometime in the early Sixties, playing with his infamous pet monkey Scatter, notorious for making a nuisance of itself at every possible opportunity. Elvis, of course, encouraged the animal's mischief-making and bad behavior.

Elvis of Hawaii; there are monkeys, of course, and a Tiki god in there somewhere. He had a huge polished cypress coffee table to rest his feet on while he watched his big-screen projection TV and ate breakfast. This was also the room where the guys waited for Elvis; waited for him to come down in the afternoon; just waited for him in general. This was also the room he used in his last year as a remote recording studio: RCA would park a sound truck in the backyard and run the cables in and Elvis would go for days. He recorded the album "From Elvis Presley Boulevard, Memphis, Tennessee" and part of the album "Moody Blue" in this room. The

put on helmets and leather jackets and gloves, to cut down on the injuries. He would try to have "war" twice a year: Christmas and the Fourth of July, if he could be home for both dates. They set the house on fire at least once. And one time, Elvis or someone really got Vernon. They left a bowl of small torpedoes – little red balls that explode when you throw them down on the pavement or step on them – out on the kitchen counter. Vernon thought it was candy and bit down on a couple of them. You can imagine the level of hilarity throughout the kitchen – once they ascertained that he was not badly hurt.

To the back a few paces is what had been the previous owner's old combination servants' quarters and smoke house (sometimes referred to as a wellhouse) which was Vernon's office. (The smokehouse part was also used by Elvis as a firing range and there are still bullet holes in the walls. They set it ablaze once with automatic fire.)

Here was where Elvis held his homecoming-from-the-army press conference. This was where all the mail and the presents poured in daily by the sackful. Ann-Margret would call here and say, "Oh, just tell Elvis that Bunny called." Elvis would straggle out here sometimes wearing his sweats to shoot the breeze and look through his mail and his "happies" (presents) that the fans were sending to him. The office looks almost exactly the same today as it did back in 1960 when Elvis walked out from the back door of the house to face the press. It is an exceedingly plain office, with old metal surplus desks, oak and glass bookshelves, and metal filing cabinets. The room is covered with cheap pine paneling. There is an old postal scale, a coffee pot, a bust of Elvis, a plastic table radio, a few pictures of him on the wall, a comfortable old Naugahyde couch (on which the secretaries would sneak naps), some kind of exotic moon-and-star deco lamp, an old-fashioned wooden hatrack. It is by far the homiest room in Graceland and that's probably because Vernon furnished it for nothing or next to nothing and saw no need to ever change it or improve upon it. The room's most distinctive feature is a wooden sign on the door. Vernon had Patsy Presley Gambill (one of the secretaries who was also Vester's daughter) paint it. This is the message, all in capital letters:

"Please read and observe. No loafing in office. Strictly for employees only! If you have business here, please take care of it and leave. Vernon Presley."

And he meant it.

All the animals used to be out here in the open. The screeching peacocks, the many dogs, the stray cats, the chickens, ducks, Scatter (the perpetually horny, alcoholic chimpanzee, eventually kept in a cage most of the time). You would almost expect to see a unicorn come prancing past. Squint your eyes here in the back of Graceland at sunset and you can almost make out the wavering images from 1957: Elvis driving up in the pink Cadillac and waving to Gladys tending her beloved chickens. There is washing hanging on the line. Elvis is ready to play a little touch football and then retire to the pool to get a Pepsi and listen to all the new tunes on his jukebox sitting right out there on the patio by his pool. The future, the future. . . it was wide open. He knew he could do anything he wanted.

Out to the Meditation Garden. There is a golden twilight across the sky and a few hushed voices around the graves. I read the names of the donors on the base of the eternal flame that burns just above Elvis' head: Tommy Henley. He worked maintenance for Elvis. Letitia Henley, Tommy's wife, who worked for Dr. Nick and acted as Elvis' private nurse. The Henleys lived in a trailer behind Graceland. Patsy Gambill, Vester's daughter and a Graceland secretary. Al Strada, one of Elvis' guys who handled wardrobe. Elvis bought him a Porsche. Felton Jarvis, Elvis' last record producer. Elvis financed a kidney transplant for Jarvis. Jerry Schilling, one of Elvis' guys, one of the few who dared stand up to Elvis when he thought he was wrong, now is a consultant to Elvis Presley Enterprises. Dean Nichopolous, Dr. Nick's son, sometimes worked wardrobe for Elvis and was a frequent racquetball partner. Elvis once "healed" him after a skiing accident. Dr. George Nichopolous, the infamous Dr. Nick, who tried to control Elvis' medication intake. His medical license was briefly suspended for overprescribing addictive drugs. He was acquitted by jury trial. Janelle McComb, longtime Elvis friend, who once asked Elvis how he would like to be remembered at his birthplace; he said he wanted a chapel in which his fans could meditate – McComb founded the Elvis Memorial Chapel in Tupelo. Joe Esposito, Elvis' right-hand man since the army days in West Germany.

Let's stroll on down to the racquetball court. This was where Elvis Presley sang his last songs. Besides the exercise equipment, there is the little piano, a stereo set and lounge chairs, a full bar, and a pinball machine with a boxing theme called "Knockout." The upstairs, now closed off, has dressing rooms, showers and a jacuzzi, and a door to the rooftop sun deck.

The actual racquetball court area is now the location of one of the most dazzling exhibits at Graceland and, for that matter, one of the most spectacular memorial tributes erected to any performer past or present, anywhere, at anytime.

The staff at Graceland know that Elvis has by now sold more than one billion records worldwide, more than anybody has ever done or likely will ever do. But, because of technical reasons having to do with RIAA (the Recording Industry Association of America) certification, and the fact that RCA's files were themselves incomplete, it was impossible to prove that. RCA awarded Elvis gold records itself, but did not petition the RIAA for retroactive certification. Nor did it request certification when a record went gold or platinum more than once.

Finally, after Graceland bought all of Colonel Parker's files, the proof was there. Graceland and RCA asked RIAA auditors to come to Memphis and see for themselves the exhaustive sales figures. So, on August 12, 1992, Graceland unveiled the remarkable wall of new gold and platinum records awarded to Elvis Presley: an amazing 110 titles that were certified gold, platinum and even multi-platinum.

As I stood, regarding the spectacular, rainbow-hued wall of new gold and platinum records in the racquetball court, I felt a sudden urge to sink to my knees and confess: "Forgive me, Elvis, for I have sinned against thee."

"Yes, my son?" I seem to hear that familiar voice trailing in from the horse pasture just outside these walls. "Yes, my son, what do you wish to confess?"

"Well, Elvis, I harbored negative thoughts about you once — inspired, I must admit, by the faithless traitors within your midst who would betray you for thirty (or a hundred thousand) pieces

The center-piece of the Presley buriel plot, the Eternal Flame, like some Olympic beacon or monument to an Unknown Soldier, stands over the graves in the Meditation Garden, adding to the sense of pilgrimage for those who visit.

of silver. And also instigated by the pointy-headed ex-professor who seemed to glorify in the, ahem, alleged occasional and of course alleged tiny indiscretions in which you may or may not have indulged or involved yourself, as it were, and so ..."

I was cut off by The Voice of Doom: "Damnit, cut the bull****! We are all human, especially me. If you have denied me, you must say three 'Heartbreak Hotels' and two 'All Shook Up's' and one 'Love Me Tender.'

"Amen, boss!" I sang out. I was rewarded by a basso-profundo heavenly laugh that seemed to shake the very ground I stood upon. I opened my eyes and shook my head to clear the misty cobwebs that seemed to have suddenly formed there. I looked around: all seemed to be normal. There was a cluster of fans gazing up at the Gold and Platinum Wall, that was all. No one was staring at me. Still, I thought, this wall really belongs in the Temple of Dendur.

EPIPHANY

On to the Trophy Room. For many, this room is an epiphany, containing as it does so many disparate elements of Elvis' life and career. If someone were to drop in tomorrow morning from Sirius and had never heard of Elvis, a walk through the Trophy Room would educate him/her/it very thoroughly.

What strikes me is that this room is a window into Elvis' heart and mind in a way that nothing else can perhaps provide. The room contains some of the things that mattered most to him in his life. I was privileged to go through Elvis' original trophy room a couple of years after he died and the feeling was the same then. By the last years of his life, possessions meant nothing to Elvis. Money obviously meant nothing to him. Cadillacs were mere coins of the realm and he tossed them around accordingly.

What he kept was clearly what mattered to him. Cars and jewelry and fancy furniture and extravagant clothes — other than the stage outfits, which were for the fans after all, not for him — all this mattered not a whit. What he kept was memories. Incredible amounts of the "happies" that the fans sent to him. Not the store-bought stuff — the cologne and all that crap. He kept the things that people had made with a little of their heart and soul thrown into them. The embroidered pillows, the carefully put-together scrapbooks, the drawings by little kids, the painstaking needle-work, little sculptures, an elaborate wooden Trojan horse, hand-stitched shirts, colorful collages. It's a celebration of folk art with one central theme: We love Elvis.

How could he not have responded to that?

The rest is, I think, easy to see. The other things he kept, he kept because: 1) they are some of his favorite toys. The badges and the guns come under this heading; 2) they validate his life and existence and career. Gold records, souvenirs of some of his greatest triumphs such as the black leather suit, the Jaycees award, the letters from presidents of the United States. They all bear witness to the fact that Elvis came this way once and that people are better off for his having done so. And that they said so while he was still alive.

In another sense, all of this proved that Elvis had done it; proved that he was, by God, truly Teddy Roosevelt's "man in the arena, whose face is marred by dust, sweat and blood."

Week after week, month after month, year after year, Elvis set sail from behind these protected gates and went forth to slay the beast and then make his triumphant return, bearing with him the spoils of war, the gold and silver and precious goods. He went out there and conquered Mammon more times than any mortal being should have to. What's left after that? Just the memories.

He knew that many of the people around him were there strictly to put the bite on him, and in the end, he really didn't care.

Besides those with their hands out ("got a handful of 'gimmie!' and a mouthful of 'much obliged' " goes the song) there were the

pack rats. Elvis knew what was going on but felt even noticing it was beneath his dignity. These were the guys who might scoop up the occasional dirty Elvis socks or underwear or scarves or dis-carded hair dryer or comb or brush and squirrel it away for that distant day when it could all be cashed in. Everything Elvis touched became an instant relic, after all. He knew that in the hotels, his tray and used dishes and silverware usually never made it back to the kitchen. Often, neither did his used linen make it back to the laundry room.

He, of course, couldn't control all that. But it was a bit discon-certing to know that no sooner had he pulled out his .45 and blasted out a 21-inch RCA TV (whose only offense had been broadcasting, say, a Robert Goulet insulting Elvis by trying to sing) and the smoking remains of the TV were hauled out, that those said remains went straightaway into the trunk of some-body's car (a car paid for by Elvis) and would be stored out of sight until . . . The Day. His X-rays were carted off, medical records had a way of vanishing, his garment bag disappeared, a hair dryer suddenly gone, his cigarillo stubs. . . where would it all end? Early on, in the Audubon Drive days, girls would beg Gladys for Kleenex so they could wipe the dust from Elvis' Cadillacs and take it away with them. Cups of water from Elvis' tap were all the rage for a while. Leaves from the driveway at Graceland were considered very desirable objects – failing all else.

But I wonder if Elvis considered the psychic minefield he walked through every day of his life – not just the people who resented or even hated him because he supported them, but all the books that would one day come bubbling out of so many who were close (or supposedly close) to him. How many notes were surreptitiously scribbled down as soon as X or Y left Elvis' side? Were there concealed tape recorders whirring away as one of the guys joked and talked with Elvis?

At any rate, the (so-called) literary output of the Elvis brigade has been fairly breathtaking thus far and there seems to be no end in sight. Books purporting to tell the real inside story of the Elvis legend have come from every imaginable source, from distant rel-atives to the pizza delivery man.

There has also been the somewhat more limited field of former Elvis acquaintances making records as a method of communicat-

The wall outside Graceland must be one of the few places in the world where middle-aged people can be found openly writing graffiti in broad daylight!

ing their experience with the King to an eager world. These have included former girlfriends, second cousins and just some of those good ol' Nashville music boys out to make a fast buck.

It's significant that Elvis' first improvements to Graceland were the walls and the music gates. Significant, because he knew that he needed them. His celebrity and stardom were such that he could never again pretend to a normal life. But also significant because in choosing the particular walls and gates that he did, he was making a very generous gesture to his fans. He was saying, in effect, "Look, you all know I have to do this to protect myself and my family, but look here, this is just a little wall and the gates aren't all that big. I don't want to shut you all out of my life completely."

These are probably the first user-friendly security gates and walls that any celebrity ever came up with. There's nothing the least forbidding about the approach to Graceland: in fact, it looks enticing and alluring, Eden-like. The gates and walls are pure symbolism. As were the gate guards for many years: various relatives of Elvis who needed work. Their main job, in the end, was to entertain the visitors. For many years, Elvis would often let the fans wander freely over the grounds.

His ultimate protection was the fans themselves. He enjoyed perhaps the closest relationship with his audience of any performer I can name. And their presence at the walls and at the gates proved that.

Over the years, the gates became the crossroads of the world for Elvis fans. Here they met, they exchanged messages, they got to see Elvis and photograph him and sometimes talk to him. And they knew, most importantly, that he approved and even liked having them here. Not for him a twelve-foot chain-link fence with razor wire on the top and slavering guard dogs and armed Rambos wandering the grounds waiting to kick your head in, like some of those celebrities; no need to name names. Elvis really was the first friendly superstar.

Look at some of the proof on the walls, the messages that are scrawled and scribbled and etched all over it. Most of them are direct expressions of love. Some are just little personal messages of how the writer has been getting along and how Elvis was helped him or her out. Some are the Elvis jungle telegraph: "Goldman is a son of a bitch." Others are more playful: "Elvis I've got your hunk of burning love between my legs."

More has gone on out here in the shadow of the walls and gates than anyone can chronicle. The gates are the magnets for Elvis' many wives and children from around the world, who show up ready to claim their legitimate place in Elvis' world. There are

Privacy or prison?
The question has been posed more than once whether the real function of the gates at Graceland was to keep the fans from Elvis, or Elvis from the fans.

the dozens of true Elvises, who arrive prepared to move into their house. There are the streakers, the strippers, the drunk collegians, the girls out on a dare, the One True Fan, the phony doctors, the fake priests, the phony terminal cancer patients, the two girls pretending to be dogs in a shipping crate addressed to Elvis, the elegant woman in a party dress who liked to pee on Elvis' driveway, and more and more. Mainly there are the true Elvis fans.

And occasionally something else. Here are two scenes from the gates:

The Elvis demon came over him when he lost count of the number of drinks he had knocked back in the dim recesses of Bad Bob's Vapors, the cavernous supper club and watering hole out on East Brooks Road that is his favorite Memphis haunt. He was hunkered down at the ninety-foot-long bar, under the Vapor's dusky red overhead lights that barely pierced the smoky vast reaches of the place. The sound of Elvis came at him again and again. Was it the phone or the jukebox or the demon murmuring to him? Elvis' voice, silky and insistent, was calling to him, calling to Jerry Lee Lewis, calling to the only legitimate pretender to the throne. The demon whispered, "Come to me, I need you, I need Jerry Lee. Come to Graceland, Elvis is in trouble. Elvis needs Jerry Lee. For nobody else understands the demands of the kingdom and the power of rock and roll."

Jerry Lee had been sinking V.O. straight up — "Coke on the side, please, Killer" — since mid-afternoon with a series of the Vapors regulars. "Buy you a drank, Killer?" "Three drinks, Killer?" He never had a shortage of friends to drink with in Memphis. And plenty of them were quick to offer the pills and powders that fueled Memphis rock and roll. Plenty of drinking and doping buddies to empathize with Jerry Lee's rotten luck over his long, ill-starred career in Elvis' shadow: "Killer, you was screwed! You shoulda been the King! They jacked you over!"

Then that November night in 1976 Jerry Lee knew he was going over the line but just couldn't stop himself. After all that V.O. and Coke and God only knew what else, he switched over to champagne. The dull red glow from the lights in the Vapors was throbbing and throbbing. There was a red shift in his brain, "Goin' to Graceland! Goin' to get Elvis! I'm comin' El, I'm comin'!"

He staggered out, through the electrically locked double set of front doors, out into the vast asphalt reaches of the 800-car parking lot, and finally found his custom Lincoln. One hand had a death grip on a bottle of Korbel; the other grasped a .38 pistol. He tossed the gun onto the dashboard, turned the ignition and burned rubber all the way out of the Vapors parking lot onto Brooks Road and hung a swerving, squealing left turn onto Elvis Presley Boulevard and set sail due south for Graceland. Only Jerry Lee, truly the sole living man capable of being King of rock and roll, could know how El felt. Only Jerry Lee could save him from himself and from the wasteful retinue of parasitic courtiers and handlers whom Jerry Lee felt to be sucking the very lifeblood out of Elvis. "I'm comin' Elvis! Hold on, brutha!"

Sacrilege and travesty! The iron gates to Graceland do not swing wide to admit Jerry Lee, the only true friend of Elvis. Even after Jerry Lee's Lincoln sort of nudges the gates, they bend not. The gatekeeper, instead of recognizing and admitting the guest, betrays him by calling the police. In the flashing red lights Jerry Lee flings the evil bottle of alcohol aside: he forgets to roll the window down first and the window shatters. His pistol is somewhere in the general field of vision. A number of police officers approach with pistols drawn. "Jerry Lee, was you fixin' to go up there and shoot Elvis?" "Hail yes, Killer!"

That's one version.

I asked Jerry Lee the truth about the gate episode. He answered straightforwardly: "Elvis had been calling me for several days— he had Linda Thompson, his girlfriend, calling me. I get on the phone with Elvis and he's saying, you got to come out here. I am so depressed I don't know what to do. He just sounded pitiful. He had called many times before but I just hadn't felt that I was in that good shape to go out to Elvis' house. I got to be honest with you, I was pretty loaded that night at the Vapors. I'd been drinking whisky pretty heavy and then I got over onto champagne, hell of a note. Then Elvis called and I said, awright, I'll go out there and straighten him out."

He laughs heartily and drains his glass. "Mistake number bigtime one! So I got into this long ole Mark I Lincoln of mine. I had a bottle of champagne between my legs. I arrived at Elvis' house. And at the Vapors Charlie Foreman had given me this .38 Derringer pistol, it's at Jimmy Swaggart's house now. It was brand new, had never been fired, beautiful gun. I took it and put it in my glove compartment. He said, 'No, you can't have a concealed weapon. Put it on your dashboard.' So I throwed it up on my dashboard and forgot about it. I whipped into the drive, the front end of that Lincoln looked like it was 30 miles long and I hit that gate. That gate shook and it looked like Elvis doin' a show. Two tons just a shakin'. The guy he had working the gate wasn't his Uncle Vester. It was a new boy and he come over there and he knocked on my window and he looked at me. I was trying to roll my window down, but instead I was puttin' my seat back. I said, 'What is this, boah?' He said, 'Well whatya want?' I said, 'Well, I wanta see Elvis Presley. Elvis called me to come see him.' This boy didn't know who I was. Now, I thought I had put down the window on the right side and I threw this champagne bottle out and the window was up so I knocked the whole window out. Well, that scared him to death. Then he saw that pistol and his eyes got this big around and he cut and run! He called the damn cops. And I sat there and the next thing I knew I was surrounded by five or six police squad cars. The cop was talking to me and I knew him and he said, ' Jerry Lee, this looks bad. What're you doin' with that pistol? Were you gonna go up there and shoot Elvis with that pistol? Were you gonna go up there and shoot Elvis with that pistol?' I said, 'Hell yes, if I can get up there! ' I figured if they were that damned stupid to ask a question like that, then I'm gonna answer 'em stupid! He said 'Well I just think the best thing to do with you is just take you downtown.' I said, 'Whatever you think. We got in the squad car and we was ridin' downtown and I said, you know somethin'? You gonna lose your job, boy, you know Elvis did call me. El's waitin' on me up there. And this boy like to got fired. A couple of 'em waitin' on me up there. And this boy like to got fired.' A couple of 'em did But he was about to make lieutenant so they let him slide. But he never pulled a stunt like that on me again. I was right. Elvis waited on me five or six hours up there. He never knew what was goin' on. Now, I did hear a different story where somebody called him and said 'Jerry Lee is sittin' down there with a gun' and Elvis said 'lock him up.' But I find that hard to believe. But I never pushed it after that. I never tried to go back anymore. I was right, son. Now am I, Jerry Lee Lewis, gonna shoot Elvis Presley? Shooo. Damn. I mean I had to sit down and explain this to Lisa Marie, you know. She asked me about this and she worships me and she really respects me. Good kid. She was really serious about this. And I told her the truth and everything. She understood."

On Elvis' birthday, 1989, I went with Jerry Lee to Graceland, where he was to appear on George Klein's radio special, broadcast live from the annex. He had been very subdued coming up the drive and seemed, in fact, to be a little apprehensive at going before Elvis' fans. But the little crowd gathered with Klein gave him a standing O when he walked in. Jerry beamed at that.

Klein of course asked him again about the gate story. "Well, Killer," Jerry Lee said with all sincerity, "you know I woudn't do nothing like that, Killer. To be honest with you, I was down there at the Vapors night club. . . So the press made a big deal out of two real personal friends that knew each other very well from the beginning and they tried to throw a monkey wrench into the spokes and tear up a friendship there that they couldn't do. They never can. Elvis Presley — you can say what you want to about the man but what you can't take away he was one the greatest entertainers ever to walk on stage."

Klein started applauding and asked. "What did you think of Elvis's version of 'Whole Lotta Shakin'?"

"I never heard it," Jerry Lee answered.

1960. Dawn comes softly to Graceland. The big wrought-iron gates covered with musical notes are still open, though the last devoted Elvis gatewatcher of the night has finally given up the vigil at the gates to go snatch a couple of hours of sleep before resuming the Elvis watch of the faithful.

Roy noses the dusty Oldsmobile up to the guardhouse at the gate and cuts the engine. It sighs into silence. It has just been driven nonstop from West Texas. Steam hisses out from under the big car's hood and is quickly swallowed up by the crisp morning air, still heavy with the hanging dew. The click of Roy's leather heels against the stone is the only sound, save for a soft, whistling, rhythmic moan coming from within the tiny guardhouse. Roy leans inside and looks around. He awakens the snoring figure, recumbent on a folding chair.

"Wake up, Uncle Vester," Roy shakes him, "It's Roy." Elvis' Uncle Vester, Vernon's brother — one of many Elvis relatives swelling the Presley payroll — struggles to consciousness.

"I'm awake, Roy," he starts to protest, but Roy hushes him. "Call Elvis. Tell him I'm here."

Vester fumbles for the phone and mumbles into the mouthpiece. Roy stands, arms crossed, and waits. He knows Elvis will still be awake, will be just beginning the long process of crashing for the night.

Vester is being passed from lackey to lackey to valet. More whispers. Roy reaches for his pack of Luckies, taps one out with a single movement, and lights it with his Zippo. He leans his head back and exhales a steamy puff of smoke into the first pink rays of sunrise, which flash off the dark lenses of his Ray-Bans.

Vester hands hims the phone.

"Elvis? Roy."

"Roy, hey, man," Elvis mumbles. How are you? Umm . . ."

"I'm fine, Elvis. Listen you told me to stop off on my way to Nashville. Well, I'm here."

A short silence ensues. "Umm, well, yeah, man, glad to see you, you know, but ahh, ummm, you see. . ."

"I have a song I wrote for you, Elvis."

"That's fantastic, man, but, umm, you know, we were all up you know, all night and, you know, there are people just laid out all over the place and umm. . ."

It's Roy's turn to lay down a short silence. "I understand," he finally says.

"Yeah, man," Elvis says with relief, "see we're goin' to Nashville tomorrow to cut an album. We'll see you then. We'll get together. You wrote a song for me, huh? Hey, man, that's great!"

"Yeah. Well, see you, Elvis. . ."

"Oh Roy, what's the song? Ummm. . ."

"Oh, we can go over that when I see you."

Roy hangs up the phone, turns on his heel, flips his cigarette butt away, and nods goodbye to Uncle Vester.

He guns the Olds and heads out for Nashville. He's driving directly into the blinding rays of the rising sun. He flips his visor down and lights up another Lucky. Cruising, humming and singing snatches of songs. With a tight little amused smile, he starts humming and then finally singing out loud his Elvis song, the one he had been ready only a few moments earlier to hand over lock-stock-and-barrel to Elvis Presley.

He sings: "Only the lonely know the way I feel tonight." The Oldsmobile begins to pick up speed and Roy can't wait to get to his session in Nashville.

One of the problems facing the new overseers of Graceland after Elvis and Vernon were gone was the specter of a real-estate ad something on the order of the following, appearing one day in the want ad sections of the *Wall Street Journal*:

FOR SALE: PRIME MEMPHIS REAL ESTATE, GATED AND WALLED 13.8 ACRES SOUTH ON HIGHWAY 51. MANY TREES. LARGE SOUTHERN COLONIAL TWO-STORY HOUSE, WELL-MAINTAINED, ATTIC AND FINISHED BASEMENT. BARN AND NUMEROUS OUTBUILDINGS. RACQUETBALL COURT, POOL, FOUNTAIN IN GARDEN. WELL LANDSCAPED. PREVIOUS OWNER, HIS PARENTS AND HIS GRANDMOTHER BURIED IN YARD. REPLY, BOX EPE, MEMPHIS.

It almost came to that. After Elvis' death the Presley estate was not rolling in money and Graceland was eating up more than half a million dollars a year in taxes and maintenance. Part of the reason was that Elvis really left no provision for such an eventuality.

To backtrack: when Elvis got out of the army in 1960 and returned home triumphantly in a private train car, he almost didn't recognize the area around Graceland. When he had left in

1958, he had lived out in the country, surrounded by rolling hills and farmland. Now, smack dab across the street from Graceland was a tawdry little strip shopping center, a church was next door, and the subdivisions were creeping closer and closer. It was getting to where a man couldn't even shoot off his guns in peace.

Neither Elvis nor Vernon was ever investment-minded, coming from the poverty they had escaped, and they did not trust the advice of others — with the occasional exception of Colonel Parker. Vernon personified the clannish, suspicious Southerner. As with many Southern men, by the time he was grown, Vernon figured that he already pretty much knew everybody he would ever need to know. And most of those were family.

He certainly wasn't going to seek out investment bankers and real estate lawyers and trust their advice. He once listened to someone expostulate to him on the wisdom of buying gold. Six months later he went out and bought a single gold piece and was very proud of his investment. His and Elvis' forays into ranching were financial disasters. Elvis' racquetball franchise was a money sinkhole. Elvis could have afforded to buy most of the land around him (who can resist real-estate advice, especially with the wisdom of hindsight) but did not. He did, in 1962, buy eleven acres of land across the street from Graceland, where his two airplanes now sit and where visitors to Graceland park. But he never did anything with it.

Partly because of advice from the Colonel and partly from Vernon's fear of the government and the haunting nightmare that the Presleys could lose everything overnight and end up in the poorhouse, Elvis had the IRS figure his tax return every year. He never really knew how much he was making or how much he could have been making. He never saw all the offers Colonel rejected for seven-figure tours in Japan or Europe or for a million dollars for one performance in England. He didn't know the figures of the deals that Colonel did make for "now money" at the expense of Elvis' future. Why he acquiesced to the royalty buy-out by RCA in 1973 will remain a mystery. In that deal, Colonel sold Elvis' record catalog free and clear to RCA for $5.4 million. Out of that sum, Elvis ended up netting less than half that amount before taxes. And he had no tax shelters, ever. When Colonel forged a five-year deal for Elvis to play the International

Hotel in Las Vegas exclusively, everyone hailed him as a managerial genius. But when Elvis went in there, as an unproven act, he was getting $100,000 a week; Colonel's five-year deal was for $125,000 a week, with no escalation clause over those five years.

There would soon be lesser lights than Elvis making more money. Colonel rejected out of hand Barbra Streisand's offer for Elvis to co-star with her in the movie *A Star Is Born*. Etc. Etc.

Elvis was also never one to take charge of his own professional destiny or to strategically plan his career or to initiate very many strong confrontations over situations he was unhappy with in his management.

All of which is to say that Elvis perhaps did not fully realize his earning potential and was not awash in money when he died. He gave freely to charities and to friends, family and strangers. Who will ever know how much he spent on things he gave away, the cars and jewels? And the loans he made to family and friends and employees that he just wrote off? When he died, his money situation was in flux.

When he died, Graceland was not only in a somewhat perilous state financially, but its neighborhood deteriorated quickly, because of the proliferation of trashy Elvis souvenir shops that took over the shopping center across the street. They were selling everything from vials of "Elvis' Sweat — His Perspiration Is Your Inspiration!" to cheap, ugly plaster busts, to those gaudy black velvet paintings, to bootleg records and tapes. What was worse, everyone just assumed that since those shops were across the street from Graceland they were sanctioned by the estate.

Things were in limbo for a while. Elvis' will had left everything to Vernon, Minnie, and Lisa Marie. After Vernon died in 1979 and Minnie passed on in 1980, that left only Lisa Marie, and her inheritance was to pass to her on her twenty-fifth birthday, February 1, 1993.

Vernon had been executor of the estate, after his death his will provided for three co-trustees/co-executors to take his place. Those were Priscilla Presley (although divorced from Elvis, she had remained close and was Lisa Marie's legal guardian), the National Bank of Commerce in Memphis (which had been Elvis' bank) and Joseph Hanks, the Presley family accountant. (Hanks retired in 1990.) When Lisa inherited the Presley Estate, she chose to keep the full manage-

The plaque at the front of the mansion confirms Graceland's status — and therefore that of Elvis Presley and rock'n'roll — as not just a leisure attraction, but part of the heritage of modern America.

ment team in place and to become part of it, with the intention of keeping Graceland open to the public for many years to come and seeing Elvis Presley Enterprises continue to grow and prosper far into the future.

Meanwhile, Colonel Parker was totally removed from any relationship with the estate by a court ruling in 1983. Over the years all hatchets have been buried and a pleasant friendship has resulted. The Colonel sold his entire Elvis collection to Graceland in 1990, including the gold suit and all his extensive files and photographs.

Priscilla Presley finally broached the subject of opening Graceland to the public in order to save it. She also wanted it preserved, just as it was, for Lisa Marie. In 1981, Priscilla hired a man named Jack Soden, an investment counselor from Kansas City whom she knew, to investigate the possibilities of opening the place up. She and Soden sat down and began discussing ways to make Graceland a viable public home tour, while maintaining as much integrity as possible. They studied various such house museums around the country, especially San Simeon (the Hearst mansion), the Getty Museum, Mount Vernon, and Monticello. There was one big advantage Graceland had: almost everything was there. There was no need, as with Mount Vernon and Monticello, to try to re-create an era with representative period furnishings. Everything at Graceland is authentic.

Another lesson came from San Simeon: visitors park off-site and are bused to the house museum. Priscilla and Jack decided that there would be no money changing hands at Graceland or on the grounds. Visitors buy admission tickets across the street and take a shuttle to the house. No hot dogs or Cokes or cotton candy or souvenir shops. They also decided to use people from the local community as docents. Looking down the road, they had Graceland get control of the shopping center across the street in 1983 and gradually, as the leases expired, removed the bootleg souvenir shops. Graceland Plaza, as it is now known, has become a staging area for shuttle buses, as well as the site of the Elvis Presley Automobile Museum, a personal Elvis museum known as "Sincerely Elvis," gift stores, a restaurant, a diner, a free theater showing an Elvis career retrospective, an ice cream parlor, and a branch of the U.S. Postal Service. Vernon had sold off Elvis' two

airplanes, the *Lisa Marie* and the JetStar, in 1978. In 1984, Graceland arranged with their current owners to have them brought to Graceland Plaza and opened to the public.

The house was opened to the public on June 7, 1982. There were skeptics who said that interest in Elvis was waning and nobody except for a limited number of dyed-in-the-wool Elvis fans would pay good money to see inside his home. Priscilla and her management team looked at it more objectively and they have been proven right. About 650,000 people a year pass through the front door. Graceland has become one of the five most visited home museums in the United States and in 1991 gained the honor of being placed on the National Register of Historic Places.

"When Elvis was a kid, growing up in very humble circumstances in Tupelo and Memphis, he said to his parents, 'One day, I'll make money, I'll be somebody and I'll take care of you. You won't have to work so hard – people will work for you. I'll buy you the prettiest house in Memphis, and I'll pay you back for all you've sacrificed for me.' And Graceland represented that to him. For Elvis, and for all of us who watched it happen, it could also be seen as a symbol of achieving the American dream. But for him on the most personal level, it was a symbol of that promise he made to his parents. Graceland was a promise fulfilled."

Built in the Georgian colonial style with Corinthian columns on the front portico, the facade of Graceland is Mississippi fieldstone. The two windows at the upper right are in Elvis' bedroom, the two upper left in his wardrobe room. The upper center window is in the bathroom suite where he died. None of the upstairs area is open to the public.

The home originally contained 10,266 square feet of space. With the Trophy Room (housing the Time Line, Hall of Gold and Big Room), the Den (Jungle Room) and annex it now has 17,552 square feet. Excluding the Racquetball Building and other structures, Graceland has twenty-three rooms (eight bedrooms) plus eight bathrooms and four half-baths.

The annex was already there when Elvis moved in, but was then a four-car garage opening to the back. A two-tiered patio and a pool were put in in 1957, the same year that Elvis built the wall and the gates. In the mid-Sixties he added the Den onto the back of the house and the Trophy Room, built over the patio which the Music Room opened onto, and the Meditation Garden. Elvis added the Racquetball Building in 1975.

The elegantly landscaped grounds were frequently semi destroyed by Elvis and his friends as they raced around on golf-carts, go-carts, three-wheelers and snowmobiles specially converted to run on the grass. It may have been a palatial estate, but it was also a playground for Elvis and his friends.

Gates

The most famous wrought-iron gates in the world were specially designed for Elvis by Abe Saucer and custom-built by John Dillars, Jr., of Memphis Doors, Inc., and installed soon after Elvis' purchase of Graceland in 1957. For the next twenty years, fans would gather at the gates hoping to catch a glimpse of Elvis as he drove through. Sometimes he would walk down to the gates, or ride down on a golf cart or a horse or some other mode of transportation, and sign autographs. Sometimes, he would have the guard open the gates to let the people in.

He would sit atop his horse or stand on a tree stump and sign autographs, pose for photos, and chat with fans. There was a sense of camaraderie among the fans at the gate as well as with the guards (some were relatives of Elvis) who worked the post. Fans hung out there even when Elvis was on tour or in Hollywood. Many people from all over the world met other people at the gates and still stay in touch today. Now that Elvis is gone, each year thousands of fans gather at the gates on the anniversary of his death for a ceremony and all-night candlelight procession to and from his gravesite.

Wall of Graffiti

People have been writing on the Alabama fieldstone wall ever since Elvis put it up in 1957 and the writing got more dense and more frequent in the years following his death. Particularly after Graceland opened to the public, writing on the wall became an obligatory thing to do. When Elvis was alive the messages were personal things like, "I love you," "Come see me, my phone number is...!" but since his death the messages have been more in tribute. The Graceland staff neither discourage it or encourage it – like Elvis they just let it happen, it's part of what Elvis Presley's Graceland is. A pressurized water system is used to thin out the writing periodically and a crew is sent out to quickly take care of any big spray-painting that might happen. One of those situations occurred when a big Elvis fan, rock star Billy Idol, happened to visit in the early Eighties. He apparently came back during the night and spray-painted a very lovely sentiment on the front wall. Lisa Marie at that time was a fan of Billy Idol, and one of her cousins on the staff took a picture of it and sent it to her. But his message, too, was eventually taken off.

The Dining Room

The Dining Room was a gathering place for Elvis and his friends and family. This is where evening meals were taken, usually served around 9 or 10 p.m. with formal china and glassware. The chinaware is in the Buckingham pattern by Noritake, chosen by Elvis and Priscilla at the time of their wedding. Lisa Marie was known to ride her tricycle round and round the table on the black marble floor. The Christmas tree was set up every year behind Elvis' chair at the head of the table, in front of the big picture window. Some say Christmas was Elvis' favorite time of year; decorations would often go up soon after Thanksgiving and stay there through his birthday on January 8.

The centerpiece of the room, the chandelier, was purchased by Elvis on an after-hours shopping spree at Belvedere Lighting in Memphis in August 1974.

Graceland was quiet when Elvis and his male entourage were in Hollywood or out on the road doing concerts, and this was the site of many a homecoming meal – usually a rowdy affair that signalled that Graceland had come back to life.

Aunt Delta, Grandma Minnie, the maids and everybody would get excited preparing for their return. Here they'd gather for the evening meal as all the wives and girlfriends would get back with Elvis and the guys. There was many a wild story, much laughter and late-night poker games, with low to no stakes.

The blue, white and gold color scheme is the one that Elvis favored for the front rooms of the house for a number of years. The main furnishings were much the same all through the years until Elvis and his girlfriend Linda Thompson redecorated in red in 1974. ("The 1974 look was red crushed velvet faux French Provincial furniture, thick blood-red shag carpet, red satin drapes, and wild appointments – Seventies kitsch in overdrive!") Even before then, though, the blue drapes were often replaced with red at Christmastime. These "formal" rooms were given a more spacious feel in the mid-Seventies when Elvis chose to add the mirrors which are such a predominant feature of both the Dining and Living rooms.

81

E ntering the hallway through the front door, visitors see the stairs ahead of them, the Dining Room to their left, while opposite, also open-plan with no dividing wall or doors, is the Living Room.

If you had been coming to visit Elvis, this is where you would have been received, where you would have waited for him to come down the stairs, to make his entrance. The sofa is fifteen feet long, the coffee table is ten feet long, both custom-made for Elvis. These and the end tables and table lamps were key elements of his decor for these rooms from the time he moved in in 1957 until 1974.

As formal as this room appears, and though, for preservation's sake, the governing phrase for employees and visitors is "do not touch," (there is even a "shoes off" rule for employees when walking on the white carpet), this room, like all rooms at Graceland, was "lived in." As in most family homes, the living room was where people relaxed, talked and just generally sat around.

Elvis and Priscilla's two Great Danes, Snoopy and Brutus, would wrestle with the pillows on the white sofa while Elvis might be in the room kicking boards in two practising karate! A somber note – it was here that Elvis' funeral service took place, with the casket positioned in front of the Music Room door.

The Living Room

Sunburst Clock *(right)*
The "sunburst" clock was an archetypal piece of late Fifties
and early Sixties decor, and typifies how the various rooms
at Graceland represent particular periods frozen in time.

Stained Glass Peacocks *(far right)*
The peacock stained-glass windows that separate the living
room from the Music Room replaced decorative glass blocks
which had been set around the archway by the original owners
and which Elvis always had covered with drapes. The peacocks
were designed for Elvis by Laukhuff Stained Glass of Memphis
in 1974. The same company did the stained-glass work around
the front door and the stained-glass billiard light in the Pool Room.
Elvis had some peacocks at Graceland, but they were only briefly
a part of the animal menagerie he had there through the years.

He donated them to the Memphis Zoo after one of them
scratched the surface of his highly polished Rolls-Royce in
which the bird had been admiring its own reflection! Apparently,
Elvis was also keen on the peacock motif as they are said to
symbolize eternal life. A superstition which he presumably was
not aware of was that they are also supposed to bring bad luck
if displayed inside the home.

Fender Precision Bass *(above)*
The Fender bass, which follows the classic lines of the solid-
bodied guitar, was not the type of instrument normally associated
with Elvis, who is usually pictured playing hollow-bodied guitars.

" He was always up to something, shooting off firecrackers or guns, running around, driving golf carts or snowmobiles. He'd pull me in a sled and scare me to death. On that long steep driveway that goes up to Grace- land he'd be pulling me up and falling at the same time. He called me Buttonhead or Yisa. He'd never call me Lisa unless he was mad at me."

LISA MARIE PRESLEY, *LIFE MAGAZINE* 1988

Lisa Marie *(left)*
The group of pictures of Lisa Marie was a gift from Priscilla to Elvis after their separation. Though father and daughter continued to spend time together regularly, Priscilla, who had custody of Lisa, also made sure that Elvis always had current photographs and didn't miss special moments he couldn't be there to share. During their marriage, Priscilla had done the same thing for him when he was out on concert tours.

Vernon Presley *(below left)*
The portrait of Vernon was a gift from him to Elvis for Christmas 1976, their last Christmas together before Elvis died in 1977.

Photo-Portrait of Elvis *(below)*
This portrait of Elvis was thumbtacked to a wall in Vernon's office out back for a while. It was framed and moved into the Living Room when the tours opened in 1982. It appears in the back-ground in the photographs and film of the famous press conference Elvis gave after being discharged from the army. The portrait is from 1957, and is what used to be called a tinted photograph, a photo made to look like a painted portrait.

The piano in the Music Room is a Story and Clark baby grand. It took its place there in 1974 and the most famous person to play it other than Elvis was James Brown, who visited him at Graceland in that last year. James Brown recalls singing gospel songs with Elvis, including a spiritual called "Old Blind Barnabas." The piano was one of three different pianos that were used over the years. Elvis' apparent favorite, the one that was there for the longest time, was a white baby grand piano with gilded trim. It was followed by a grand piano done in gold leaf, which Priscilla gave to Elvis in the Sixties. It was too big for the room, so he eventually got rid of it. Then came the black Story and Clark. Elvis was a pretty good piano player and he played on some of his records. He enjoyed playing for his own pleasure both at home and in hotel suites or wherever. He and the guys and the different musical back-up groups he worked with would sing and play to wind down after concerts in Vegas and elsewhere. At Graceland in the Music Room, Elvis and friends would sing and play all kinds of music for fun, including lots of close harmony, gospel and R&B. Elvis also had some quiet, private moments alone at the piano. Some of the songs you might have heard him play at different times at home would be "Unchained Melody," "Blue Eyes Crying In the Rain," and the Irish ballad "Danny Boy." One time at Graceland Jerry Schilling and the guys were downstairs in the basement playing pool. Jerry heard music and walked up the basement stairs and into the entrance way of the living room. Elvis was at the piano, playing and singing "You'll Never Walk Alone," in there all by himself and just giving it everything he had. Jerry said it was the most beautiful thing he had ever heard. He just stood there watching him. Elvis noticed him and looked up and smiled, and then just dove back into the music. Even those who were closest to Elvis and knew him inside and out, knew the good and the bad, could still be swept away by his artistry, his voice, and his sheer charisma.

The Music Room

Story and Clark Piano *(right)*
The baby grand piano currently in the Music Room is just one of several on which Elvis entertained fellow musicians and friends when they visited the mansion over the years. Although he was forever associated with the guitar, Elvis in fact played more piano privately, and was certainly more accomplished on the instrument.

Music Room Mirror *(below)*
The wall mirror in the Music Room illustrates the fact that a lot of things were kept; things weren't thrown away and trashed over the years. This mirror dates back to the house on Audubon Drive that Elvis and his parents lived in just before moving to Graceland. A reporter snapped a picture of Gladys Presley trying on a new hat in this very same mirror back at the Audubon Drive house in 1956.

The Stairs

The stairway in the hall leads to the upper floor of the house which is out of bounds to visitors and most employees. Only certain management staff, maintenance staff and family members are allowed upstairs. The upper floor consists of Elvis' private bedroom, bath, wardrobe room, and office, another bath and dressing area, and his daughter's bedroom and bath. The semicircular railing at the top of the stairwell was originally open. The windowed wall (one-way glass) was installed by Elvis for quiet and privacy.

The stairs themselves sometimes resembled stadium bleachers (risers) with friends sitting on them as they watched Elvis and the guys do karate practice and demonstrations in the foyer. The stairs were also the site of many a grand entrance by Elvis, as he would descend from his private master suite to greet his guests. On one such descent, his daughter, Lisa, caused Elvis to collapse on the stairs in laughter. She was playing in the foyer and noticed her father coming down the stairs. She stopped what she was doing, and looked up at him, threw her arms up in the air, and screamed "Ailvis! Ailvis!" in perfect fan mimicry, learned from having seen Elvis' concerts and having ridden through the crowds at the mansion gates with her father. She then walked off into the dining room without another word.

Prior to Elvis' funeral, his body lay in state at the foot of the stairs. Vernon Presley, for a brief period, allowed some of the thousands of fans who were at the gate to walk up and step inside the foyer to view the body.

The chandelier over the stairs is the largest one of three that Elvis bought on August 16, 1974, exactly three years before his death. Identical in design but smaller is the one hanging over the Dining Room table. Both are made of Italian cut glass, in the Maria Theresa design, while the third chandelier is actually Strauss crystal and is hanging in the foyer just as you come in the front door.

Mirrored Staircase

At the end of the hallway, the door to the right leads to the private quarters of Elvis' Aunt Delta, while a sharp left (opposite the "bird room" door, a store-room where Elvis once kept a pet myna bird) leads the visitor down the mirror-lined basement staircase which has an almost kaleidoscopic effect.

Portrait

A portrait of Elvis hangs at the bottom of the stairs. It was based on a snapshot that was taken of Elvis while he was stationed in Texas during his days in the U.S. Army.

Guitars

Elvis owned scores of guitars over the years, but gave many of them away – he was even known to hand them to members of his audience from time to time. As a result, the Presley Estate inventory includes just fifteen, the total he had at the time of his death.

The spectacular shot of the whole collection on the stairs was created specially for this book, and although some of these guitars can be found on display in Graceland exhibits, others have remained in storage. They include the Gibson J200 that is displayed in the Time Line, that featured in the film *Loving You (below center and bottom right on stairs)*, and a later version of the same guitar that carries a personalized ELVIS PRESLEY engraved on the neck, which is exhibited in the "Sincerely Elvis" collection *(below right and bottom left on stairs)*.

Other guitars in the stairs shot include the double-neck red Gibson *(second bottom)*, the "Chet Atkins Country Gentleman" Gretsch *(top)* and the Burns twelve-string *(third bottom, right)*.

This shot represents only the second time ever that Elvis' guitars have all been gathered together in this way; the only other time was when Graceland put them in a one-night only exhibit in connection with a rock'n'roll pops concert featuring the Memphis Symphony Orchestra a few years ago.

The violin at the front of the shot is something of a mystery. What is known is that it is a Stradivarius copy and was found in the back of one of Elvis' closets upstairs in his private suite. Members of his family have confirmed that he could "play a lick or two on the fiddle," which of course is how the instrument is referred

to in country music.

It was in forging the link between country music and blues, both guitar-based traditions, that Elvis almost single-handedly helped define rock'n'roll in the mid-Fifties.

As is acknowledged elsewhere, technically Elvis had no pretentions to being a master of the guitar, but as a straightforward rhythm player came to epitomize its use in rock music. Right from his debut album cover *(below left)* Elvis' image was that of the "guitar man."

His backing groups throughout his career always included strong lead guitar players, from Scotty Moore with the original Sun line-up to James Burton in his sensational touring band of the Seventies.

Guitar-Toting Rocker
From earliest publicity shots through movie stills and literally hundreds of record covers worldwide to his days in Vegas, Elvis is best remembered as the quintessential guitar-toting rocker.

T he TV Room, which from the Fifties housed televison, hi-fi stereo and movie equipment, was decorated in its present style in 1974 by an interior designer, Bill Eubanks, who also decorated the Pool Room across the hall, and Elvis' office upstairs.

"It's frozen in time. You could have easily seen a picture of a room like this on the cover of a top decorating magazine in the mid-Seventies. All the chrome, glass, super graphics and chrome arc lamps, the sectional furniture − all of these things were very much 'in' at the time. So were the mirrors and mirrored ceiling. These features also helped open the room up, make it feel larger and less closed in."

Elvis decided that he wanted the TCB lightning bolt worked into the design somehow, but he also required that the wall unit remain intact, meaning the stereo, the three television sets, and the built-in jukebox. Elvis and his girlfriend, Linda Thompson, wanted the room to feel bright, cheerful, and more open. Beyond that, the decorator had a free hand in coming up with ideas, all subject of course to Elvis and Linda's approval.

The TCB Logo

"The TCB logo, which also appears on his tombstone, on the famous ring, the tail of the *Lisa Marie* jet, on the tail of the Jet-Star... everywhere. TCB – 'Takin' Care of Business' – in the Sixties and on into the Seventies was a common saying in black pop culture, then it made its way into white pop culture. For instance there was a white rock band, Bachman Turner Over-drive, that did a song called 'Taking Care of Business.' It was just something that people were saying, and Elvis and the Guys would use it. By 1970, for what-ever reason, Elvis wanted some kind of signature or logo to represent him and his organization, some kind of saying to go with it. We've always said that TCB and the lightning bolt meant 'taking care of business in a flash.' Where he got the lightning bolt idea to begin with is arguable. There's a lightning bolt on his Army insignia for the battalion he was in. It could have come from that, possibly not. A lightning bolt was a symbol of the West Coast mafia, and Elvis' group had been dubbed the 'Memphis Mafia' by the press. So, maybe that had something to do with it. Or it could have just meant 'in a

flash.' It could be all of those things.

There are several stories about how the design came to be. The one that we tend to go with is that in the early Seventies, it must have been 1970, Elvis and Priscilla and everyone were on a plane, probably coming home to Memphis from California, and they got into this conversation about Elvis wanting a logo, Priscilla took out a pad and they sketched some things, and Elvis had Saul Schwartz of Beverly Hills, a jeweler there that he did some business with, design the first TCB necklaces. These were gold pendants on a chain, which Elvis would give to his entourage, and his close male friends and family.

It was a symbol of belonging to his inner circle. Members of the band and his male singers had them too. Soon thereafter he developed TLC (Tender Loving Care) pendants in the same design, for the women. The TCB became his signature, his logo through the years, and the TCB and TLC necklaces were highly coveted, a real symbol of being close to him. An interest-ing side note – one time for an exhibit we asked Priscilla if we could have hers and Lisa's TLCs and we were surprised to find out that they never got one from Elvis. And it says a lot about him, about Elvis and how he felt about them, because Priscilla said that she had asked about it and Elvis told her that the TLCs and TCBs were for everybody else. He considered them on a level above everybody else."

The Bar *(left)*

With its crushed-ice maker and refrigerator, the bar in the TV Room was always well-stocked – "for all of the guests, all of the friends, entourage and what-have-you. Elvis wasn't really big on drinking. It would be wrong to say he never drank, but he wasn't what would be called a drinker."
He did drink a lot of Pepsi Cola, and on stage it was usually Gatorade or Mountain Valley Spring Water.

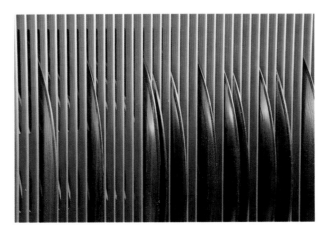

Home Jukebox *(above)*

The built-in jukebox was not custom made, they were actually sold commercially in the late Fifties. It took one hundred singles which were chosen by flipping little levers – either all of them or particular selections. It's wired for sound throughout the house, and even outside. Much of Elvis' own record collection is in this room – country, pop, jazz, classical and opera, but mostly R&B and gospel. Some of the discs go right back to his high school days, so his friends say.

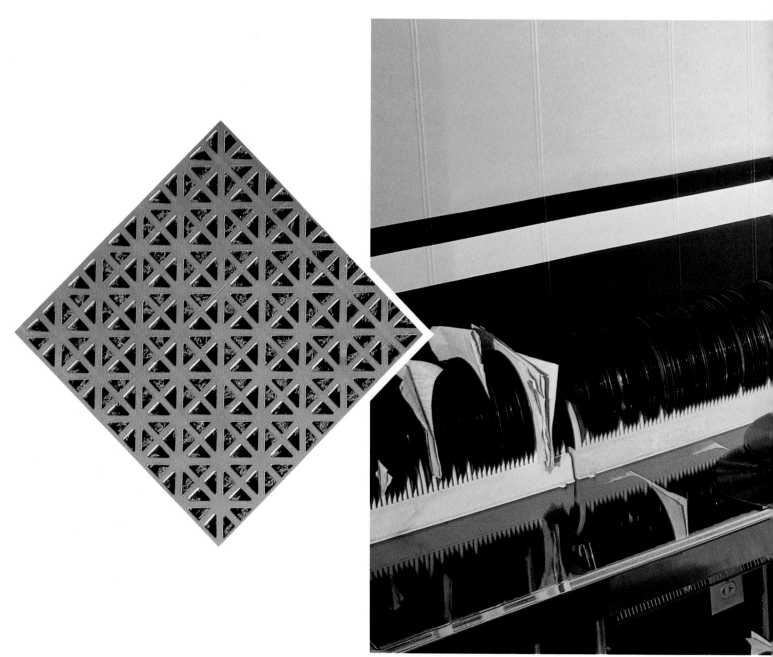

Home Movies

The framed fabric panel alongside the bar is hinged and can be lifted to accommodate a movie projector, which is operated from the projection room. Here was stored Elvis' collection of films and home movies, including 16mm prints of all his Hollywood films, though he rarely watched his own movies.

Elvis also rented local movie theaters on a regular basis. He and his guests could see first-run films they rented at the film exchange as well as old favorites. He particularly enjoyed the Monty Python films, *Patton* was a favorite, as were the Peter Sellers' *Pink Panther* movies. He showed some films over and over again, so often that he could recite all of the dialogue along with the actors.

TV Sets

Elvis got the idea for the three TV sets in a row from hearing a story about President Lyndon Johnson having three TVs in a row at the White House so he could watch all three network news programs at one time. Elvis was known on occasion to watch three football games or sporting events all at one time. He would put the game he was most interested in on the center screen, with the sound up, and the two games or programs that he was less interested in on the TVs on either side, with the sound down. As well as sports he enjoyed variety or sitcom shows; among his favorites were *The Dick Van Dyke Show*, *I Love Lucy* and *Rowan and Martin's Laugh-In*.

Decorated by Bill Eubanks (in collaboration with Elvis and Linda Thompson) in 1974, the most spectacular feature of the Pool Room is without a doubt the fabric used to cover the sofas, walls and ceiling. It took something between 350 and 400 yards of fabric, and three workmen about ten days to hang it.

The fabric is stapled to the ceiling, and hangs from rods on the walls. The room, with its French, Oriental, and turn-of-the-century European influences, is an example of the Seventies American trend toward eclectic decorating, mixing styles of various eras and countries. A similar "retro" trend has emerged in the Nineties.

None of the furniture is antique. Most was chosen to complement the general decor, including the three reproduction Louis XV red leather chairs. All the pictures are either prints, some signed by the artists, or – like the Toulouse Lautrecs – just regular commercial reproductions.

Pool Table

The pool table, so far as anyone knows, goes all the way back to 1957 when Elvis bought Graceland. He liked 8-ball and rotation and was pretty good. The tear in the felt remains from a mishandled trick shot by one of Elvis' friends, and confirms the philosophy that when Graceland was opened to the public things should be left as much as possible as they were.

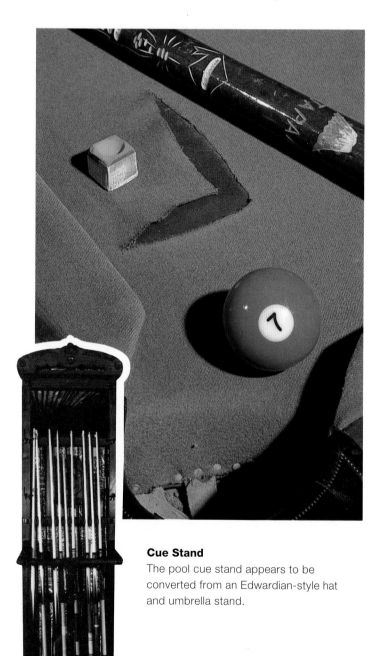

Cue Stand

The pool cue stand appears to be converted from an Edwardian-style hat and umbrella stand.

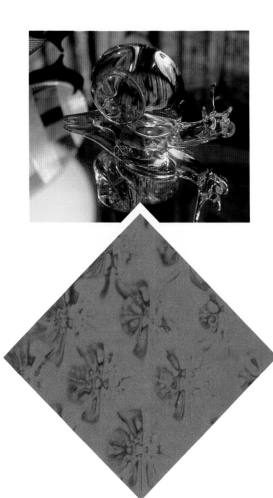

(previous pages)
The brass-over-wood **campaign trunk** – on which rest ostrich plumes – contains extra pool balls, the remaining stock of pool chalk and other accessories. The richly patterned **curtains** reflect the ornate feel of the entire room, as do the scores of decorative ornaments, like the **glass butterfly** and **snail**. On top of the trunk rests an **antique chalice** in red cut glass.

"Tiffany" lightshade
The lightshade over the pool table, the work of Laukhuff Stained Glass in Memphis, was done in the revived Tiffany style, which was popular in the mid-Seventies.

The Jungle Room

T he room was added on to the house in the mid-Sixties. It functioned first as a screened-in porch, then it was closed in completely and made into a family room or den. It looked like a typical American family room of that time, with regular den-style furniture.

Legend has it that Elvis' father had been out and about and came to Graceland one day, talking about this really hideous furniture he had seen in a store called Donald's in Memphis, and how it was just bizarre and only somebody crazy would buy it. Apparently, unbeknownst to Vernon, Elvis had seen that same furniture at that very store and had liked it. It reminded him of Hawaii, particularly things he had seen at the Polynesian Cultural Center there. He loved Hawaii. He had made several movies there, did several important concerts there, and he vacationed there. He was very into Hawaiian culture.

Todd Morgan explains, "This kind of furniture was sort of a fad in this area. I'm from a small town of 2,500 people in Arkansas and I saw furniture exactly like this in the furniture store in my hometown. I remember being a kid thinking this stuff would be really cool for my room, if my parents would buy it for me."

So Elvis saw the furniture and liked it, went on a little thirty-minute shopping spree and – presumably to his father's horror – bought a whole roomful of it.

Another design feature that was popular at the time, at least in California, was the use of carpeting on the ceiling. Elvis later realized that it made the room quite good acoustically, and as well as using it for preliminary rehearsals before he went into the recording studio, he eventually recorded the greater part of two albums in the Jungle Room – "From Elvis Presley Boulevard, Memphis, Tennessee" and just over half of the "Moody Blue" album, which included his last single "Way Down." RCA would park their equipment truck in the backyard and run wires into the room. The recording sessions usually took place at night and would often last until dawn.

115

"Monkey" Chair (far left)
The big "monkey chair," typical of the exotic theme of all the
Jungle Room furniture, is so enormous that one of the windows
had to be removed to get it into the room. Lisa Marie was
known to take naps in it when she was a little girl.

Welcome to Hawaii (left and above)
From relatively early in his career Elvis played Hawaii – in fact it
was the only location where he ever performed officially outside
the North American mainland – and this was on a 1957 date
there. The fans' expressions say it all, some presenting him with
garlands (leis) in welcome. These welcomes must have occurred a
number of times throughout his career – 1957, 1961, the "Aloha"
concert – and at least a couple of other occasions.

Indoor Waterfall (far right)

"You couldn't go to a hotel or a restaurant or almost any public building in America at that time without encountering an indoor waterfall. These were also becoming popular in people's homes as well. In the Sixties Elvis had this waterfall put in the room. It was done by a guy named Bernard Grenadier, who was Marty Lacker's brother-in-law. Marty Lacker was part of Elvis' entourage. The story goes that Bernard Grenadier had the room curtained off so the work couldn't be seen while it was in progress. He had an agreement with Elvis, that Elvis wouldn't look, that the drapery wouldn't come down until the project was complete. Elvis was like a kid when special things were going on, he loved surprises and fun things happening. He was very curious. Elvis was also notorious for not being able to keep a secret. But he apparently remained true to the agreement and they had a little ceremony one night and unveiled it. Elvis was really pleased. It tended to get the carpet wet

so the waterfall wasn't turned on very often through the years. We tend to have the same problems today!"

Telephones (below)

The red telephone is part of the intercom phone system for the various rooms in the house, while the green multi-line telephone is part of the regular phone system for the house. These are both original, both still working, and they are both in their original position in the room.

Feathered Mirror Frame
The mirror above the Jungle Room stereo system is another example of exotic texture, framed in real pheasant breast feathers, with peacock feather accents.

(previous pages)

Much of the attraction of the room's decor seems to be tactile, as with the fake fur on the **bar stools** and the **long-backed chair**, and the pressed orange velvet **lampshade**. Likewise, the carved wood on all the furniture spares no attention to detail, from animal-head features to totem-style engravings.

Ornamental Animals

Through the years Elvis owned many different pets of all kinds. At one time or another Graceland has been home to dogs (chows, poodles, Pomeranians, Great Danes, etc.), horses, mules, chickens, ducks, peacocks, monkeys, a chimpanzee, turkeys, and a myna bird. In the Jungle Room, Elvis indulged this fascination further with a menagerie of ornamental wildlife.

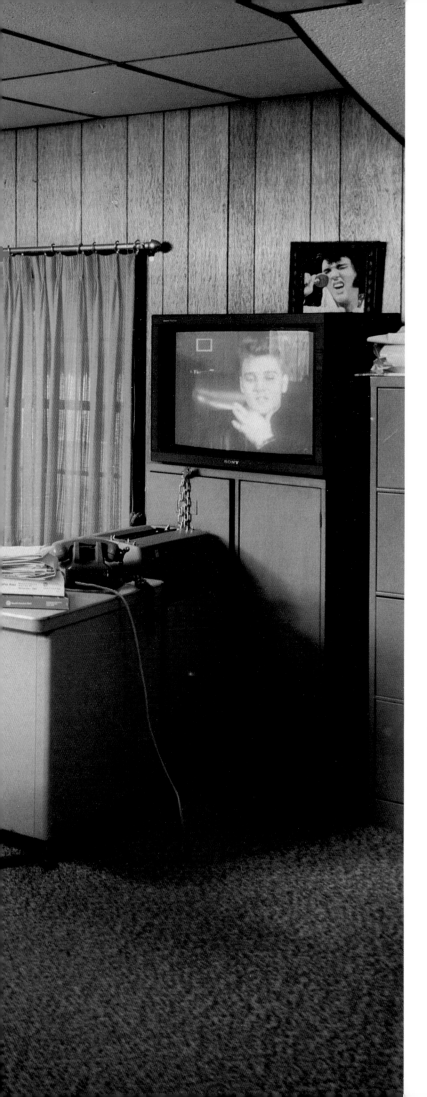

The Office

The office building was already there when Elvis bought Graceland. It was probably the maid's quarters or groundskeeper's quarters originally. It was always the office when Elvis lived at Graceland. Colonel Parker who was Elvis' career manager, had an office in Madison, Tennessee, just outside Nashville, and he would have an office at whatever movie studio Elvis was working in. But this was the office for Graceland, for all the business on the home front. Vernon ran the office and had a staff of secretaries. They would handle fan mail and all the household and personal bills that came in. Elvis gave a press conference sitting at his father's desk in this office on March 8, 1960, the day after he returned from his army tour of duty in Germany. In photographs and in the video that now plays in the office, you can see that it is the same desk, the same blotter, the same lamp, the same filing cabinets, the same card files on top of the filing cabinet. Luckily, Vernon was very tight with money and didn't throw a lot away. This of course was the opposite of Elvis, who was a big spender, and resulted in some colorful arguments when Vernon tried to get his son to curb his spending. But Elvis clearly knew that his father would watch every nickel and dime. He often kidded Vernon about being tight, but he also said that he was the one person he could trust to handle the business. Vernon made some minor changes over the years, but the office remained essentially the same. All the office equipment and such is the genuine article.

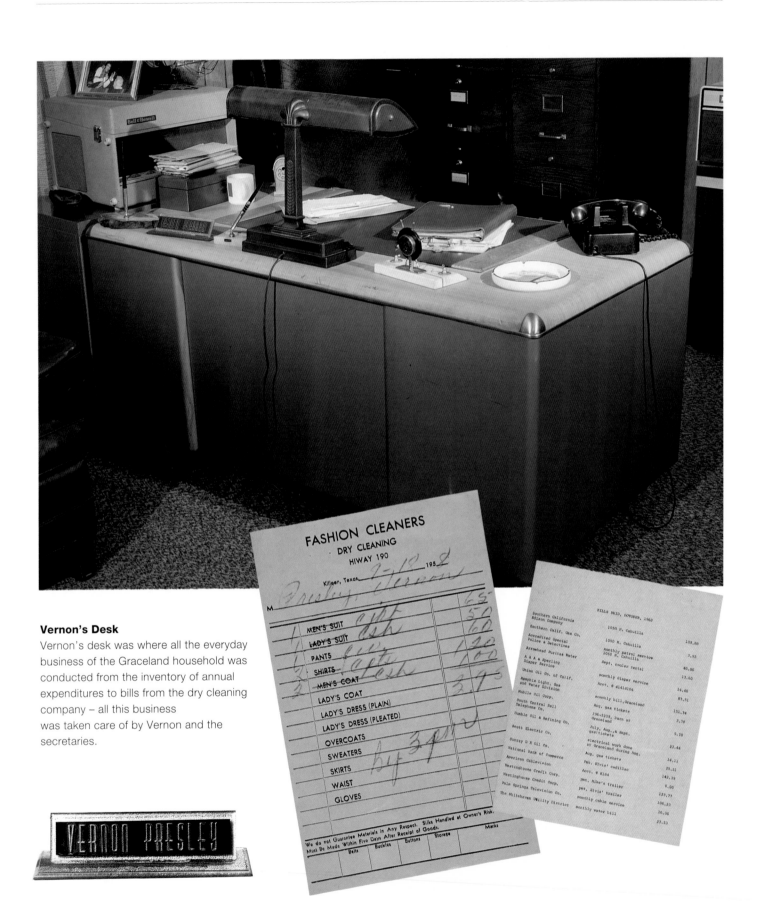

Vernon's Desk

Vernon's desk was where all the everyday business of the Graceland household was conducted from the inventory of annual expenditures to bills from the dry cleaning company – all this business was taken care of by Vernon and the secretaries.

Vernon's Door Sign

The sign on Vernon's office door came about because Elvis would sometimes sleep during the day and be out and about at night – he kept weird hours, at least compared to the rest of the world. And a lot of the times the guys, the entourage, would be at a loss for something to do while they just hung out and waited for Elvis to get up, or wait on Elvis to come downstairs and tell them what he wanted them to do. Some of them would loiter in the office with the secretaries or with Vernon or whatever, just for a lack of anything better to do; also there was the problem of anybody who came to Graceland to make a delivery at the office wanting to hang around and see if they could catch a glimpse of Elvis. Vernon got tired of all of that, and the work of the secretaries was being interrupted constantly by the human traffic. Priscilla says she might have had something to do with that sign too, because she would get bored when Elvis was out in Hollywood making movies and she would pass the time of day there talking to Patsy Presley Gambill, Elvis' double first cousin who was the lead secretary. So Vernon had Patsy hand-letter the sign.

Office Press Conference

Two candid shots of Elvis sitting at Vernon's desk during the famous 1960 press conference and film interview he held after leaving the U.S. Army.

The "Moon and Stars" Lamp *(right)*
The lamp on the office refrigerator is
real Fifties kitsch with moon, stars and
the suggestion of a rocket ship in there.
During a 1990 photo shoot for *Rolling
Stone* magazine, one of the satellite-
looking objects just shot off for no
apparent reason as the lamp was
being photographed.

Office Equipment
The ordinary office equipment, such as
the simple **air conditioner**, **telephone**
and **adding machine**, seem caught in a
time-warp, like props from the set of a
Fifties movie.

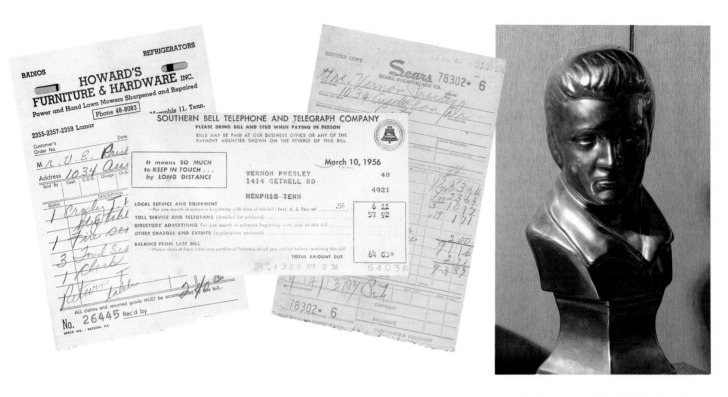

"Years ago people often smoked and cured meats in a smoke house at home, and that's what they were used for when the Moore family lived at Graceland, but for all the years that Elvis was there it was just utilized for storage. The stuff hanging from the ceiling is stuff we just left in there when we cleaned these rooms out. We cleaned them out in order to create an exit from Vernon's office when we made that part of the tour. There was like a week or two in the Sixties, probably about 1964, when Elvis and the guys had decided they would use the Smoke House as a firing range. What they did is set up telephone poles as a backdrop inside the Smoke House and put up police targets. Then they would stand out in the backyard and put all of their guns and ammo out on a table. They'd shoot through the door of the Smoke House, toward the target, assuming that everyone could at least manage to shoot well enough to get the shot through the doorway. Nevertheless there are a lot of bullet holes in the bricks around the outside of the door."

The Smoke House

Storage Space

Every house has its junk room, and
Graceland is no exception. The rusting
bric-a-brac in the Smoke House includes
an old carriage lamp and a broken bicycle,
plus the used ammunition from Elvis'
target practice.

"On one occasion, a neighbor called the police to report a disturbance involving gunfire. A cop came up to check it out. Elvis managed to turn on his charm as usual, and the cop stayed awhile, taking a turn shooting, then left."

The barn was there when Elvis bought Graceland; he had horses, mules and such over the years, but really got into horses about 1966. For a surprise he bought Priscilla a black horse with a white spot on one of its legs, so it got the name Domino. From then he got into horses in a

big way. (Before that most of Elvis' horse riding had been confined to his movie roles.) His favorite horse of all was Rising Sun, a golden palomino quarterhorse, who died at the age of twenty-five in June 1986. Elvis bought him in 1967, and for a while the barn had written on its front door "The House of Rising Sun" relating the horse to the song "The House Of The Rising Sun." When Rising Sun died he was actually buried in the pasture facing the rising sun.

Saddle and Chaps *(far right)*
The saddle was made for Elvis by his long-time employee and good friend Mike McGregor, who also worked security and did a lot of Western-style leather work and some jewelry work. The black-and-white leather chaps feature a winged "G" logo at the bottom. This was the logo for the Flying Circle G ranch which Elvis bought in the Sixties and enjoyed for a couple of years when the horse hobby got too big for Graceland to contain it.

"The window in the background is to Aunt Delta's bedroom. It had been Elvis' parents' room, then Grandma Presley's (or 'Dodger' as Elvis nicknamed her). Elvis was known to ride up to his grandmother's window and just sit there and talk to her for a long time. Another story is that once Elvis was out back leading Lisa Marie around on her pony and decided that Grandma needed to see that. So he took Lisa on the back of her pony through to the kitchen and in front of Grandma Presley's bedroom door. Just about the time he got in there, Grandma said, 'Oh son, you know animals aren't supposed to be in the house.' No sooner did she say that than the pony relieved herself on the kitchen floor! Just another great moment at Graceland."

Bear *(right)*
A candid picture taken around 1970 by a newspaper photographer; it's shot from the Highway 51 side of the stone wall, and Elvis is riding Bear, the Tennessee Walking Horse, that eventually died while Elvis was on the road.

The horses

There are four horses currently stabled at Graceland. Though his favorite individual horse was his palomino, Elvis seemed to be a big fan of Tennessee Walkers. He was fascinated with the way they moved. He once took riding instruction and was quite impressive on horseback. He had a Tennessee Walking Horse named Bear, which died while he was on a concert tour. The guys had to keep the news from him until the tour was over because they knew he would be upset. **Ebony's Double** was sired by the World Champion Tennessee Walking Horse of 1962, Ebony Masterpiece, and Elvis bought him from G.L.L. Farms in 1975. Out to pasture from 1975 until 1983, then retrained over a period of forty days, Ebony's Double was exhibited at the Tennessee Walking Horse Celebration in Shelbyville on September 3,1983. He was formally retired that night after a performance to a medley

of Elvis music. That night Priscilla introduced a new award called the "Graceland Challenge Trophy in Memory of Elvis Presley" for junior (four-year-old) Walking Horse World Champions.

  Memphis, photographed for this book in 1992, died in early 1993. He, like Rising Sun, had been part of the Sixties stable. **Sun's Reflection** is related distantly to Rising Sun and was acquired by Graceland after Rising Sun's death. **Ebony's Secret Threat** belongs to Priscilla and is currently being boarded at Graceland. She bought him on the Shelbyville trip in 1983. **Mare Ingram** is a grade mare (mixed breed) about which there is little known except that she was named Mare Ingram after the then-Mayor of Memphis, Bill Ingram.

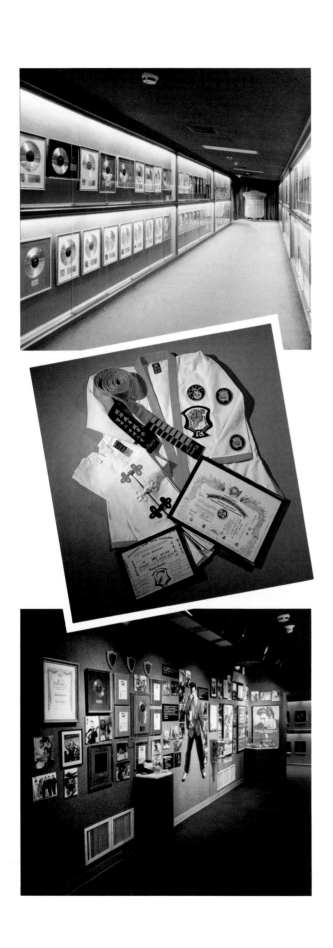

The Trophy Room

When Elvis bought Graceland in 1957, he had a large patio constructed where the Trophy Room is now. It was constructed in two levels, with the lower level featuring the pool that is there now. Elvis and his friends partied on the patio, which had a jukebox housed in its own little glassed-in hut and a brick barbecue grill. In the mid-Sixties, Priscilla gave Elvis a slot car track that he set up in the basement — slot cars were very popular at the time. He put a roof over the patio and closed it in to house a much larger, much more elaborate track for himself and the guys to enjoy. The track was one-level and took up a great deal of space in the building. Elvis tired of the hobby after a few months and removed the track, reportedly giving it to a children's home. Some of the cars and equipment, and some track (probably track from the one Priscilla gave him) are part of the estate inventory. When he got rid of the big track, Elvis turned the building into a Trophy Room and storage area. Up until that time, he had displayed his gold records in the TV Room. As a Trophy Room, the building had built-in glass wall cases (the same ones that are there now) and free-standing glass display cases. Some say he even talked of eventually opening the room to the public so they could see what they had made possible for him. When Graceland was about to be opened for tours in 1982, the trophy room was emptied. Items were selected to go back on display and the rest was put in storage. The jewelry-store-style floor cases were removed and put in storage, and the railed island was installed, as was the wall that now displays the portraits. Elvis had his gold records displayed in the first set of wall cases in what is now called the Big Room. These records were moved into the hallway cases to create a "Hall of Gold." The hallway and its cases were already there, but the floor had to be raised to meet the level of the rest of the building, because it still had a patio floor. In fact, if you were to remove the floor of the entire building, you would find the original patio surface still intact.

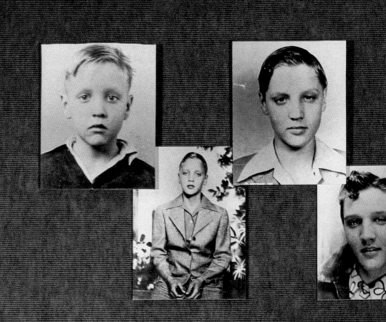

he Time Line, as it is known in the tour guide vocabulary, starts with a wall display of various pictures and documents tracing Elvis' early years.

Top left is the most famous childhood shot of Elvis, aged around two or three, with his parents. The reason his mouth is crooked in the picture is that just as it was taken he bit down on a peanut. An enlarged, colorized version of this shot, with the parents cropped out, was used for the cover of his 1971 album "Elvis Country," with a black-and-white of the whole photo printed to the side. Below that there is a copy of Elvis' birth certificate.

The photograph to the left of the central painting is a group shot of Elvis with his class at Milam Junior High in Tupelo; below that are two photographs of Vernon and Gladys, one with the ten-year-old Elvis.

The first three pictures above the painting were taken before the move to Memphis, the fourth is from Elvis' early teens in Memphis. The color photograph to its right is a shot of Elvis' grandmother, Minnie Mae Presley. Below the painting, the shot of Elvis on the bicycle is probably pre-Memphis, the one with the brick building is at Lauderdale Courts where the family lived for a while, and the one where he is sitting on the sidewalk curb shows him with a girlfriend.

To the right are, top to bottom, his high school ROTC certificate (Reserve Officers Training Corps, a school-based cadet corps), his high school diploma and the Class of '53 composite picture.

The far right row of photographs features, from the top, Elvis in his high school ROTC uniform, a group shot of the ROTC class at Humes High, Elvis as a teenager leaning against a car, and Elvis with two teenage friends in Memphis.

Elvis' Birthplace

The painting of Elvis' birthplace in Tupelo, Mississippi, was a gift from a fan. Vernon Presley and his brother Vester built the fifteen-by-thirty-foot, two-room "shotgun" house for about $180 shortly before Elvis was born. Years later Elvis remarked that the little house would practically fit in his living room at Graceland. They lived in the house for several years, then moved to other parts of Tupelo before finally settling in Memphis in 1948. The Tupelo house is open for tours and is part of a small park, Elvis Presley Park, which includes a chapel built in his memory in 1979. When a picture of the house appeared in a newspaper article during the publicity surrounding Elvis' receiving the "Ten Outstanding Young Men of the Nation" Award, longtime family friend Janelle McComb asked Elvis what kind of monument, if any, he would like to see built in his honor one day in Tupelo. In an instant he said "a chapel for my fans to meditate in." At the urging of Vernon Presley after Elvis died, Janelle headed up the fundraising drive to build the chapel. Also on the site is a community center Elvis helped to fund, which now houses a museum in tribute to him.

Gold Suit *(left)*

The gold suit is the one featured on the cover of the album "50,000,000 Elvis Fans Can't Be Wrong – Elvis Gold Records Vol. 2." It was designed and manufactured for Elvis by Nudies of Hollywood, who over the years has wardrobed scores of stars including Roy Orbison, Bob Dylan, and a great many names from the country music fraternity. It is possibly the most famous performance costume in the history of entertainment. It is interesting to note that Elvis had the most famous suit in the world and he drove the most famous car in the world, the pink Cadillac. These Elvis items and others like them have become icons of an era of American popular culture, recognized by people of all ages throughout the world.

Gibson J200 *(above)*

The guitar that is displayed with the gold suit is the 1956 Gibson J200, which Elvis used frequently on and off stage and in his movies. The oldest guitar in the Presley Estate inventory, it was used on stage in the Fifties, sometimes with the personalized leather cover that is also exhibited. It appears in many, many photographs – including the poster for *Loving You* – and apparently was one of his favorites. It was also one of several guitars used in the 1968 "comeback" television special.

Although Elvis was no great guitar player, he helped establish the guitar as a symbol of rock'n'roll. His image became the stereotype for early rock'n'roll stars worldwide, even if they could hardly play the guitar. That's not to say that Elvis was no good on the instrument, but he certainly was no virtuoso, nor did he claim to be.

Love Me Tender and *Loving You* Film Posters

Despite the film being in black-and-white, the film posters for Elvis' debut, *Love Me Tender,* were run in full color. The film was a straight Civil War drama rather than the rock musical that most fans would have expected. Nevertheless Elvis managed to sing four songs in the movie, the title track topping the U.S. charts for four weeks. His follow-up picture, *Loving You*, on the other hand, was a full-blown Technicolor production with seven songs that included four chart entries. The theme was more as expected with Elvis playing a contemporary rock'n'roll singer in a storyline that frequently paralleled his own life; the band featured throughout was called the Rough Ridin' Ramblers and included Elvis' regular trio of Scotty Moore, Bill Black and drummer D.J. Fontana. Elvis' vocal backing group, the Jordanaires, also appeared.

Film Ephemera

Elvismania was such in the mid-Fifties that his early films like *Loving You* and *Love Me Tender (above, left and right)* were re-released within a year of their first appearance. His first two Paramount movies for Hal Wallis were even repackaged as a double bill *(above)*.

Army Discharge (above)

Elvis returned to the U.S.A. from West Germany and was discharged from active service in March 1960. During his two years of service he had not done any professional work, except for a very brief recording session on a leave while still in the United States, though there had been plenty of offers. To make up for lost time, soon after his return Elvis appeared on a special "Welcome Home Elvis" edition of Frank Sinatra's TV variety show. For the nine minutes he was on screen Elvis was paid $125,000.

More hit records followed, and his new film – appropriately titled *GI Blues* – was a monster smash, as was the soundtrack album. Elvis was certainly back, and the parents, the educators and the preachers who had often

Army Fatigues

Elvis' original fatigues from his time in the U.S. Army. He was probably the most publicized and most photographed soldier in U.S. Army history, but as much as possible he tried to be a regular G.I. He could have served in the special services or the USO as a performer, as other entertainers had done in the past, or he could have tried to avoid service altogether. But he and the Colonel were perfectly aware that if it looked like he was getting some kind of preferential treatment, the press would have eaten him alive. Far better to "soldier on" and come out at the other end with his reputation, if anything, enhanced.

derided him in the past were now on his side. "Elvis the Pelvis" was considered a respectable, regular, "All American" guy.

Certificate of Achievement *(far left)*

Elvis with his Certificate of Achievement from the Spearhead Armored Division, on his discharge from the U.S. Army. The press conference was held at Fort Dix, New Jersey, and among the press people visible at the top of the picture is Tina Louise (in the white hat), who later played the fictitious movie star Ginger Grant in the TV comedy series *Gilligan's Island* and was featured in many Hollywood movies including *God's Little Acre* and *The Stepford Wives*.

"The first time that

I appeared on stage, it

scared me to death. I really

didn't know what all the

yelling was about. I didn't

realize that my body was

moving. It's a natural

thing to me. So to the

manager backstage I said,

'What'd I do? What'd I do?'

And he said, 'Whatever it is,

go back and do it again.' "

ELVIS, 1972

MODERN SCREEN

King of Fan Mail Award

presented to

ELVIS PRESLEY

in recognition of

his meteoric rise to fame, a fame evidenced

by the enthusiastic and spontaneous

acclamation of countless thousands

of loyal fans

presented by

DELL PUBLISHING COMPANY, INC.

1956

"King of Fan Mail" Award *(above)*
A *Modern Screen* magazine "King of Fan Mail" award was presented to Elvis in Memphis in 1956 for holding the world record in reception of fan mail. As far as was physically possible – and it became more and more difficult over the years – Elvis tried to remain accessible to his fans, whether backstage after a show or, as pictured *(right)*, on the film set. This was taken, probably by a fan, during the shooting of *Love Me Tender*.

Dog Tags *(far right)*
These so-called dog tags were in fact described on the packet as "sweater holders," a Fifties device for holding a girl's sweater in place cape-style. Just one example of the extent to which Elvis merchandising was to be found virtually anywhere and everywhere. These and the other merchandise material are part of a collection bought by Graceland from fans Craig and Barbara Canady. Barbara had collected Elvis items from childhood and her husband Craig helped her with her collection after they were married. In all, it covers Elvis through from the Fifties to Seventies, and the bulk of it is in storage.

Lipstick and Perfume *(above left and right)*
The Elvis Lipstick and "Teddy Bear" perfume are some of the earliest examples of Elvis souvenir items. In the first six months of Elvis souvenir merchandise availability it is said that it grossed over $22 million. Elvis and Colonel Tom Parker were pioneers in celebrity merchandising, and the King was seldom rivalled by others in the amount and variety of goods that could be bought bearing his name or image.

Elvis Bubble Gum Cards *(above center)*
Bubble gum cards are something of an American institution; they had long been a craze for baseball fans, and the Elvis series launched in 1956 pioneered their use of rock and roll stars. Later editions appeared over the years, the very latest being an extravagant, aggressively marketed series of 660 cards produced in 1992 and 1993.

Sun Records

The original-release Sun singles displayed in the Time Line are on loan from a collector, and all bear the now-familiar Sun Records logo.

"I'm Left, You're Right, She's Gone" was written by Stanley Kewsler and Bill Taylor (based on a Campbell's Soup jingle!) and recorded by Elvis on December 18, 1954. The artist credit reads "Elvis Presley with Scotty and Bill," referring to bass player Bill Black and guitarist Scotty Moore. As with many of Elvis' early Sun sides, there were no drums on the session.

RCA Signing (opposite right)

From left to right, Colonel Parker, Gladys Presley, Elvis, Vernon Presley, and two officials of RCA Records on the occasion of his leaving Sun Records of Memphis and signing with the giant RCA.

RCA Contract

(opposite below)
Dated November 15, 1955, this is the contract that moved Elvis from Sun Records to RCA. Note that Elvis' father, Vernon, has cosigned. The age limit for such agreements was then still twenty-one, so Elvis was considered a minor.

Live 1957 (opposite far right)

In action, 1957, (left to right) guitarist Scotty Moore, Elvis, D.J. Fontana on drums and Bill Black on bass.

As can be seen from many of the pictures of Elvis in action, right from the early days of his career he performed as many numbers without a guitar around his neck as with, although he came to personify the guitar-strumming rock'n'roll star.

The Hall of Gold stretches for nearly 80 feet and is lined on both sides with gold and platinum records, and many other awards presented to Elvis from all parts of the world. In this hallway there are scores of gold and platinum records, representing various sales figures. The countries represented include Norway, Japan, the former Yugoslavia, Australia, South Africa, the United Kingdom, Sweden, Germany, France, Canada, Belgium and The Netherlands.

The sales requirements for being awarded gold and platinum records have changed over the years and vary from country to country; also, many of these recordings have achieved gold status more than once, although they were often only recognized for an award the first time. The new collection of gold and platinum in the Racquetball Court is an attempt to put this right in terms of the sales of records since Elvis' death and unrecognized sales during his lifetime.

The awards case contains, among other awards, an elaborate trophy from South Africa for "ten million sellers" from 1956 to 1960; an Australian *Everybody's* award which looks rather like an Oscar, for Elvis' acting in *GI Blues* (though it is dated 1968 for a film released in 1960); and a Japanese trophy which features the RCA Victor trademark dog "Nipper," recognizing outstanding sales of "It's Now Or Never" in Japan.

Other trophies in the case include the Las Vegas Musical Star of the Year Award, the 1971 Memphis Music Award, awards from *Cashbox* and *Photoplay* magazines, and a silver cup from the Elvis Presley Fan Club of Great Britain with a color picture of Elvis receiving the cup from fan club organizer Todd Slaughter.

TV Console

The TV and stereo console that is normally on display at the entrance to the Hall of Gold was a gift from RCA Records shortly after Elvis got back from the army. It has a plaque on it commemorating the fact that up to that point Elvis had sold more than fifty million records. At the time an item like this was the epitome of luxury, and the black-and-white photograph shows an excited Elvis supervising the delivery of the console to the front door of Graceland in 1960 as the Colonel looks on.

A Lifetime of Awards

Among the many trophies on exhibition in the Hall of Gold is the first Grammy Award to be made to a rock'n'roll artist, although, significantly, it was for Elvis' interpretation of gospel songs. The first Grammy Awards ceremony was on May 4, 1959, and recognized recording achievements of 1958. The starting and ending dates for eligibility for an awards period and the date of the ceremony have changed through the years. It was many years into the life of the awards before rock music started receiving its due recognition – the industry was very different then. In fact, some of Elvis' most important music, historically, was recorded before these awards existed. Awards and the way they are determined have received a lot

of criticism from the music-buying public and from within the industry itself. Still, they are considered important, and the Grammys are considered among the most prestigious, if not the most prestigious, of all music awards. Elvis never attended a Grammy Awards ceremony, most likely on the advice of the Colonel, who liked to keep Elvis out of such highly public, "everybody-else-does-it" events for his own strategic reasons.

The Video Platinum Award

The video award brings things right up to date. Elvis was getting video awards in the Nineties, and the one shown here was for a documentary the Elvis Presley Estate made with the Disney company, Buena Vista Home Video, which went platinum.

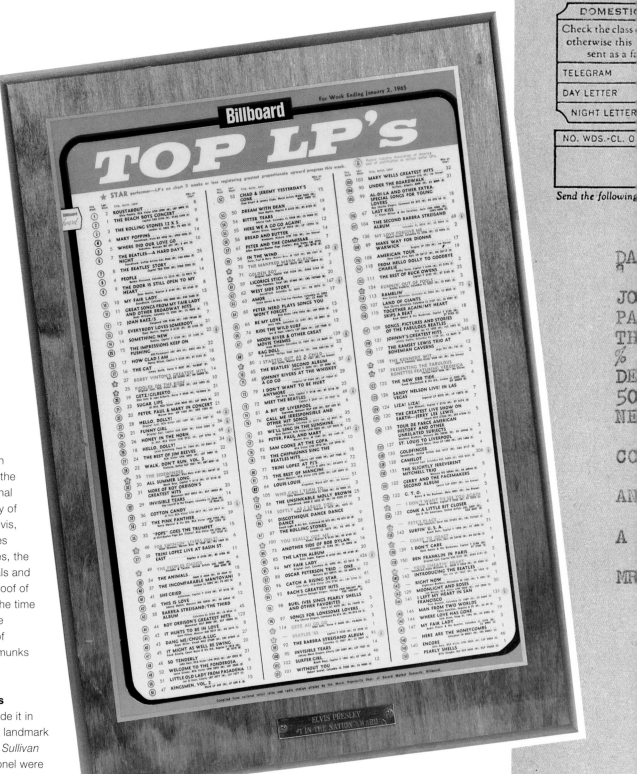

Billboard Chart

The *Billboard* chart from 1964 puts Elvis' continuing popularity in the context of the British beat invasion of America. He was one of the few American stars who had been around prior to the Beatles' U.S. breakthough in 1964 who remained at the top despite the phenomenal competition from the army of U.K. groups. Alongside Elvis, the *Billboard* chart features such names as the Beatles, the Rolling Stones, the Animals and Manfred Mann. Further proof of the Beatles' influence at the time is in two U.S. entries – the Supremes' album "A Bit of Liverpool" and "The Chipmunks Sing The Beatles' Hits"!

Telegram to the Beatles

When the Beatles first made it in America – like Elvis with a landmark TV appearance on the *Ed Sullivan Show* – Elvis and the Colonel were among the first to congratulate them on their historic achievement.

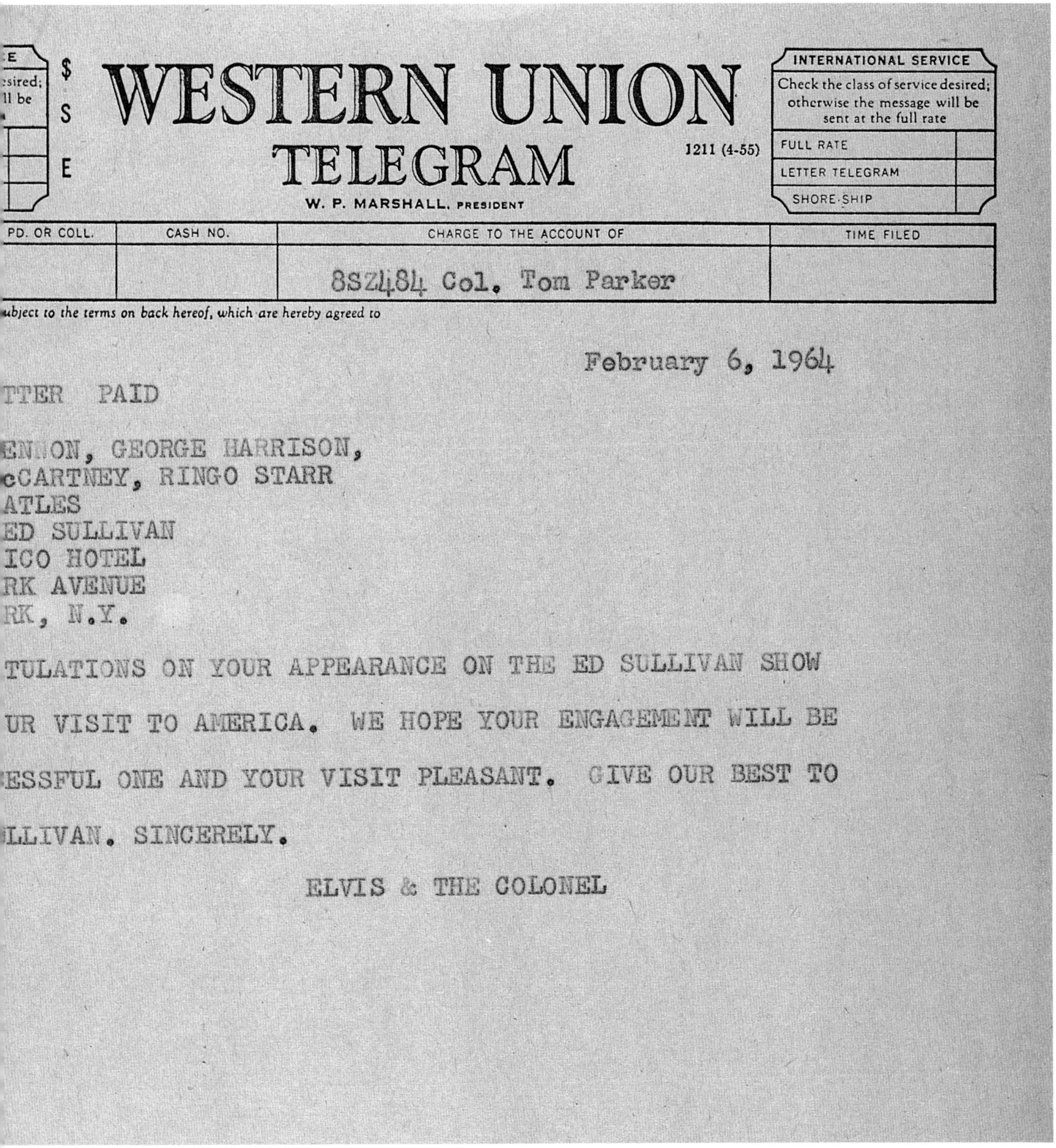

WESTERN UNION
TELEGRAM

W. P. MARSHALL, PRESIDENT

1211 (4-55)

INTERNATIONAL SERVICE

Check the class of service desired; otherwise the message will be sent at the full rate

FULL RATE

LETTER TELEGRAM

SHORE-SHIP

$

S

E

PD. OR COLL.	CASH NO.	CHARGE TO THE ACCOUNT OF	TIME FILED
		8SZ484 Col. Tom Parker	

ubject to the terms on back hereof, which are hereby agreed to

February 6, 1964

TTER   PAID

ENNON, GEORGE HARRISON,
cCARTNEY, RINGO STARR
ATLES
ED SULLIVAN
ICO HOTEL
RK AVENUE
RK, N.Y.

TULATIONS ON YOUR APPEARANCE ON THE ED SULLIVAN SHOW

UR VISIT TO AMERICA. WE HOPE YOUR ENGAGEMENT WILL BE

ESSFUL ONE AND YOUR VISIT PLEASANT. GIVE OUR BEST TO

LLIVAN. SINCERELY.

ELVIS & THE COLONEL

The Big Room

What has come to be known as the Big Room houses by far the greatest number of items of Elvis memorabilia in the entire Graceland complex. As the visitor turns left at the end of the Hall of Gold, he or she comes to the first portion of the collection which includes items from Elvis' Hollywood career, from early draft scripts to front-of-house posters, scores of civic awards from cities, counties and states across America, and numerous other presentation items – plus his and Priscilla's wedding clothes. Of special interest, and certainly valued highly by Elvis when he received them, are the scrapbooks and other mementos assembled by fans and sent to Graceland over the years.

Then there are the paintings of Elvis, again done largely by fans and donated to the collection as a tribute to the King. The third part of the Big Room, walking back parallel to the first section, features on one side Elvis' large collection of police and sheriff badges, an array of his many firearms, and more presentations from various civic bodies. Opposite this are a selection of the elaborate stage clothes – including the celebrated *Aloha from Hawaii* outfit – designed by Bill Belew (with the amazing variety of belts that were worn with them), one of Elvis' karate outfits, more awards, guitars and the fabled TCB ring.

Film Scripts

Elvis had the original film scripts from every one of his movies. Some on display have unfamiliar titles because the films started production under working titles that changed when the films were finished. At some point he had leather or leatherette binders ordered for all of them so they could have a uniform look. He stored them in the Trophy Room, and some of the them have Elvis' own handwritten annotations and notes in the margins; others have telegrams and notes stuck in them; they represent the unglamorous side of moviemaking as a real job.

In 1960, after his army discharge, Elvis had a triumphant return to Hollywood with his new film *GI Blues*. A light comedy/drama with eleven songs, it was well received by both public and critics, though his next two movie vehicles, *Flaming Star* and *Wild In the Country,* were not quite so successful, probably due to the fact that they had more dramatic stories, which Elvis personally welcomed; he had aspirations, never to be fulfilled, to be a serious screen actor like his idols James Dean and Marlon Brando. Elvis was getting into the pattern of releasing two or even three movies a year (in 1964 there were four!) In 1961 *Wild In The Country* was swiftly followed by *Blue Hawaii*, which was probably his biggest box-office smash. It had lots of music, lots of girls, a fight or two, a light script, and an exotic location – it became a predictable formula that was to be followed fairly closely by his films in the Sixties. In all Elvis made thirty-one films – twenty-seven of them between 1960 and 1969.

Kid Galahad **Robe**

One of Elvis' more dramatic roles was
in the 1962 release *Kid Galahad* in which
he played an up-and-coming boxing star.
Based on a *Saturday Evening Post* story
from the Thirties, it was first filmed in
1937 as *The Battling Bellhop* with
Edward G. Robinson, Bette Davis
and Humphrey Bogart.

For his fight scenes Elvis was coached
by former junior welterweight champion,
Mushy Callahan, who was assisted by Al
Silvani, a former trainer and corner man
for boxing legends Floyd Patterson, Jake
LaMotta and Rocky Graziano.

The *Kid Galahad* boxing robe is one
of the few examples of Elvis' movie
costumes on display at Graceland. This
is because most of the costumes
remained the property of the film studios
and because many of those Elvis owned
were cut into fabric swatches and placed
in record album packages as promotional
items in the early Seventies.

Gretsch "Chet Atkins" Guitar (center)
One in Graceland's inventory of guitars, the mahogany-colored Gretsch guitar is an edition named after Chet Atkins, the legendary guitarist, and one of his big instrumental hits. It was called the "Chet Atkins Country Gentleman" guitar.
It appears in the photograph (top left) of Elvis playing his 1970 engagement in Las Vegas. He is wearing one of his two-piece karate-style outfits and appears to be in the middle of one of the monologues that were a feature of his shows, when he would tell stories, reflect on the past and joke with his audience. Some of these narratives have made their way onto various albums over the years, and provide an interesting insight into the man's character.

Film Guitars (top right)
The green guitar was made by Burns of London; a 12-string, it was featured in the film *Spinout* released in 1966. The double-neck red Gibson appeared on some of the publicity material for *Spinout* and the 1964 film *Girl Happy*, though it is hard to spot in either film. The guitar itself would be considered a genuine collector's item, even if it had not belonged to Elvis Presley.

Martin D-28 Guitar (bottom left)
The Martin D-28 acoustic guitar is one that Elvis used during his last year of concert tours, 1977. There is a crack in the instrument that was made while Elvis was still using it. There are pictures of him with it on stage before and after it was damaged, but no story has emerged to explain what actually caused the crack in the instrument.

Acoustic Gibson (bottom right)
The acoustic Gibson guitar with ELVIS PRESLEY set in the neck is a 1960 J200 similar to the one from 1956 on display in the Time Line. It is the second oldest guitar in the entire Graceland collection, and both J200s were featured in the '68 TV special.

Priscilla's Wedding Dress

Priscilla's wedding dress was, surprisingly, just an off-the-rack dress. She fell in love with this particular gown and that was that. Elvis and Priscilla were married on May 1, 1967, at the Aladdin Hotel in Las Vegas. He had turned thirty-two the previous January and she was about to turn twenty-two on May 24. Elvis' Best Men were Joe Esposito and Marty Lacker, who were members of his regular entourage. Priscilla's Maid of Honor was her younger sister Michelle Beaulieu. The ceremony was performed by Judge David Zenoff, a Nevada supreme court justice. A breakfast reception with a five-and-a-half-foot tiered wedding cake followed, during which the bride and groom met the press.

After honeymooning in Palm Springs for a couple of days, they returned to Memphis. They had a second reception for relatives, friends and staff who had not been able to attend the first in Vegas. Although there was not a repeat ceremony, the couple did wear the wedding clothes again.

Elvis' Wedding Suit

Elvis' suit was in a paisley-style fabric fashionable in the late Sixties. Over the years it has faded from its original black.

The Awards Ceremony Suit

On January 16, 1971, Elvis was honored by the United States Junior Chamber of Commerce when he accepted their award for being one of the "Ten Outstanding Young Men of the Nation" for 1970. The award is a highly prestigious national honor, which has recognized doctors, lawyers, ambassadors, heads of state, activists, educators, professors, and entertainers. It recognizes young men of thirty-five or under, who achieve something of importance, but part of the qualification for receiving it is also civic involvement or humanitarian and charitable efforts.

For a man who had received considerable criticism in his early career, and was clearly conscious of his humble upbringing, we can imagine how Elvis felt to be recognized in this way by the "establishment."

On display with the trophy and matching medallion are the tuxedo Elvis wore at the formal ceremony, held in Memphis that year at the Ellis Auditorium, and a transcript of part of his acceptance speech. As well as photographs of the award ceremony, there is also the original sketch by designer Bill Belew when he began work on the tuxedo.

The Ellis Auditorium, incidentally, was the same place where Elvis attended gospel singing when he was young, where his high school graduation took place, and where he performed charity concerts back in 1961.

Today, the award is known as the "Ten Outstanding Young Americans" award as women are included in the Jaycees and therefore are eligible for consideration for the honor.

The list of past honorees includes Howard Hughes, John F. Kennedy, Robert F. Kennedy, Richard Nixon, Leonard Bernstein, Orson Welles, Pat Boone, Jesse Jackson, Joe Louis, Henry Kissinger and hundreds more.

"When I was a child, ladies and gentlemen, I was a dreamer. I read comic books, and I was the hero of the comic book. I saw movies, and I was the hero in the movie. So every dream I ever dreamed has come true a hundred times . . . I learned very early in life that 'Without a song, the day would never end; without a song, a man ain't got a friend; without a song, the road would never bend – without a song.' So I keep singing a song. Goodnight. Thank you."

ELVIS' ACCEPTANCE SPEECH AT THE JAYCEES AWARD CEREMONY, 1971

"King of Fan Mail" *(above left)*
An Elvis concert in Memphis in 1956 is interrupted for the presentation of the "King of Fan Mail" award.

Key to the City of Pontiac *(above right)*
As Elvis Presley became more and more an establishment figure, almost an American institution rather than the figure of youthful rebellion he had been in the Fifties, he was increasingly feted by civic bodies, local mayors, state governors and so on.

The plaque with the key to the City of Pontiac was typical of the scores of such awards showered on him during the latter part of his career, several examples of which hang in a case in the Big Room.

Car Buyer Award
One of the more unusual awards given to Elvis was the one proclaiming him "The World's Greatest Car Buyer" by a local Memphis automobile dealer. After Elvis had been on one of his famous spending sprees, the dealer obtained the names of those for whom Elvis had bought a car and listed them on a plaque which he gave to Elvis. There are thirty-one names (plus one blank) on the plaque – some spending spree!

TO
ELVIS PRESLEY
IN APPRECIATION FOR THE WONDERFUL
MUSIC AND GREAT TALENT THAT YOU
HAVE PROVIDED TO THE PEOPLE OF
SAN ANTONIO, TEXAS
AUGUST 27, 1976

Billboard
1973
Trendsetter
Award
ELVIS PRESLEY
Col. TOM PARKER
For creating the first worldwide TV concert
which was beamed via satellite to 1.5 billion people
in 40 countries

Texas Plaque *(above)*

Quite often, apart from the kudos conferred on the donors, Elvis was given plaques and such for the simple reason that people enjoyed what he did and the pleasure he brought to their lives. This one in the shape of the State of Texas is inscribed: "In appreciation for the wonderful music and great talent that you have provided to the people of San Antonio, Texas. August 27, 1976."

The King's Crown *(above)*

The crown was a gift from a fan. This was handed to him as he was making his final bows, about to leave the stage of the *Aloha from Hawaii* concert. Behind the crown is an award presented to Elvis and the Colonel in recognition of the record number of viewers that the satellite broadcast attracted.

Personal Letter from President Nixon

Elvis visited President Richard Nixon on December 21, 1970, and was presented with a Federal Narcotics Officer's badge to add to his vast collection of police badges and certificates.

After talking to Vice President Agnew, Elvis had voiced his concern to the president about "the drug culture, the hippie elements, etc." in a hand-written letter. He offered his services as a "federal agent at large" so he could use his influence as an entertainer to campaign against hard drugs.

He subsequently showed up at the White House unannounced, and talked his way into meeting Nixon in the Oval Office. After presenting the President with a commemorative World War II Colt .45 pistol encased in a wooden box, he received his much sought-after Narcotics Bureau badge. Elvis also persuaded the President to meet his two bodyguards, Jerry Schilling and Sonny West, and talked him into giving them presidential souvenirs too!

In 1975 Nixon requested that Elvis perform at the White House, only to have Colonel Parker quote a fee of $25,000. The White House replied that performers were never paid to appear there, to which Parker retorted that Elvis never performed for free!

THE WHITE HOUSE
WASHINGTON

December 31, 1970

Dear Mr. Presley:

It was a pleasure to meet with you in my office recently, and I want you to know once again how much I appreciate your thoughtfulness in giving me the commemorative World War II Colt 45 pistol, encased in the handsome wooden chest. You were particularly kind to remember me with this impressive gift, as well as your family photographs, and I am delighted to have them for my collection of special mementos.

With my best wishes to you, Mrs. Presley, and to your daughter, Lisa, for a happy and peaceful 1971,

Sincerely,

Richard Nixon

Mr. Elvis Presley
Box 417
Madison, Tennessee 37115

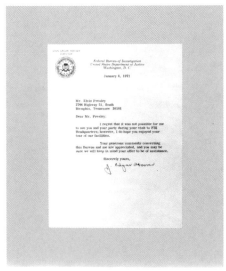

Letter from J. Edgar Hoover *(above)*
A letter from legendary FBI boss Hoover
(left) with Richard Nixon) referring to Elvis'
visit to the bureau headquarters in
December 1970.

Meeting Richard Nixon
Elvis is holding two pictures – one of Lisa
Marie, and one of himself, Priscilla and Lisa
Marie – which he is about to show to the
president.

Fans' Scrapbooks

Fans sent Elvis scrapbooks and other homemade personally decorated items throughout his career. They range from the hand-painted to the embroidered to the carved. Elvis thought as much – possibly more – of these personal gifts as he did of all the civic awards presented to him over the years. At one point, Elvis had his entire scrapbook collection put on microfilm for posterity.

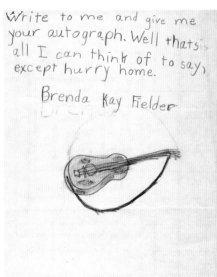

Dear Elvis,

I have a fan club for you. You are my favorite
I am seven years old. singer, I have all of your records, and we
play them all the time. I saw all of
your movies, and "Loving you" four
times. A friend of ours got a piece of
your rotten tree for me. I have
lots of pictures of you. I have
a picture framed of you sitting
by your swimming pool, and I
sleep with it every night. I
would like for you to call me,
and I will pay for it. My
number is Cy8-2060. I would
like for you to visit me. My
address is 927 Battery Lane.
Nashville Tenn. Please don't get
married because I love you.

Write to me and give me
your autograph. Well thats
all I can think of to say,
except hurry home.

Brenda Kay Fielder

"Elvis for President"

The "Elvis for President" campaign was
a publicity gimmick thought up, presumably
by Colonel Tom Parker, to coincide with
the 1956 presidential election.

Ralph Cowan Portrait

The only portrait that Elvis ever commissioned was the life-size one done by Ralph Cowan in 1969. Cowan had painted many celebrities and heads of state, and Elvis saw an example of his work on the cover of the Johnny Mathis "Heavenly" album. Cowan was living and working in Las Vegas at the time, and Elvis was in town and sought him out. He commissioned the portrait, then turned up one afternoon saying he was there for a sitting.

The painter explained he didn't always work from sittings, he would often just take Polaroids of his subject to work from, and he'd seen enough by watching Elvis walk across the casino.

Elvis responded, "You mean I let the band have the afternoon off for nothing?" He paid the $10,000 fee in advance to get the work started. When he turned up to collect the painting, it wasn't quite finished, but Elvis was so pleased with it he took it as it was, with the paint still wet. Elvis later paid another $8,000 for foreign and U.S. reproduction rights.

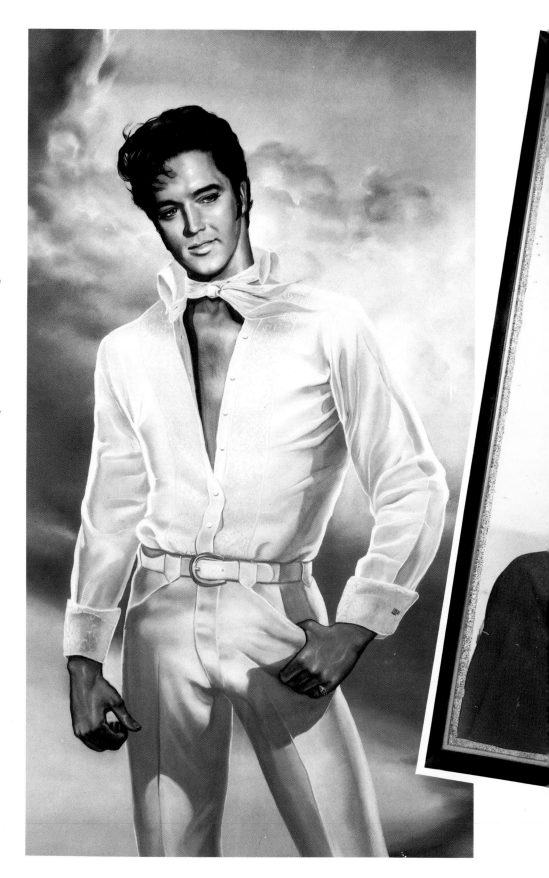

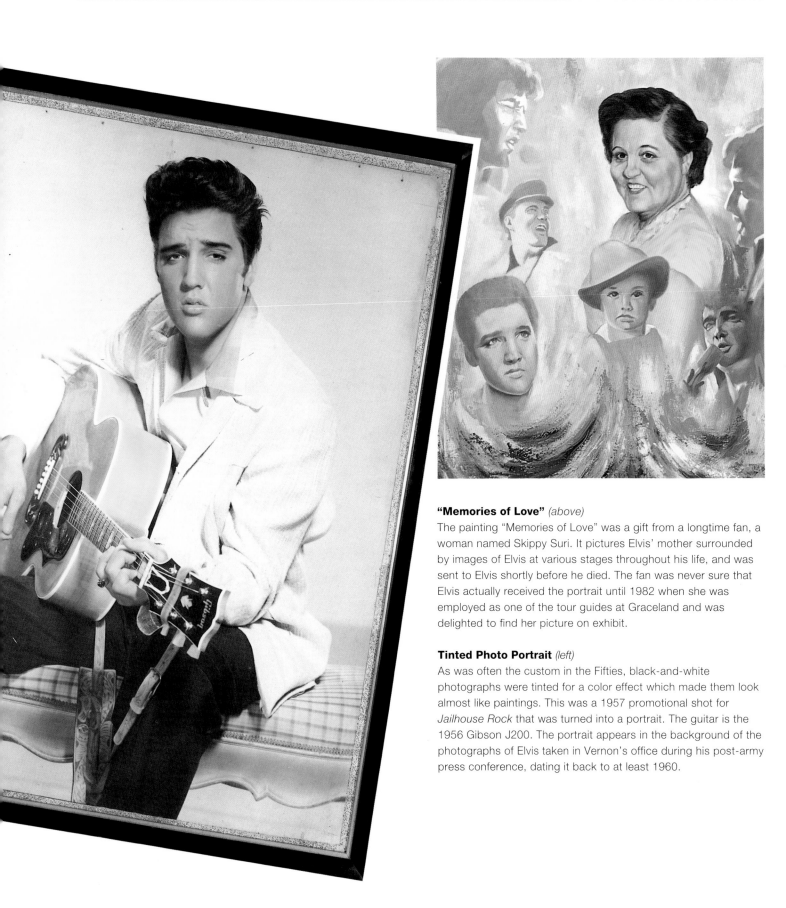

"Memories of Love" *(above)*

The painting "Memories of Love" was a gift from a longtime fan, a woman named Skippy Suri. It pictures Elvis' mother surrounded by images of Elvis at various stages throughout his life, and was sent to Elvis shortly before he died. The fan was never sure that Elvis actually received the portrait until 1982 when she was employed as one of the tour guides at Graceland and was delighted to find her picture on exhibit.

Tinted Photo Portrait *(left)*

As was often the custom in the Fifties, black-and-white photographs were tinted for a color effect which made them look almost like paintings. This was a 1957 promotional shot for *Jailhouse Rock* that was turned into a portrait. The guitar is the 1956 Gibson J200. The portrait appears in the background of the photographs of Elvis taken in Vernon's office during his post-army press conference, dating it back to at least 1960.

Tupelo, Mississippi 1957 *(top)*
On the occasion of Elvis' performance for
the Elvis Presley Youth Recreation Center,
Elvis poses with state troopers.
Denver, Colorado *(above)*
In the mid-Seventies, Elvis receiving one
of his many honorary memberships from a
local police force – in this case, complete
with the whole uniform.

"Because of the nature of the work
he was involved in, Elvis was very
often in contact with police and
security people. He started collecting badges and, of course, word
spread. Somebody was always
presenting him with a badge back
stage or in his suite, making him
an honorary this or that, induct-
ing him into various security,
police and law enforcement
fraternities. We've had badge
collecting enthusiasts, such as
the actor/comedian Dan
Ackroyd, who came through and
was just blown away by the part of the
collection that we display (there's more in
storage). He asked if we realized that
nobody has this widely varied a collection,
or has all these memberships or all these
important signatures that Elvis had."

Narcotics Bureau Badge *(above)*
The Narcotics Bureau badge presented
to Elvis by Richard Nixon in 1970.

185

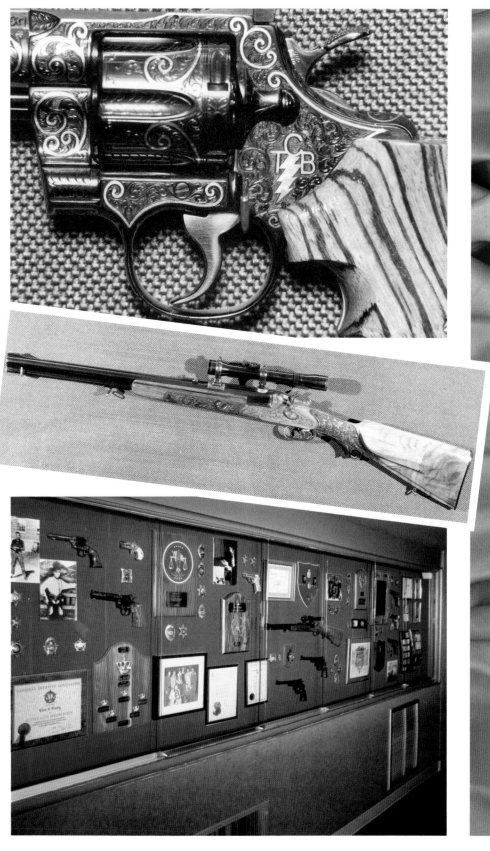

Firearms Collection

Allied to his badge collection is his array of firearms.

Detailed *(opposite)* is Elvis' familiar TCB logo engraved on a **Python 357 pistol**, an "over and under" **20-gauge shotgun and .22 rifle combination**, and the **firearms display** in the Big Room. The group shot features *(clockwise from top)* a **Colt .45 automatic**, the turquoise-handled **Colt .45** which has "E" engraved on one side of the grip and "P" on the other (said to be one of Elvis' favorites), the **Python 357** and a small pearl-handled **Derringer**.

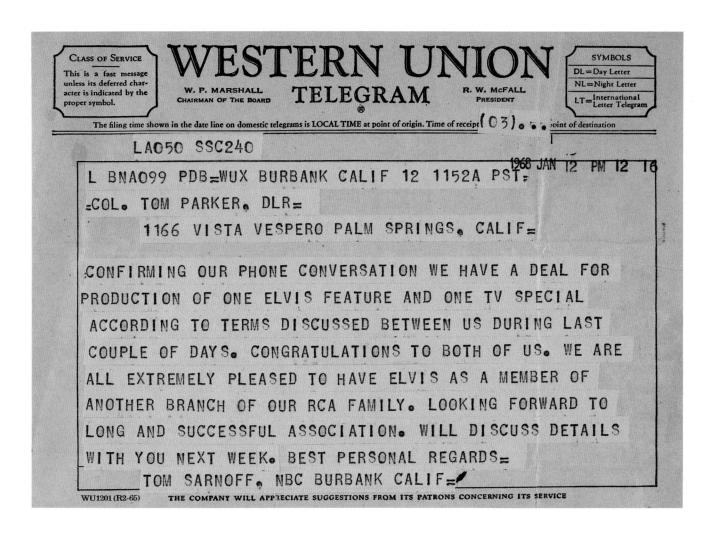

"The Comeback Special"

The leather suit which Elvis wore on his 1968 "comeback" TV special was designed by Bill Belew who went on to be the main designer of Elvis' stage and personal clothes through to the end of Elvis' life. Commonly referred to as the "68 Special" or the "68 Comeback," the actual name of this landmark television show was simply *Elvis*. That one word said it all.

The Sixties had brought about great changes that Elvis had helped pave the way for over a decade earlier. But tucked away in Hollywood making movies, or at Graceland in a world of his own creation, Elvis had become less and less a part of the current pop cultural scene.

Elvis had been making one movie after another through the Sixties, and many of the records he put out in these years had been movie soundtrack albums. In the early Sixties, the films and film-related records had been wonderfully successful, but as the Sixties wore on, these movies and records, though still profitable, were not nearly so successful as they had been. The public was growing weary of the "Presley formula." The weariest of all was Elvis himself. Elvis had reached the supreme level of frustration

and unhappiness with the state of his career. He had hoped to become a serious actor, but Hollywood and his management had had other ideas, and Elvis had gone along with them.

By the summer of 1968 it had been more than seven years since Elvis had appeared in front of a live audience. (The last time had been his 1961 benefit concert in Hawaii to help fund the building of the U.S.S. *Arizona* memorial at Pearl Harbor.) Elvis had missed the closeness of his audience, the energy and excitement of live performing. He was ready for a change.

In June, 1968, Elvis was set to tape a television show to be aired on December 3 on NBC as a Christmas special. What the Colonel basically planned was Elvis coming out in a suit and spend the hour singing holiday songs and say "Merry Christmas and goodnight." Typical holiday television fluff. But Steve Binder, the young, innovative producer/director of the show, knew that Elvis' first performance in front of a live audience in more than seven years, and his first television appearance in more than eight years, was a more important event than that. Elvis knew it too. He and Steve had a different kind of show in mind.

After all those years in Hollywood away from the public, and

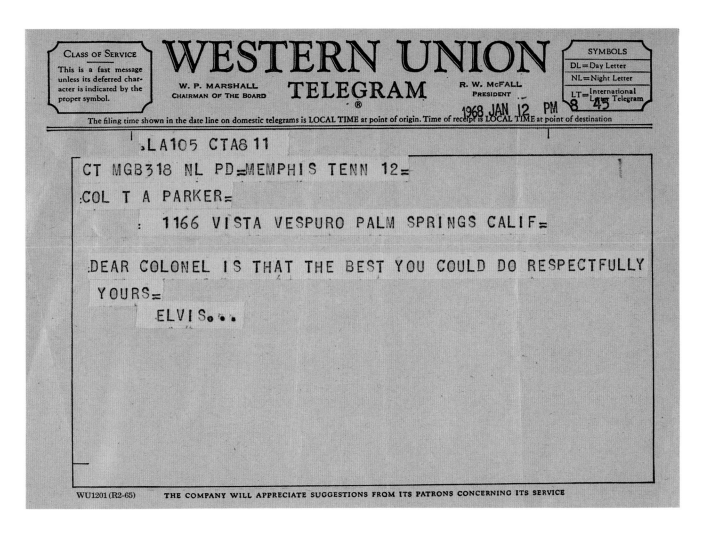

CLASS OF SERVICE

This is a fast message
unless its deferred char-
acter is indicated by the
proper symbol.

WESTERN UNION

W. P. MARSHALL
CHAIRMAN OF THE BOARD

TELEGRAM

R. W. McFALL
PRESIDENT

SYMBOLS

DL=Day Letter

NL=Night Letter

LT=International
Letter Telegram

1968 JAN 12 PM 8 45

The filing time shown in the date line on domestic telegrams is LOCAL TIME at point of origin. Time of receipt is LOCAL TIME at point of destination

LA105 CTA8 11

CT MGB318 NL PD=MEMPHIS TENN 12=

COL T A PARKER=

1166 VISTA VESPURO PALM SPRINGS CALIF=

DEAR COLONEL IS THAT THE BEST YOU COULD DO RESPECTFULLY

YOURS=

ELVIS...

WU1201 (R2-65)   THE COMPANY WILL APPRECIATE SUGGESTIONS FROM ITS PATRONS CONCERNING ITS SERVICE

with all that was happening in music, Elvis had to prove that he could still rock with the best of them. His reputation and, very likely, the future of his career were riding on this show.

The show was taped over several days in late June at the NBC studios in Burbank, California. Some of the taping was in front of a live audience, other portions were not. It was aired on NBC December 3, 1968, and was sponsored by Singer (the sewing machine company). It was the top-rated program of the week, capturing about a third of the national viewing audience, and was one of the top-rated specials of the year. The executive producer was Bob Finkel. Bones Howe served as musical producer.

The show opened with Elvis singing a hot version of the gutsy "Trouble," which he had first performed in his most critically acclaimed film, *King Creole,* in 1958. Then, Elvis was reunited with two of his original Fifties band members, guitarist Scottie Moore and drummer D.J. Fontana. They sat together on stage in the round, along with several friends and associates of Elvis for an informal jam session. Steve Binder had the idea for this portion of the show from watching Elvis and his friends singing, jamming, and swapping stories off camera in real life. Notes had been

made about some of the stories and songs that had been a part of this natural activity, and Elvis and the guys recreated this for the camera in front of a live studio audience. Segments of the session were woven throughout the special.

There were also sequences of Elvis taking the stage alone and performing many of his greatest hit rock'n'roll songs and ballads, such as "Hound Dog," "Don't Be Cruel," "Jailhouse Rock," "All Shook Up," "Love Me Tender," and "Can't Help Falling in Love."

For the group jam session and for the solo stage performance segment, Elvis wore the two-piece black leather outfit that had been specially designed for the show by Bill Belew, who also designed all the other wardrobe Elvis and the cast wore in the show. The look evoked the era of James Dean, Marlon Brando and the "motorcycle" films of the Fifties, the era when Elvis had first been proclaimed the "King of rock and roll." Photographs of Elvis in this suit are the most commonly thought of images to represent this television special.

In the jam session segment, Elvis speaks of the gospel origins of rock'n'roll. This leads into the gospel music portion of the show, which has Elvis wearing a two-piece burgundy suit, singing

NATIONAL BROADCASTING CO., INC.
NBC COLOR CITY
3000 W. ALAMEDA AVE., BURBANK, CALIF.

374

"ELVIS"
starring
ELVIS PRESLEY
IN COLOR
Children Under 12 Will Not Be Admitted

STUDIO 4
Thursday
June
27
1968
Show Time
6:00 PM
GUESTS
SHOULD
ARRIVE
5:00 PM

374

"Where Could I Go but to the Lord," "I'm Saved," and "Up Above My Head," backed by the black female group, The Blossoms, and accompanied by a troupe of dancers – all of this for a rousing gospel production number.

Toward the end of the special Elvis appears in a lengthy production number that, through song, dance, karate, and various situations, traces a young man's journey from a struggling guitar player, through all the challenges, dangers and compromises on the path to his dreams of success and superstardom. Something is lost along the way. Once the dream is achieved, the man realizes that he remains unfulfilled, that he has abandoned his true self. He decides to return to his roots, where he was happiest. He sings, "I'll never be more than what I am . . . a swingin' little guitar man." The parallels to Elvis' own life are clear and deliberate, and his doing the 1968 special represents his own return to his roots, to his true self.

At the end of the show, Elvis appears alone, wearing a simple white two-piece suit, standing in front of the towering backdrop of red lights that spell "Elvis," singing a brand-new song, specially written for the show, called "If I Can Dream."

When the writers first came to Elvis to play a run-through of the song for him, he loved it. In a studio rehearsal of the song, a little-known story is that Elvis turned the lights out and sang it alone to the tape of the band playing it and literally writhed on the floor with passionate emotional energy. Only a handful of people in the studio booth witnessed this amazing performance. More than a hint of this emotional charge is evident in the performance of "If I Can Dream" that is seen at the end of the television show.

Elvis was not inclined to sing "message" songs as such, but "If I Can Dream" was a rare example of a number that seemed to be both topical and apt in the way that it reflected Elvis' view of his life at the time.

Elvis was nervous about the show and wondered if he could still cut it after so many years away from the stage. But soon after he got out there, his confidence was clearly in place. He was a lean, youthful-looking thirty-three years old, and the polished maturity in his voice and the sophisticated stance in his presentation wowed his audience. He poured his heart and soul and every ounce of energy he had into this show, and gave himself a physical and vocal workout like he hadn't had in years. He had never looked or sounded better. It was obvious that he was enjoying it. It was the

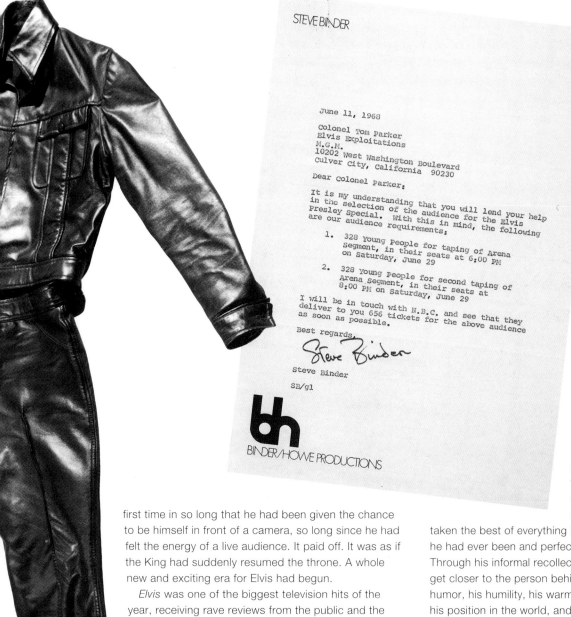

STEVE BINDER

June 11, 1968

Colonel Tom Parker
Elvis Exploitations
M.G.M.
10202 West Washington Boulevard
Culver City, California 90230

Dear Colonel Parker:

It is my understanding that you will lend your help
in the selection of the audience for the Elvis
Presley Special. With this in mind, the following
are our audience requirements:

1. 328 Young People for taping of Arena
    Segment, in their seats at 6:00 PM
    on Saturday, June 29

2. 328 Young People for second taping of
    Arena Segment, in their seats at
    8:00 PM on Saturday, June 29

I will be in touch with N.B.C. and see that they
deliver to you 656 tickets for the above audience
as soon as possible.

Best regards,

Steve Binder

Steve Binder

SB/gl

BINDER/HOWE PRODUCTIONS

first time in so long that he had been given the chance
to be himself in front of a camera, so long since he had
felt the energy of a live audience. It paid off. It was as if
the King had suddenly resumed the throne. A whole
new and exciting era for Elvis had begun.

Elvis was one of the biggest television hits of the
year, receiving rave reviews from the public and the
critics alike. Later rock writer Greil Marcus remembered the 1968 special this way:

"It was the finest music of his life. If ever there was
music that bleeds, this was it."

Said another rock writer, John Landau:

"There is something magical about watching a man
who has lost himself find his way back home . . . He
sang with the kind of power people no longer expect
from rock and roll singers."

The NBC special has come to be regarded by
many as the ultimate showcase of Elvis Presley as an
artist and a man. As a performer he combined the
raw, sensual, fiery qualities of his early days, with the

polish and poise he had gained
through the movie years of the
Sixties, and he looked absolutely
magnificent. It was as if he had
taken the best of everything he was at the moment and everything
he had ever been and perfectly blended it all for this performance.
Through his informal recollections of his past, he lets the viewer
get closer to the person behind the legend. We see his sense of
humor, his humility, his warmth, his sense of amazement over
his position in the world, and his excitement over this fresh start
in his career. We even sense the thinly veiled expression of the
professional frustration and unhappiness that led him to this
moment. After this show everything in Elvis' life and career
changed.

The soundtrack album went to number eight on *Billboard*'s
pop album chart, and "If I Can Dream" was Elvis's most successful single in several years. The home video of the 1968 show is
one of the most popular in the Elvis catalog today, and the show
airs frequently in syndication around America and overseas.

In the Eighties, a cable television special called "One Night with
You" was produced by Steve Binder. It was comprised mostly of
footage from the "black leather" jam session, most of which had
not been included in the original television special.

"Aloha from Hawaii" Jumpsuit

Elvis made television and entertainment
history with his *Elvis: Aloha from Hawaii -
Via Satellite* special. It took place at the
Honolulu International Center Arena on
January 14, 1973. Sponsored mainly by
Chicken of the Sea tuna, the show was
broadcast live at 12:30 a.m. Hawaiian time,
beamed via Globecam Satellite to Australia,
South Korea, Japan, Thailand, the
Philippines, South Vietnam and other countries. It was seen on a delayed basis in
around thirty European countries. A tape of
the show was seen in America on April 4
on NBC-TV. The live broadcast in January
attracted 37.8% of the viewers in Japan,
91.8% in the Philippines, 70% in Hong
Kong, and 70-80% of the viewers in Korea.
The April showing in the US attracted 51%
of the television viewing audience, and was
seen in more American households than
man's first walk on the moon. In all, it was
seen in about forty countries by 1 billion to

Elvis called designer Bill Belew and told him he wanted a jumpsuit for the Hawaii special that would say "America" to the world-wide viewing audience. Bill told Elvis that, except for the United States flag, he could think of nothing other than the American eagle.

1.5 billion people. Never had one performer held the world's attention in such a way.

Elvis did a complete, untelevised rehearsal show for a packed house on January 12, then did the actual television special on the 14th. After seeing a video-tape of the rehearsal, Elvis decided to have his hair cut and restyled for the satellite broadcast. This difference in hairstyle provides a basis for the Elvis aficionado to distinguish between photos from the rehearsal show and photos from the actual TV special.

Both shows were a benefit for the Kui Lee Cancer Fund in Hawaii. There was no set ticket price for either performance. Audience members were asked to donate what they could afford. Elvis, the musicians, and the crew worked for free – Elvis even paid to get in himself. (This was a tradition Elvis and the Colonel had for benefit shows.) Proceeds from merchandise sales were also donated. It was projected that the shows would raise $25,000 for the fund, but Elvis proudly announced during the satellite broadcast that $75,000 had been raised.

Kui Lee was a Hawaiian composer who died of cancer while still in his thirties. After Elvis announced the sum raised for the Kui Lee Cancer Fund, he sang a Kui Lee song that became an Elvis classic, "I'll Remember You." Elvis had been singing it in concerts during this period and first recorded the song for the movie *Spinout* in the late Sixties.

The Program

Elvis' recording of the theme song from his 1965 movie *Paradise, Hawaiian Style* played over the opening credits, scenes of Elvis' helicopter arrival, and his walking among the fans. The concert opened with Elvis' band playing his introduction for his Seventies shows, "Theme from 2001."

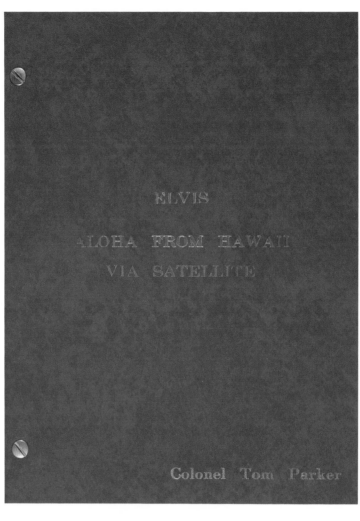

Everything about the show was special – even Elvis' costume, designed by his regular designer, Bill Belew. Bill would come up with various designs and have the clothes made and sent to Elvis, who would choose what he liked and make suggestions about the design elements. There were only a few occasions when Elvis asked for a specific design. One of those was the *Aloha* show.

Elvis' Jumpsuits

Elvis had been wearing jumpsuits on stage since 1970, and they had become quite elaborate by the time of this show. For the past year or two he had been wearing studded, hip-length capes and heavy studded leather belts with his jumpsuits. For the American Eagle jumpsuit, Bill first designed a huge

He sang "See, See Rider," "Burning Love," "Something," "You Gave Me a Mountain," "Steamroller Blues," "My Way," "Love Me," "Johnny B. Goode," "It's Over," "Blue Suede Shoes," "I'm So Lonesome I Could Cry," "I Can't Stop Loving You," "Hound Dog," "What Now, My Love," "Fever," "Welcome to My World," "Suspicious Minds," "I'll Remember You," "Long Tall Sally/Whole Lotta Shakin' Goin' On," "An American Trilogy," "A Big Hunk o' Love," and "Can't Help Falling in Love."

The show was one hour. It was lengthened to ninety minutes for the taped broadcast in the US in April with Hawaiian scenery shots that rolled while Elvis, inset onto the screen, sang "Blue Hawaii," "Ku-u-i-po," and "Hawaiian Wedding Song" from his 1961 hit movie, *Blue Hawaii*, plus "Early Morning Rain." Elvis and the band waited and came back out on stage in the empty arena after the live show to shoot these inserts.

The show was produced by Marty Passetta and featured a dramatic backdrop of flashing lights. Elvis was in top form physically and vocally. This was probably the pinnacle of his superstardom. In fact, that night, he redefined the term superstar. It was one of the great moments of his career.

calf-length cape. During preparations for the show, Elvis tried working with this cape, but it was just too cumbersome to use. So out went the emergency order for another cape in the usual size. Elvis tossed his belt into the audience after singing "An American Trilogy." He then surprised everyone by tossing the cape out as he finished his closing song.

Elvis wore the suit several more times after that, so he had a second belt and a second short cape made. The original unused big cape and the second belt are in the Presley Estate inventory. Elvis gave the second small cape to a friend. The man who caught the cape tossed out at the show sold it to a private collector who still has it. No one seems to know for sure who caught the belt tossed out at the show and what its current whereabouts are. The black customized Gibson J200 guitar Elvis played in this special was a favorite of his at the time. At a 1975 concert he handed it to a fan in the audience, who kept it for many years, then sold it to a collector. The American Eagle jumpsuit is on permanent display at Graceland, along with the white corduroy suit he wore in the helicopter arrival scenes, and a crown a fan gave to Elvis during his final bows that night.

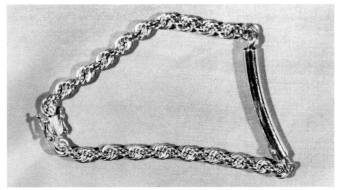

TCB Ring *(right)*

"Elvis had this custom-made in 1974 or '75. It's made of gold, black onyx, and 16 carats in diamonds. The big diamond alone is over 11 carats of that total diamond weight. This ring is probably one of his most famous pieces of jewelry. There was a point when he had the large diamond removed. He called his jeweler Lowell Hayes late at night, wanting to have an engagement ring made for Ginger Alden and he needed a big stone. It's hard to get a big stone like that, you don't just have those lying around your jewelry shop, so in order to get the ring made as quickly as he wanted it made for Ginger, they took the big diamond out of the TCB ring and put it into Ginger's ring, which we understand she still has after all these many years. They put in a paste or cubic zirconium to replace the large diamond in the TCB ring. Elvis never got around to replacing the fake diamond with a real one."

18-Carat Gold Rolex *(above)*

The inscription on the back of the watch indicates that it was a gift from the Houston Livestock Show Officers when Elvis played six shows to a total of 207,494 people at the Astrodome in 1970. So vast is the auditorium in Houston that the Livestock Show was actually going on at the same time as Elvis' appearances.

The Show Officers made a gift of a similar watch to the Colonel at the same time.

Bracelet *(top)*

The bracelet has Elvis' name on top of the bar while underneath the bar is his nickname, "Crazy." This was his nickname within his inner circle of guys, his entourage of "Memphis Mafia." Elvis would give bracelets like this to all the guys with their name on top and their nickname within the group inscribed underneath. So the guys all got together and gave Elvis this one. The nickname "Crazy" was a term of endearment because of his crazy antics from time to time, although most of the time the guys addressed him as Elvis, "E" or just "Boss."

Jumpsuit Flares

The flared legs on all of Elvis' jumpsuits were pure Seventies. After the Hawaii spectacular, his caped and studded costumes continued to become more elaborate and, for that reason, a lot heavier.

Virtually all the jumpsuits and stage outfits are made of 100 percent wool gabardine from Milan, Italy. The stones, selected by Bill Belew on his Paris buying trips, were generally from Austria or Czechoslovakia. Bill Belew used this fabric because of its ability to move with the body and still keep its shape and good looks. (He had noticed that ice-skaters' costumes were made of the same material.) The metal studs on the costumes are generally brass or silver.

Because of their longterm work together, fittings were seldom necessary, and Elvis rarely came up with a specific design – he left it to Bill Belew, and features he liked would appear again and again.

Bill liked the Italian sleeve designs, and the look of stand-up collars from the Napoleonic period. He says that the capes and belts came about because Priscilla suggested that the various capes and belts that Elvis was wearing in his casual wardrobe might be incorporated into his stage wear.

Bill designed a lot of Elvis' personal clothes as well as virtually all his stage outfits, from 1968 until the end.

Cape

The first capes in 1971 and '72 with just the metal studs were not that heavy, but the ones with metal and rhinestone studs in '73 and '74 certainly were. Probably the heaviest outfit of all was the white outfit with red stones. Elvis began to phase out the use of capes on stage towards the end of 1974; this was not just because of the weight, discomfort and impracticality, but also because when he wore them on stage members of the audience would reach out for them, they were too easy to grab, leading to instances when he would almost be pulled off of the stage.

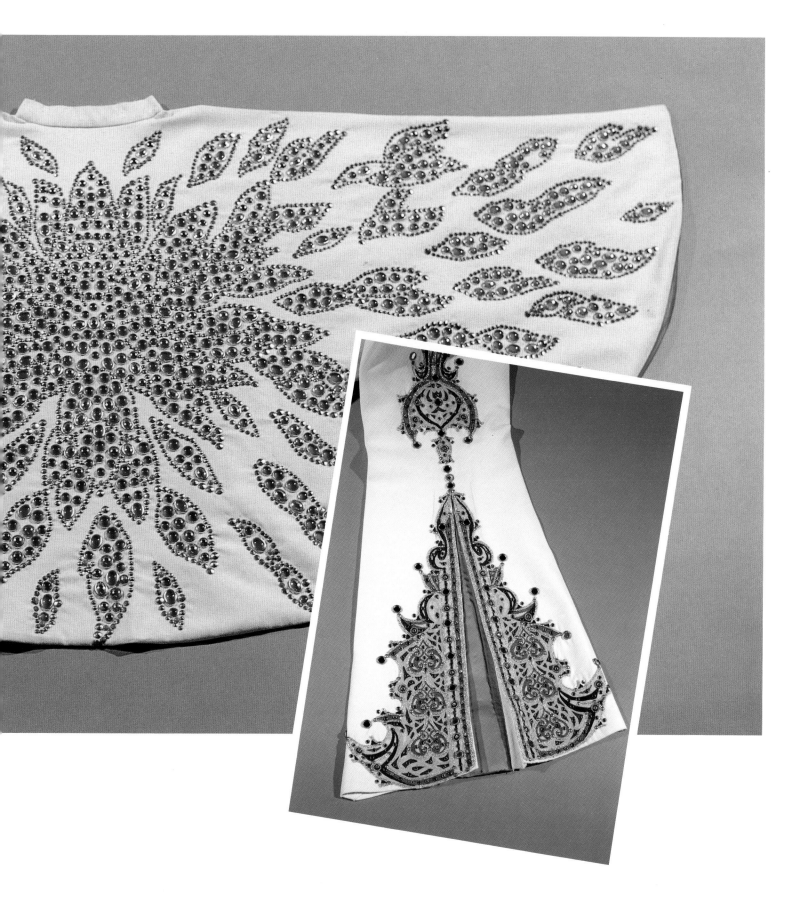

Gold Belt

Elvis was presented with a spectacular gold belt as an award for his record-breaking 1969 engagement in Las Vegas at the International Hotel, where he broke all existing Las Vegas attendance records. The International was the biggest showroom in Vegas at the time, and he was only the second headliner to perform there. Barbra Streisand had opened the showroom, and his engagement followed hers. Business went up by ten percent or so all over Las Vegas whenever Elvis was in town, such was his drawing power for the city. And most of their promotion was a reaction to all the ticket sales rather than an effort to sell tickets. His shows invariably sold out. The 1969 engagement was four weeks and fifty-seven shows. It was his return to the live stage after wrapping up his movie contracts and after the success of the '68 special.

The belt itself is gold over sterling silver, with animal designs which resemble (but are not) the signs of the zodiac. Elvis later had stones added to it, including diamonds, rubies and sapphires. Pictured *(left)* is the manager of the hotel presenting Elvis with the belt.

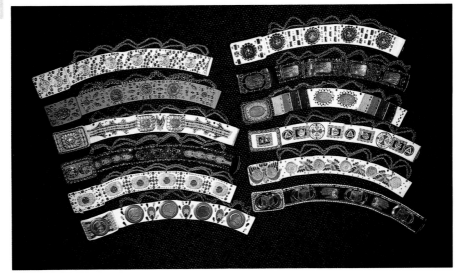

E lvis had been physically active most of his life, though not so much in the last few years. His doctor was a racquetball enthusiast and got Elvis interested in the sport. Elvis had the 2,240-square-foot Racquetball Building constructed in 1975.

Elvis was last in the building on August 16, 1977. He had come home from the dentist sometime after midnight. He, his girlfriend Ginger Alden, his cousin Billy Smith, and Billy's wife, Jo, casually hit a few balls on the court, nothing strenuous, and settled in the lower lounge. Elvis played and sang at the piano. Two of the songs that morning were "Unchained Melody," and "Blue Eyes Crying in the Rain." It was the last time he would play the piano. Shortly after, Elvis returned to his master suite upstairs at the mansion. He was to leave on the next leg of his 1977 tour that night and would be sleeping during the day. He made a few last-minute preparations with his staff for the tour and retired. Within a few hours he had died.

The upper lounge features a weight equipment workout area, lounge furniture, a pinball machine, and a bar with refrigerator.

The lower lounge features a state-of-the-art stereo (for its time), lounge furniture, a Schimmel piano, and a half-bath. A glass viewing wall separates the lower lounge from the racquetball court.

The Racquetball Building

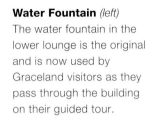

Water Fountain *(left)*
The water fountain in the lower lounge is the original and is now used by Graceland visitors as they pass through the building on their guided tour.

Shower Bath *(left)*
and **Jacuzzi** *(lower left)*
Upstairs in the Racquetball Building (not open to the public due to logistics) are showers and a restroom/dressing area for Elvis' friends, and a separate suite for Elvis that includes a lounge area with a massage table, and an an elaborate bathroom with a Jacuzzi whirlpool and a large five-head shower/steam bath.

RCA Display

On August 12, 1992, RCA and the Recording Industry Association of America (RIAA) posthumously awarded to Elvis 110 gold, and platinum and multi-platinum albums and singles, the largest presentation of gold and platinum records in history. Included was a gold award for the boxed set, "The King of Rock and Roll," for which there had been enough advance orders to prompt the RIAA to give it gold status – in fact, it went platinum soon after that. RCA also presented an elegantly designed, nine-foot, etched-glass trophy sculpture to recognize him as the greatest recording artist of all time. This, to say the least, was the high point for Elvis Week 1992, the week that marked the fifteenth anniversary of his death.

Officials from RCA, the RIAA, and Elvis Presley Enterprises, the press and more than 90 Elvis fan club presidents attended a special unveiling ceremony in the Racquetball Building, while a large group of fans watched it live on closed-circuit television in the visitor center plaza.

It is estimated that Elvis Presley has sold in excess of one billion records worldwide, more than any individual or group in the history of recorded voice. About half of these sales have been in the U.S., about half elsewhere. Yet in the world's record books and other fact books, Elvis is not listed at the top. The reason is that the authors of these books of lists typically consult with the RIAA for their information. The RIAA is the official body to which record companies report record sales and request the awarding of gold and platinum records to their artists. Elvis' RIAA certifications had badly needed updating for a long time.

The RIAA came into existence in 1958. Elvis had many gold records before that time that had been awarded in-house from his record comapny, RCA. However, RCA, for the most part, did not request retroactive RIAA certification of these records. Also, over the years, they did not often request additional certification when the records went gold or platinum more than once.

Colonel's Data

However, for RCA to go back and make it right, they had to present actual sales figures to the RIAA. That was not possible as pre-computer-age files on Elvis' sales were misfiled, incomplete, lost, and scattered. But, after BMG took over RCA, there was a new and energetic focus on all things Elvis-related. Around this same time Graceland bought Colonel Parker's lifetime collection of files, photography, and memorabilia. The Colonel's files were more complete and were well-organized. RCA and Graceland worked together to bring auditors from the RIAA to go through the Colonel's files. The auditors were able to locate sales figures to prompt an amazing number of new certifications. In the ceremony, RCA and the RIAA not only presented the new certifications, but also re-awarded those that had been certified in the past. Together, this totaled 110 titles. But, even if they had presented only the updated certifications (60 or so), it still would have been the largest presentation in history.

The records are hung on a black-fabric-covered false wall built at the back of the Racquetball Building. The nine-foot glass sculpture award rests on the floor at the center of the wall display. The court has been partially carpeted to give visitors access for viewing. Part of the floor remains bare so that visitors can see what the original hardwood court floor is like. The records will remain in the Racquetball Buillding indefinitely. There is no space in the Trophy Room for all of it, and there is no other location available.

World Leader

With 110 titles of albums and singles certified as either gold, platinum, or multi-platinum, Elvis stands at number one on the list of certifications, with more than twice as many certifications as any of the nearest contenders. As of August 1992, the Beatles come in at number two with 41 titles, followed by the Rolling Stones with 39, Barbra Streisand with 37, and Elton John with 37. (These gold and platinum awards for all these artists are for U.S. sales alone; complete and accurate figures for total sales worldwide are almost impossible to obtain.)

It is important to note that 110 reflects the number of titles. One award was presented for each title, whether it was gold, platinum, or multi-platinum. Multi-status is indicated on the engraved identification plate on each award. Any platinum album or any platinum single has to have achieved gold status twice to go platinum, and some of these titles are multi-platinum. So, if Elvis were given separate awards to reflect two golds for each platinum, and a separate platinum for each time a platinum went platinum again, there would be 162 more awards for a total of 272!

(see page 256)

The Meditation Garden

The Meditation Garden was inspired by Elvis' fascination with various Eastern religions and philosophies in the Sixties, and was built then at his request. It was never intended to be his place of burial, it was just a private retreat that he enjoyed for quiet times alone or for private conversations with someone close.

Elvis' mother was buried at Forest Hill Cemetery in 1958; in 1977 when Elvis died he was placed in the mausoleum there and they moved his mother from the grave into the mausoleum at Forest Hill. Shortly thereafter, on October 2, 1977, after Vernon Presley got special clearance from the city, he had Elvis and Gladys moved to Graceland. Since then, Grandma Presley and Vernon Presley have died and been buried in the garden. Also there is the plaque in memory of Elvis' twin brother Jesse Garon, who was stillborn and is buried in Tupelo, Mississippi.

The staff at Graceland are continually amused, year in and year out, by how many visitors still say they expected to see a guitar-shaped swimming pool. This is one of those legends that has just stuck, although Elvis never had a guitar-shaped pool; it seems it got mixed up in various journalists' minds back in the Fifties with Liberace's piano-shaped pool or possibly the guitar-shaped pool built by country singer Webb Pierce, and crept into articles about Elvis in that way.

Elvis wasn't really that enthusiastic about swimming. He more often than not just used the poolside for sunbathing, with a bag of ice, a pitcher of cold water and an electric fan. One night Elvis was out around the grounds at night and he heard splashing noises coming from the pool; he walked over and found a couple of young men, apparently fans from the neighborhood, who had jumped the fence and were swimming around the pool. He just said "y'all be careful" and walked on and left them there to enjoy their swim.

The Presley family graves in the Meditation Garden *(left to right)*: **Minnie Mae**, **Elvis**, **Vernon**, **Gladys** and the plaque for Elvis' twin **Jesse**.

Elvis and Priscilla (*right*)

Elvis in the Meditation Garden not long after it was built in the mid-Sixties. Very few people get photographed fifteen feet away from where they will eventually be laid to rest, and Elvis had no such intention when he had the garden constructed. With him is an unusually blond Priscilla, and behind them, Jerry Schilling and his then-wife Sandy.

Stained-Glass Windows

The meaning of the four nineteenth-century Spanish stained-glass windows that decorate the back wall of the garden has long been the subject of speculation. The Moorish feel to the imagery gives a religious bias to one's interpretation, and the present function of the garden encourages this; when built it had no reverential theme as such.

104 S. Main St.
Bel Air, Md.
May 14th. 1960

y;

Perhaps this will be the strangest letter you have ever
because you are a christian boy, I do not believe you will

Here in this community where I live there are many modern
on a tiny plot of ground, there is a tiny church and mostly
re are from little towns scattered throughout the deep South.
It brings a little bit of home to those who are from the
word of THE LORD as preached from the HOLY BIBLE.
Havimg heard you sing many of the old time Hymns and
a fine christian boy you are , I have a favor to ask of you.
Young peopletoday look up to you, not only because of
my record and your recordings but because you have not turned
e christian way your precious Mother brought you up in.

JUst a few lines written by you , encouraing young
ne to Church, would do more to bring them to GOD than anything

Will you take just a few minutes of your valuable time
short note to be displayed in our Church telling the young
ple not to forget to come to Sunday School and Church.
Thank You Son and may I hear from you?
God will bless you I know.
Sincerely your freind
MRS. ELIZABETH LEE RIGOR.

The Family Monument

The garden includes the original Presley family monument from the Forest Hill Cemetery that was bought to go along with the family plot, which was purchased when Gladys died.

The introduction of the monument to the Meditation Garden added a sacred element which had not previously been apparent, and which became a focus for pilgrims of various persuasions once the mansion and the garden were open to the public.

Although a tiny minority, there were those who sought to venerate the memory of Elvis to the point of it being almost an act of religious faith.

The car in front of the Automobile Museum is becoming the most photographed car in America, yet it never belonged to Elvis and has no known history of any importance.

It was an old junker, a two-door hard-top Cadillac Seville. A couple named King had The King's Heartbreak Hotel Restaurant in Memphis. They cut off the top of the car and painted it pink, and made it into a salad bar for their restaurant, which was done in an Elvis and rock and roll theme. It was down the street from Sun Studio. The couple divorced and Graceland bought a lot of their fixtures to use in a restaurant in the visitor plaza. When the car museum was being designed in 1989 it was decided that

the car would make a great attraction. It has been renovated and weatherproofed, put out front and now people get their pictures taken in front of it all day long.

The most celebrated automobile in the Elvis Presley collection, the pink Cadillac Fleetwood 250 h.p. eight-cylinder four-door, has always been known as his mother's car, though actually it always belonged to Elvis. It was certainly Gladys' favorite, but she didn't drive or have a license. It was originally blue, and Elvis had it painted pink. Elvis always said that this would be a car he would always keep and he did just that. It has become a universal symbol of Fifties America and rock and roll, and one of the most famous cars in the world.

Cadillac Eldorado '56

The legend behind the '56 purple Cadillac Eldorado goes like this: Elvis walks into the showroom of the dealership and is looking at the car – which was white at the time – and is very interested in it. (At that time he probably wasn't quite as famous as he was about to get, and still looked a little strange with his sideburns and his loud clothes.) Apparently the salesman more or less snubs him, ignores him, which miffs Elvis, as you can imagine, so he leaves the showroom and he's out on the lot when he notices this older black gentleman washing the cars there on the lot; Elvis walks up to the gentleman and asks him if he minds telling him how much he gets paid doing the job. The old gentleman tells him, and Elvis says, "Come with me," and takes the old guy back into the showroom and asks to see the manager. He says "I'm Elvis Presley and I'm interested in buying this car. I have the money for it and I'm going to buy it and I want you to give whatever commission that your salesman would have got, had he treated me right, to this gentleman here."

Not long after the purchase Elvis decided he wanted the car painted purple. He walked out of the house to the front where the car was parked and squashed a handful of grapes on the fender and said "I want it that color." The local firm that had done the customizing of the pink Cadillac for him earlier did the paint job on the purple Cadillac; when the car was delivered to Elvis, the customizers had sprinkled grape Kool-Aid on the purple carpet so it would even smell purple when they delivered it to him! All of this might not be absolutely true, but it's a great story.

"While I was driving a truck, everytime a big shiny car drove by it started me sort of day-dreaming. I always felt that someday, somehow, something would happen to change everything for me. I would daydream about how it would be."

ELVIS PRESLEY

1973 Stutz Blackhawk

Elvis' first Stutz in 1971 had the distinction of being the first one manufactured for sale after the prototype car. Legend has it that it was originally ordered for Frank Sinatra, but Elvis charmed the salesman out of it so he could have the first one. The car was badly wrecked in California in July 1971 in a multi-vehicle accident when it was being driven by a livery driver to be washed. Elvis had the car partially restored, but ended up storing it out behind Graceland and not using it anymore. It was fully restored just prior to the opening of the Elvis Presley Automobile Museum in 1989.

The 230 hp 1973 Stutz Blackhawk III was purchased by Elvis in September 1974 for $20,000. It had a red leather interior with 18-karat gold-plated trim throughout. Late at night on August 15, not long before he left Memphis for the next leg of his 1977 tour, Elvis drove this car to his dentist for an appointment, and returned to Graceland not long after midnight, on the morning of August 16. He died less than twelve hours later. The last time he drove through the gates of Graceland he was at the wheel of this car.

Red Harley *(above)*

The red Harley was one of the last motorcycles that Elvis acquired. It is a customized 1976 Harley-Davidson Electra-Glide 1200, with a 1200cc, 54 horsepower engine. It was the Bicentennial Model with which the company commemorated the 200th anniversary of the American Declaration of Independence. Early on Elvis became an honorary member of both the Memphis Motorcycle Club and the American Motorbike Association.

'57 Harley *(left)*

The 1957 Harley-Davidson Hydro-Glide was owned and enjoyed by Elvis for a short while in the late Fifties. Elvis idolized James Dean and Marlon Brando. Brando, particularly in *The Wild One,* had popularized the motorcycle among American youth in the early Fifties, even before the advent of rock and roll. Elvis got caught up in the spirit of the motorbike, and he would tool around Memphis, often being chased by fans in cars when they saw him on the street. He owned and enjoyed motorcycles all of his adult life, and Harleys were his favorite.

A blow-up of the picture *(left)* hangs in the lobby of the Automobile Museum at Graceland, and when visitors ask who the blonde is, the guides usually reply "Miss Ellaneous" because her identity is unknown.

In front of Graceland *(far left)* soon after the filming of his second movie, *Loving You,* when he had just moved into the house, Elvis poses with one of his Harleys and actress Yvonne Lime, who had a very small speaking part in the film and whom he dated briefly afterwards.

1971 Mercedes

The White 1971 Mercedes Benz 280 SL roadster was a gift from Elvis to Priscilla, purchased on December 8, 1970. Priscilla drove this car – which had a top speed of 118 m.p.h. – for a long time. It was a personal favorite of hers. Priscilla sent it from her home in California to Graceland for permanent display in 1989. The car has a detachable hardtop as well as a rag top.

1975 Dino Ferrari 308 GT4 Coupe

The Ferrari represents a rare occassion when Elvis bought a used car. He bought it with one easy payment of $20,583. He was known to drive this car as fast as 165 m.p.h. on the highway. Elvis often drove fast, but he also drove well, and passengers generally felt safe with him. Elvis sometimes got pulled over by the cops when out driving his various cars, but they usually got an autograph and a good look at Elvis' car, enjoyed a friendly chat, and let him go without a ticket.

Pink Willys Jeep *(above)*

The pink 1960 Willys Jeep was purchased by Elvis on July 12, 1960, for $1,812, less the $300 allowed on the golf cart he traded in, plus $33 sales tax. It was for a long time thought to be the pink jeep used in a scene in the movie *Blue Hawaii,* but this proved to be incorrect. It was used primarily by the security guards to patrol the grounds at Graceland in the Sixties, and they were sometimes known to give fans rides around the grounds when Elvis was away.

Golf Cart *(below)*

There was a fleet of golf carts that Elvis had that he and the guys, the wives, and the girlfriends enjoyed driving around the Graceland estate. The elegantly landscaped grounds were frequently damaged in this way. Elvis gave Lisa Marie a Harley-Davidson golf cart, which she loved to ride around the mansion grounds with her cousins and friends – just like Daddy. It was a present from her father in 1976, the last Christmas they were to spend together.

Highway 51 Drive-In

In the center of the Automobile Museum is the drive-in movie feature that runs scenes from Elvis' movies. It attempts to recapture the feel and style of a classic American drive-in movie of the Fifties and Sixties, complete with a mock snack bar at the back.

"Elvis Presley Boulevard is just part of Highway 51 that runs south into Mississippi. We couldn't come up with a name for our mock drive-in; we experimented with song titles and all kinds of things, then we found that there used to be a Memphis drive-in called Highway 51 Drive-In, and it just seemed like a name that made sense."

Drive-In Speakers

The speakers are genuine vintage drive-in movie speaker boxes, the kind that were hooked onto car windows.

Chevy Seats

The seats in the Highway 51 Drive-In are real 1957 Chevy seats with new covers on them that are faithful to the original design.

'56 Continental

The '56 Continental was the car that Elvis kept the longest, other than the pink Cadillac. For whatever reason, he got rid of it in the last year of his life. Absolutely loaded with gadgets, it's a real collector's item, even if it hadn't belonged to Elvis. It is a Continental Mark II, made before they were put under the Lincoln umbrella. Elvis was photographed in it at various points; for instance, on a date with Natalie Wood when he went to court to defend himself for hitting a gas-station attendant. During the early Sixties Priscilla would use the car to drive to school. Elvis kept the car until 1976 and now Graceland has the vehicle on lease from its current owners.

Gas Station

The final display in the Elvis Presley Automobile Museum features the back end of a red 1959 Cadillac Coupe de Ville in a mock-up of a typical American gas station from the Fifties and Sixties. The Coupe de Ville was the all-time classic Cadillac, its long, low lines exuding luxury and glamor, and it certainly had the most spectacular tail fins and rear lights in an era when such details typified car design. To make it apparent that this is not actually one of Elvis' own cars cut up for the display, the dummy license plate says "NOT HIS."

APPLICATION FOR LIABILITY INSURANCE UNDER AUTOMOBILE ASSIGNED RISK PLAN

IMPORTANT

This application must be filled out in duplicate and accompanied by the investigation fee or deposit premium prescribed in the Assigned Risk Plan. Every item must be completed and answers typewritten or written legibly in ink.
If you are eligible for insurance under the Plan, the allowance to the producer of record for services rendered in connection with this application will be paid by the company to which the risk is assigned.
This application does not constitute a binder of insurance. Coverage becomes effective only in accordance with the terms of the Plan.

1. Full name of applicant **Elvis** (First) **Aron** (Middle) **Presley** (Last) 1a. Date of birth **Jan. 8, 1935**

2. Address **1414 Getwell** **Memphis** **Shelby** **Tennessee** (No., Street, Town, County, State)

2a. All previous addresses—past three years **365 Alabama St — 2410 Lamar, Memphis, Tenn.**

3. Occupation **Entertainer** 3a. If applicant is a married woman, give husband's occupation Business **Stage, Radio, TV, Moving pics**

4. Name of employer **Self** Address of employer **1414 Getwell, Memphis, Tenn.**

5. Will applicant operate motor vehicles of his employer **Yes** If Yes, give name of carrier insuring such vehicles _____

6. Description of motor vehicle(s) for which coverage is desired: (If necessary, use separate sheet)

Year and Make	Model	Body Type	Size Type if Truck	Serial No.	Motor No.	Registration No. and State
1955 Cadillac 60	Fleetwood					
1956 Plymouth	Station Wagon					

7. Is motor vehicle owned by and registered in the name of the applicant **Yes** If not, explain _____

8. Motor vehicle will be principally garaged in **Memphis, Tenn.** (Town) **Shelby** (County) **Tenn.** (State)

9. Purposes for which motor vehicle will be used are **Travel to show, radio, TV engagements**

10. Is applicant (or anyone who usually drives the applicant's motor vehicle) required to file evidence of financial responsibility with any state? _____ If Yes, give the following information:
Name _____ Relationship to Applicant _____ Type of certificate required: Owner's ☐; Operator's ☐
State _____
Give motor vehicle case number, if any, and reason for requiring filing _____

11. Is a filing required to comply with (a) I.C.C. regulations _____ (b) State regulation _____ (c) Local ordinance _____
If Yes, list states and cities requiring such filings, radius of operation and limits of liability required by each _____

11a. If no such filing required, and applicant is a truckman or bus operator, indicate radius of operation _____

IF APPLICANT IS AN INDIVIDUAL, QUESTIONS 12a to 12f MUST BE ANSWERED FOR EACH PRIVATE PASSENGER AUTOMOBILE DESCRIBED IN ITEM 6

12a. State number of operators of the automobile resident in the applicant's household or employed as chauffeur of the automobile? **2** Indicate estimated mileage during next 12 months **100,000** miles.

12b. Is there any operator of the automobile under 25 years of age resident in the applicant's household or employed as a chauffeur of the automobile? **Yes** [If No, skip to question 12d].

12c. There are no such operators of the automobile under 25 years of age except the following: (If necessary use separate sheet)

NAME	AGE	Percentage of estimated annual mileage driven by this person	Is this person married?	If married, does this person have legal custody of a child resident in the household?
Elvis Presley	21	50%	No	
W.S. Moore	24	50%	Yes	No

12d. Is the use of the automobile required by or customarily involved in the duties of the applicant or of any other person customarily operating the automobile, in his occupation, profession or business, except in going to or from his principal place of occupation, profession or business? **Yes** [If Yes, skip to question 12f.]

12e. Is the automobile used in driving to or from work, or part of the way to or from work (for example to a depot or station), one day a week or more, or as part of a car pool or other share-the-ride arrangement? _____ If answer is "Yes" state one-way road milage car is driven _____ miles.

12f. If the automobile is owned by a person residing on a farm, is the owner or anyone who customarily operates the automobile engaged in any occupation other than farming? _____

13. The following insurance companies granted automobile liability insurance to applicant during the immediately preceding thirty-six months **Bankers Fire & Marine Ins.Co.—Interstate Fire & Casualty Co.**

14. Does applicant (or anyone who usually drives the applicant's motor vehicle) owe any broker, agent or company any automobile liability insurance premium contracted for during the immediately preceding twelve months? **No**

15. Has applicant (or anyone who usually drives the applicant's motor vehicle) either as the owner or operator, been involved in ANY motor vehicle accident during the immediately preceding thirty-six months? **Yes** (If Yes, give for EACH accident name of operator and relationship to applicant, date, place and description of accident. If necessary, use separate sheet)
W.S. Moore, Employee, Sept. 2, 1955. 15 mi S Texarkana, passing pickup truck which turned left into car driven by Moore.

16. Has applicant (or anyone who usually drives the applicant's motor vehicle) any mental or physical disability? **No** (If Yes, give name of person and relationship to applicant, describe disability, indicate what special equipment, if any, is installed on the motor vehicle and how operator's license is restricted) _____

W.C. 3230

17. Has applicant _____ any time during _____ one who usually drives the applicant's motor veh_____
EACH item and if bail was forfeited, answer "Yes bail" for that item. _____ immediately preceding thirty-six months for any _____
Driving a motor vehicle while under the influence of _____ icating liquor or narcotic drugs _____

stop and report when involved in an accident _____ No _____ (h)
ising out of the operation of a _____ No _____ (i) (j)
at an excessive rate of speed _____ No _____ (k)
or damage to property results

in a reckless manner where _____ No _____ (l)
e to property results therefrom
of revocation or suspension of _____ No _____ (m) A
e without state or owner's _____ No _____ (n) A
of the above questions, give the following infor_____

_____ Location of court _____

gistration suspended or revoked? _____ If

d to obtain automobile liability insurance in _____

NS 19 TO 21 INCLUSIVE TO BE ANSWERED _____
WHO DOES NOT OWN A MOTOR VE_____
sed operator. _____ If Yes, is spouse under
marily operate an automobile in his occupatio_____
spouse will operate: Commercial _____; pr
26 INCLUSIVE TO BE ANSWERED ONLY IF
F FINANCIAL RESPONSIBILITY AND DOES
nt's household own a motor vehicle? _____
ned by member of household: (If more tha_____

Size Type if Truck	Serial No.	Mo

is or her relationship to the applicant: _____

ility insurance? _____

insuring the vehicle, and the policy numbe_____

WERED ONLY IF APPLICANT IS A MEMB_____

, where do you maintain a permanent famil_____
t family residence, please give an addres_____

rd for this insurance _____

E ON THIS APPLICATION IS MAD
ired information will prejudice your applicati_____
on is answered correctly before you sign th_____

ve statements are true.

_____ 19 _____

do hereby certify that I am a licensed _____

_____ expiring _____
have explained its provisions to the ab_____
y the applicant. In the event the poli_____
turn premium to the insured, I agree u_____

Address_____

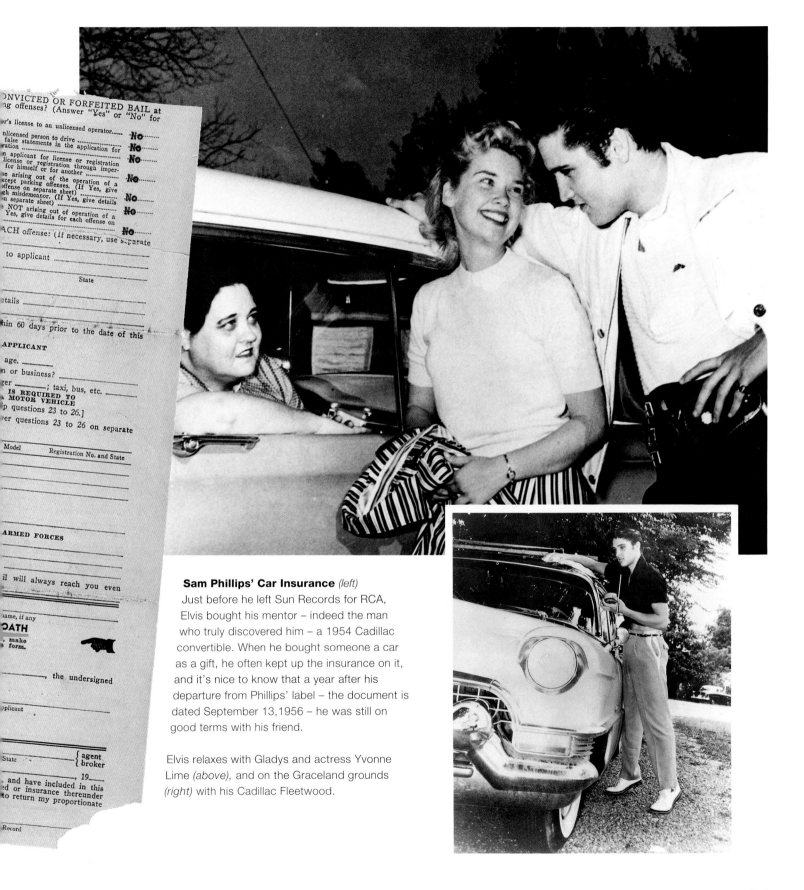

Sam Phillips' Car Insurance *(left)*
Just before he left Sun Records for RCA, Elvis bought his mentor – indeed the man who truly discovered him – a 1954 Cadillac convertible. When he bought someone a car as a gift, he often kept up the insurance on it, and it's nice to know that a year after his departure from Phillips' label – the document is dated September 13, 1956 – he was still on good terms with his friend.

Elvis relaxes with Gladys and actress Yvonne Lime *(above),* and on the Graceland grounds *(right)* with his Cadillac Fleetwood.

Elvis with the obligatory stretch limo *(top)* – every Seventies superstar had to have one.
The shots above include *(left and center)* the Stutz Blackhawk, in which the last pictures of Elvis were taken.

Motorcycle Display

In keeping with the Highway 51 Drive-In feature and the mock gas station, the entire Automobile Museum is built in the style of a typical American small town of the Fifties, complete with sidewalks, billboards, street lamps and simulated trees.

The remarkable collection of Harley-Davidsons and other spectacular motorcycles is complemented with examples of Elvis' own biker clothing, helmets, and the familiar peaked cap, which is to be seen on many photographs. From the days of Gene Vincent through the Shangri La's "Leader Of The Pack" to modern-day punks, the black leather motorcycle jacket has long been a rock'n'roll icon, and one which Elvis embraced in both his leisure time and, most famously, in the opening part of the 1968 "comeback" TV special.

Other less conventional vehicles on display include dune buggies, golf carts and the Jetstar automated snow-sled *(left)*, most of which Elvis utilized as toys rather than for any serious practical use.

"Sincerely Elvis" is the name of the exhibit located on the Graceland visitors plaza, a few doors down from the Automobile Museum and across the highway from the mansion itself. It features a wide variety of items, mostly relating to Elvis' personal, off-stage life. Visitor demand, however, led to the inclusion of a display of stage costumes and related items, as a supplement to what is on show in the Trophy Room at the mansion.

The gold telephone was one of the phones on Elvis' bedside night table, upstairs at Graceland.

Among Elvis' baseball memorabilia are two balls autographed by star players.

A stereo and reel-to-reel tape console of Elvis' is surrounded by a small cross-section of his huge collection of albums, which gives a hint of his broad taste in music. The LPs displayed range from jazz by Duke Ellington through gospel, classical and country records to recordings by Dean Martin, Tom Jones, the Jordanaires and Sam Cooke.

TV Set *(right)* **and Night Table** *(below right)*
The TV set and night table were used in Elvis' bedroom at Graceland when he first moved in, in 1957. The bedroom TV set, a very Fifties design, appears to be housed in a wardrobe cabinet, possibly converted for use as an entertainment center. It complements the bedroom night tables (and other pieces that are in storage) which likewise must have looked very modern and contemporary in the late Fifties.

Gold Boxing Gloves (above)

Elvis and boxing champion Mohammed Ali were mutual admirers. There is a pair of gloves in the Graceland archive, autographed to Elvis from Ali, one of which says "Elvis, you are the greatest." On one occasion Elvis gave Ali a rhinestone-studded cape to wear; however, he lost the fight when he wore this gift from Elvis. He never wore it again.

Elvis and Ali (right)

At the Las Vegas Hilton hotel in 1973, Elvis is wearing a Hawaiian pendant around his neck which was given to him in appreciation of his making the *Aloha From Hawaii* concert, a benefit for the Kui Lee Cancer Fund – in fact, he wore it on the show.

Football Memorabilia

Elvis was a big sports fan, but football was a special favorite. In his early days his favorite team was the Cleveland Browns and in the later years he liked the Pittsburgh Steelers. He was really into football. He knew all of the players' statistics, the histories of the teams, and who played what position; he was genuinely well versed in football, which was a great passion for him through the years.

In the TV Room the three sets enabled him to watch three football games at once, and he would watch the main game he was interested in on the center screen with the sound up, the side two with the sound turned down.

He played football frequently, touch football games with his entourage and with friends, and sometimes they would hire a local stadium after hours for private matches both in Memphis and out in Los Angeles, the team carrying the EPE (Elvis Presley Enterprises) logo on their shirts. The game plans would be meticulously worked out by Elvis and the guys, and some of these are still preserved in the Graceland archive.

EPE Football Team (left)

Probably taken in California, the Elvis Presley Enterprises football team, which included Elvis, of course (second left, back row), Sonny West (far left, middle row), Red West (second right, middle row) and Alan Portis (far right, middle row).

The pictures (top left, center bottom and top right) were taken at an informal practice session with Elvis and the guys, in Memphis in the early Sixties.

Football Plays (below)

The football plays, little hand-drawn diagrams of game tactics, were found in storage at Graceland, and date from the days of the great EPE football games of the early Sixties.

It's not clear who drew them, but it certainly wasn't Elvis as he is mentioned in the notes – for example: "EP can't catch too good, but when he does watch him. He's shifty and fast, we can pick this one off if the linebackers are alert."

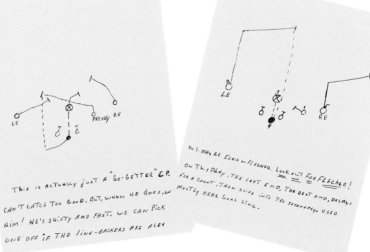

237

"I've never gotten over what they call stage fright. I go through it every show. I'm pretty concerned, I'm pretty much thinking about the show. I never get comfortable with it, and I don't let the people around me get comfortable with it, in that I remind them that it's a new crowd out there, it's a new audience, and they haven't seen us before. So it's got to be like the first time we go on."

ELVIS INTERVIEW FROM

MGM DOCUMENTARY

ELVIS ON TOUR 1972

Onstage
Las Vegas, early in 1970, wearing a karate-style outfit with the Gibson J200 guitar.

Tour Trunks, Amp and Guitar Case (left)
An Elvis concert tour was typified as much by the hardwear as by the spectacular costumes, and the "Sincerely Elvis" exhibit includes some of the airline trunks that were used to carry equipment, wardrobe and other things needed on the road.

The Fender guitar amps and the Martin guitar case were just part of the essentials that had to be transported from venue to venue when an Elvis concert trek was in gear.

Personalized Gibson (right)
The personalized Gibson guitar on display in "Sincerely Elvis" was a gift to Elvis from a fan.

Jumpsuits

The Bill Belew jumpsuits in "Sincerely Elvis" include a white outfit studded with red rhinestones *(right)* from some of Elvis' 1973 and 1974 concert appearances, and the "claw" outfit *(center)* which Elvis wore during shows in 1975, which incorporates elements of American Indian design.

Design Sketches *(far right)*

The two sketches were acquired from Bill Belew in 1974. They are examples of preliminary design ideas which Bill would show to Elvis when working on a new concept for an outfit.

That's the Way It Is *(below)*

Another Belew stage suit, worn at the Las Vegas International Hotel in the summer of 1970, in the MGM cinema documentary.

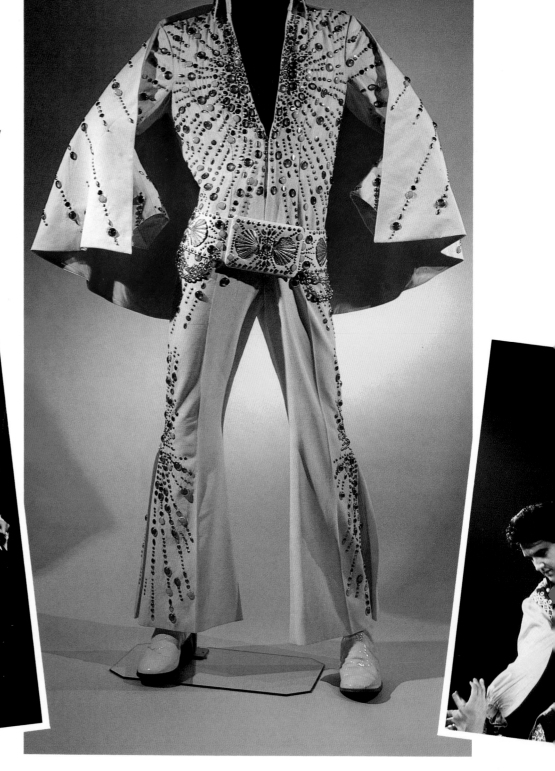

Aircraft

The Convair 880 was manufactured in December 1958 by General Dynamics in San Diego, California. Elvis purchased the plane on April 18, 1975, for $250,000 and then spent over $800,000 having the plane customized to his personal specifications, which reduced the seating capacity to twenty-eight. He named the aircraft *Lisa Marie* after his daughter and had the registration number changed to N 880 EP. His personal TCB logo is painted on the tail. He nicknamed the plane "Hound Dog One" and referred to it as "The pride of Elvis Presley Airways" and his "Flying Graceland."

Elvis used the plane from November 1975 to August 1977, and it was being prepared for his next tour to depart from Memphis on August 16, 1977, the day he died.

Following Elvis' death, the plane was sold by the Presley Estate to International Airmotive Inc., its last flight being from Fort Lauderdale, Florida, in February 1984, back to Graceland.

The JetStar, built by Lockheed of Georgia, was the first in a series of executive class jets with four engines. Elvis purchased it in September 1975 for $899,702, had the registration changed to N 777 EP and nicknamed it "Hound Dog Two."

The exterior of the aircraft is white with red accents, like the *Lisa Marie*. The customized interior has blue carpet, off-white overhead and seats in Florida lime and sunshine yellow. Cabin comforts in the ten-passenger plane include a heating oven, bar, hot galley, private lavatory, three tables and a Sony stereo system.

Gold Wash Basin
The wash basins to be found in the two half-baths of the *Lisa Marie*, are made of flecks of 24-carat gold, with brass fixtures imported from Spain.

Cockpit of Smaller Plane *(right)*
The little plate in the cockpit of the smaller plane says: "O God. Thy sky is so great and my plane is so small." The pilot's name, believe it or not, was Milo High.

JetStar Main Passenger Cabin *(left)*
The JetStar was designed as an intercontinental business jet, with features only found on larger commercial airliners, such as dual landing gears, thrust reversers and "stand-up" headroom throughout the cabin.

JetStar Data
LENGTH: 60 FEET, 6 INCHES
WINGSPAN: 54 FEET, 6 INCHES
TAIL HEIGHT FROM GROUND: 20 FEET, 6 INCHES
CRUISING SPEED: 550 M.P.H.

The Bed

The Graceland staff get a lot of jokes about the seatbelt on the bed. FAA regulations state that all seats on an airplane must have a seatbelt, and a bed is, technically, a seat.

Elvis' private bedroom has a closed-circuit TV, a reading chair and a pull-out desk. Nightstand has sky phone, intercom phone, lamp and control switches for the room. Off the bedroom is Elvis' private half-bath.

Gold Wash Basin

Like those in the half-baths, the blue wash basin at the tail end of the *Lisa Marie* also features flecks of real gold.

Lisa Marie Data

LENGTH: 129 FEET, 4 INCHES

WINGSPAN: 120 FEET

TAIL HEIGHT FROM GROUND: 36 FEET, 3 INCHES

CRUISING SPEED: 615 M.P.H.

MAXIMUM ALTITUDE: 41,000 FEET

TOWER CALL NAME: "880 ECHO PAPPA"

RANGE: 3,000 MILES

HORSEPOWER: 44,800 LBS. THRUST

Lisa Marie Cockpit

The pilot for this plane was Captain Elwood David. He and three others were the constant standby flight crew for Elvis.

Conference Room

On-board meetings were held at the conference table on the *Lisa Marie* jet. Meals were taken at this table, and part of Lisa Presley's ninth birthday was celebrated around the table. The green chair at the back of the Conference Room is beside a desk and controls for a quadraphonic eight-track stereo system, an international sky phone, and an intercom phone to contact cockpit and make passenger announcements.

Front Lounge

The front lounge was the favored place for everyone to "hang out" while in flight. It has gold-plated seatbelt buckles and appointments, suede, leather, and tweed seats, leather-topped tables and two closed-circuit televisions.

Rockabilly's

Tennessee
1-ELVIS
MEMPHIS

TENN
77
8-16

TENN
35
1.8

©1987 ELVIS PRESLEY ENTERPRISES INC

ADMIT
ONE

HOUSE

DO NOT
DETACH

NO REFUNDS

Anniversary

GRACELAND

NO RAINCHECKS

ADMIT
ONE

TROPHY
ROOM

DO NOT
DETACH

TIME _____ 0181253 _____ TOUR NO. _____

THE KING

Hea
H

RES

There had been various proposals over the years, ever since Elvis came out of the army a "respectable" member of the community, for the City of Memphis to honor their most famous resident in some way. One of the main campaigners was Mayor Bill Ingram (after whom Elvis jokingly named one of his horses Mare Ingram). Finally, the Memphis City Council officially changed the name of a two-mile section of Highway 51 in late June 1971. The first actual sign went up in January 1972, after a ceremony outside Graceland with Mayor Wyeth Chandler (Ingram's successor) and Vernon Presley.

For some time after the road name changed, Elvis could not get used to the idea, especially when he heard crime reports on the radio such as "robbery on Elvis Presley." He would say, "Man, they're gonna think I'm doing that stuff!"

The restaurant sign, like the car outside the Automobile Museum, was acquired from King's Heartbreak Hotel Restaurant in midtown Memphis. It has caused some confusion over the years, with the name suggesting the restaurant is part of a hotel of the same name — people come in looking for the check-in desk.

Other Graceland ephemera ranges from the ELVIS number plates on the shuttle buses that take tourists over the road from the visitor's plaza to the mansion, to the actual tour tickets — the one illustrated opposite was the design used throughout the Eighties and only recently changed.

Cinema Sign *(left)*

The Bijou is the name of the little cinema in the vistors' center which tourists can visit for free. It shows a 20-minute program *Walk a Mile in My Shoes*, a retrospective of Elvis' career.

Rockabilly's Diner *(below)*

Rockabilly's Diner, also at the visitors' center, is an accurate recreation of a typical Fifties diner, complete with a vintage Wurlitzer jukebox – full of Elvis Presley singles of course!

The steel-tube furniture, plastic decor and pastel color scheme are all evocative of the days when the rock and roll revolution first took place, with Elvis at its forefront.

Around the walls are signed pictures from celebrities who have made the pilgrimage to Graceland over the years – a collection that grows by the month – and pictures of Elvis with various celebrity friends.

Albums

Elvis Presley ....Gold
Elvis ....Gold
Loving You ....Gold
Elvis' Christmas Album (1957 package)....................2x Platinum
Elvis' Golden Records, Vol. 1 ....5x Platinum
50,000,000 Elvis Fans Can't Be Wrong (Elvis' Records, Vol. 2) .... Platinum
G.I. Blues...Platinum
His Hand in Mine...Platinum
Blue Hawaii ....2x Platinum
Girls! Girls! Girls! ....Gold
Elvis' Golden Records, Vol. 3 ....Platinum
Roustabout ....Gold
How Great Thou Art...2x Platinum
Elvis, NBC TV Special ....Gold
Elvis' Gold Records, Vol. 4...Gold
From Elvis in Memphis ....Gold
Elvis: From Memphis to Vegas, From Vegas to Memphis...........Gold
On Stage, February 1970...Gold
Worldwide 50 Gold Award Hits ....Platinum
Elvis' Christmas Album (1970 package).....................Platinum
Elvis, That's the Way It Is ....Gold
Elvis in Person at the International Hotel ....Gold
Elvis Country ....Gold
You'll Never Walk Alone ....Gold
Elvis Sings the Wonderful World of Christmas............2x Platinum
Elvis Now ....Gold
He Touched Me ....Gold
Elvis As Recorded at Madison Square Garden ....2x Platinum
Elvis Sings Burning Love and Hits from His Movies, Vol. 2...........Gold
Aloha from Hawaii ....2x Platinum
Elvis, A Legendary Performer, Vol. 1..........................Gold
Pure Gold...2x Platinum
Elvis, A Legendary Performer, Vol. 2..........................Gold
From Elvis Presley Boulevard, Memphis, Tennessee.............Gold
Welcome To My World ....Platinum
Moody Blue..2x Platinum
Elvis in Concert ....Platinum
He Walks Beside Me ....Gold
Elvis, A Legendary Performer, Vol. 3..........................Gold
Memories of Christmas ....Gold
The Number One Hits...Gold
The King of Rock and Roll..Gold

Singles

Heartbreak Hotel/I Was the One ....Platinum
I Want You, I Need You, I Love You/My Baby Left Me ....Platinum
Hound Dog/Don't Be Cruel ....3x Platinum
Love Me Tender/Any Way You Want Me ....2x Platinum
Too Much/Playing for Keeps ....Gold
All Shook Up/That's When Your Heartaches Begin ....2x Platinum
Teddy Bear/Loving You...Platinum
Jailhouse Rock/Treat Me Nice ....2x Platinum
Don't/I Beg of You...Platinum
Wear My Ring Around Your Neck/Doncha'
  Think It's Time...Platinum
Hard Headed Woman/Don't Ask Me Why ....Platinum
I Got Stung/One Night ....Platinum
A Fool Such As I/I Need Your Love Tonight ....Platinum
A Big Hunk o'Love/My Wish Came True ....Gold
Stuck On You/Fame and Fortune ....Platinum
It's Now or Never/A Mess of Blues ....Platinum

Are You Lonesome Tonight/I Gotta Know ....2x Platinum
Surrender/Lonely Man ....Gold
Feel So Bad/Wild in the Country.................................Gold
His Latest Flame/Little Sister ....Gold
Can't Help Falling In Love/Rock-a-Hula Baby.............Platinum
Good Luck Charm/Anything That's Part of You.............Platinum
She's Not You/Just Tell Her Jim Said Hello...................Gold
Return to Sender/Where Do You Come From................Platinum
One Broken Heart for Sale/They Remind Me Too Much of You ....Gold
Devil in Disguise/Please Don't Drag That String Around...............Gold
Bossa Nova Baby/Witchcraft ....Gold
Kissin' Cousins/It Hurts Me..Gold
Viva Las Vegas/What'd I Say..Gold
Ain't That Loving You, Baby/Ask Me ....Gold
Crying in the Chapel / I Believe in the Man in the Sky ....Platinum
I'm Yours/Long Lonely Highway ....Gold
Puppet on a String/Wooden Heart...............................Gold
Blue Christmas/Santa Claus is Back in Town...............Gold
Tell Me Why/Blue River...Gold
Frankie and Johnny/Please Don't Stop Loving Me ....Gold
If I Can Dream/Edge of Reality....................................Gold
In the Ghetto/Any Day Now ....Platinum
Clean Up Your Own Back Yard/The Fair Is Moving On ....Gold
Suspicious Minds/You'll Think of Me ....Platinum
Don't Cry Daddy/Rubberneckin' ....Platinum
Kentucky Rain/My Little Friend ....Gold
The Wonder of You/Mama Liked the Roses ....Gold
I've Lost You/The Next Step is Love ....Gold
You Don't Have to Say You Love Me/Patch It Up ....Gold
I Really Don't Want to Know/There Goes My Everything................Gold
Burning Love/It's a Matter of Time ....Platinum
Separate Ways/Always in My Mind ....Gold
Way Down/Pledging My Love.......................................Gold
My Way/America..Gold

Extended Play Singles

Elvis Presley ....Gold
Heartbreak Hotel..Gold
The Real Elvis..Platinum
Elvis Presley ....Gold
Elvis, Volume 1 ....2x Platinum
Love Me Tender ....Platinum
Elvis, Volume 2 ....Gold
Peace in the Valley ....Platinum
Loving You, Volume 1 ....Gold
Loving You, Volume 2..Platinum
Jailhouse Rock ....2x Platinum
Elvis Sings Christmas Songs.......................................Platinum
King Creole, Volume 1 ....Platinum
King Creole, Volume 2 ....Platinum
Follow That Dream..Platinum
Kid Galahad ....Gold